When we do move we can move in all directions at the one time, personally I envisage creating an atmosphere of mass emotion trying to use it as best we can and as soon as we can to assert pressure from all angles on the Brits.

Bobby Sands (24 August 1979).

The hunger-strikes, at a great cost to our H-Block martyrs and their families, smashed criminalisation and led to the success of the electoral strategy, plus the revamping of the IRA.

Gerry Adams (Bobby Sands Memorial lecture 1985).

BROADENING THE BATTLEFIELD

LIAM CLARKE

BROADENING THE BATTLEFIELD

The H-Blocks and the Rise of Sinn Féin

Gill and Macmillan

Published in Ireland by
Gill and Macmillan Ltd
Goldenbridge
Dublin 8
with associated companies in
Auckland, Dallas, Delhi, Hong Kong,
Johannesburg, Lagos, London, Manzini,
Melbourne, Nairobi, New York, Singapore,
Tokyo, Washington

0 7171 1476 7
Print Origination in Ireland by Wellset Ltd
Printed in Great Britain

Contents

Thanks...

There are many whose assistance, patience or frankness has helped this book along. Some won't want a mention and to any omitted in error, my apologies.

The list includes Pat McGeown, Joe Austin, Mary McDermott, Jim Prior, Fr Dennis Faul, Paddy and Theresa Devlin, Fr Tom Toner, Mary Sheehan, Liam McCloskey, Bertie McCaffrey, Jackie Donnelly, Jimmy Drumm, Billy McQuiston, Fr Alec Reid, Canon Arlow, the Lynch family, Pat McCusker, Gusty Spence, Tommy Little, Andy Tyrie, Sam Walker, Terry Harkin, Jim Sullivan, Sam Wilson and Seamus Harrison.

Thanks to the various prisoners (past, present but hopefully not future), Sinn Fein members past and present, solicitors, prison staff, policepersons and others who have helped with particular insights or recollections of events. I am also grateful to Danny Morrison who, if he didn't help at least spoke his mind and saved me time, and Alfie Doherty who kept me right despite his misgivings.

I have been assisted with documents and other materials by, amongst others, Robert Bell of the Linenhall library, Maurice Neil of *Sunday News*, Graham Hurley at *TV South*, Raymond Fitzwalter of *World in Action*, Walter McAuley at *Belfast Telegraph*, Brendan O'Brien (formerly of *Today Tonight* and now with the *Irish Independent*), Martin O'Hagan (at *Fortnight*), Barrie Penrose (Sunday Times), the NIO and Adrian Robinson of the RUC. Fergal Tobin of Gill and Macmillan was understanding way beyond the call of duty when I ran into problems or got diverted into other projects.

Finally I am indebted to my wife Kathy who listened to me, helped with research, read drafts, spotted howlers, gave encouragement and put up with it all.

Needless to say not everyone mentioned above will agree with my interpretation of events and nobody except myself is responsible for any errors that have crept into the text despite their help or advice.

Introduction

IRA activity is part of the status quo in Ireland. Republican violence, whether actual, remembered or threatened, has been a part of the social wallpaper throughout the history of the two present Irish states. It is soaked into their civil societies and their values. Attitudes to it feed the roots of the agreed political traditions. Provided it can be held within limits, the 'acceptable level of violence', this apparently subversive undercurrent is a stabilising factor, a fact of life which can be relied on and around which the existing order has, of necessity, grown up.

In the south the IRA and the Irish Citizen Army were the forcing houses from which the main political parties had emerged until the *in vitro* birth of the Progressive Democrats in 1986. In Ulster the IRA, actual and potential, has frequently been the bogeyman with which the unionist poor have been marshalled behind their ideology of siege by their prosperous leadership. For nationalists the IRA with its bombs, its martyrs, its ideals and its claim to a truth beyond mere politics has also acted to reproduce and legitimise the existing political alliances along community and sectarian lines.

Throughout this period of state building the IRA itself has not stood still or remained immune to the influence of social currents around it. Republicans sometimes speak of the IRA as a vacuum cleaner which absorbs all available talent. Its role for Northern Catholics has often been that of a funnel through which all desire for change, all forms of discontent, bitterness and anger can be directed into the narrow, and historically ineffective, outlet of physical force nationalism. It combines romantics, socialists, traditionalists, bigots, and misfits in an armed conspiracy where the common denominator is agreement that force should, as a matter of principle, be used against the British presence in Ireland.

The belief in force, the ideology of sacrifice and duty that go with it, are essential to IRA thinking and for long periods in the organisation's history 'politics' has been a dirty word, synonymous with sellout and compromise.

'The leadership of the IRA', its training manual states, 'is the lawful government of the Irish Republic.' Its claim to this title and its authority to do whatever it thinks necessary does not depend on votes or popular acclaim. It lies in the dead generations, first principles, destiny and the bald fact that British soldiers are present in Ireland. Even the most politically sophisticated of present-day Sinn Fein representatives stress that in its own lights the IRA needs no mandate and will continue its operations, win or lose, to the best of its ability, whether people like it or not.[1]

At nearly every stage of the IRA's development it has been evident to some of its members that this approach, however pure, principled and emotionally satisfying, is one which the authorities can handle. All experience shows that their chosen battleground of pure force is one on which republicans can be isolated and defeated. Various reactions were possible to this realisation, ranging from despair through a mythology of glorious defeat to an attempt to broaden the battlefield into other areas of life. The problem is how to achieve this without undermining the alliance of differing views which made up the republican movement.

The years since 1976 have been one such period of soul searching, leading to the drive by the Provos in the '80s to broaden their base, to turn Clausewitz on his head and to make politics the extension of war. To understand their problems in doing this it is useful to look back at how the Provisionals themselves emerged from the last, more thoroughgoing, attempt to bring the IRA beyond the battlefield of force.

Characteristically this occurred at a period when the IRA was isolated and defeated after the 1956-62 border campaign. The IRA had been comprehensively routed when its Harvester offensive, waged by flying columns against border installations and police stations, ran out of the support necessary to sustain it. As in previous campaigns the lessons of defeat were teased out by the vanquished in the prisons. This time a new and distinctively left-wing strategy began to emerge in which the use of force was no longer a principle. Instead the emphasis was on building towards state power by mobilising different strands of opinion around democratic and social demands.

In the republic the IRA revitalised Sinn Féin (its political wing) and became involved in a range of issues from tenants' struggles to fish-ins on preserved waters and attacks on the homes of foreigners who owned Irish estates. In the North it co-operated with the Communist Party of Ireland and others to set up the Northern Ireland Civil Rights Association, a body aimed at undermining sectarianism through popular and democratic reforms. This was to create the space in which class-based politics could be built up and more fundamental change would eventually be achieved. More immediately NICRA caught the idealism of the first generation of Catholic and working-class students to benefit from the introduction of free third-level education. Emotionally attuned to the chic student radicalism of the late '60s in Europe and the US, movements like People's Democracy grew up. They were far keener than the more cautious and thoughtful IRA veterans for physical confrontations with the unionists and the police. Republicans within NICRA sought to minimise street confrontation, correctly calculating that, if the issue was reduced to one of force, marches would shrink and the mass movement so patiently built around the Civil Rights demands would shatter.

This tactic met with initial success (in the North some unionists went so far as to join NICRA, which achieved most of the reforms it demanded) and was consequently perceived as profoundly subversive by large sections of the establishment, North and South. In states where the existence of the state itself, 'the national question', had always been the secure centre of politics, and the threat of armed insurrection was constantly available to rally support behind the existing order, social issues were now being raised in terms that were hard to refute. Loyalist hardliners, who longed for the old simplicities, treated the Civil Rights movement as a cover for the IRA, and in a sense it was but not in a way which they wished to understand. A pattern of savage attack and pogrom grew up as attempts were made to re-establish the familiar sectarian battle-lines and to beat the new and unfamiliar social debate off the streets. The IRA, by and large, tried to sit this out, attracting bitter criticism for failing to fulfil its traditional role as defender of Catholic areas. The critics, often old sweats who had drifted out of the IRA in disillusionment, lacked the resources to make their discontent effective.

In the South, too, nostalgia for the simplicities of an IRA which confined its activities to shooting up border RUC stations and knew how to keep its nose out of the everyday issues of social control, mixed easily with concern for the fate of Northern Catholics. Sections of the establishment set about funding the Northern nationalists and even met with former IRA leaders, offering money to those prepared to confine their activities to Ulster and forget about politics.[2]

This struck a chord with many of the older republicans in the North as well as enraged youth in the hard-pressed nationalist ghettos, but not with the IRA leadership. It wanted to maintain the pressure in the south and believed that a return to physical force would only serve to dissipate the powerful new alliance of interests building up in NICRA. In these circumstances the southern funds handed over provided the initial 'float' for the emerging Provisionals, putting full-time workers on the road, and providing resources to get the organisation moving.

The result, as so often before when the primacy of physical force came under question, was a split in the IRA into Officials and Provisionals, a split which many believed at the time would not last but which proved durable precisely because it raised in a particularly sharp form the fundamental internal contradictions of Irish republicanism in the latter half of the twentieth century. Its effect was for years to confine the Provisionals to the traditional narrow ground of pure force and to marginalise the new issues which the left-wing leadership, who continued in the Officials, had pioneered. Its lessons were not forgotten when the Provisionals themselves saw the need to make changes in order to survive.

On 6 February 1971 Provisional IRA gunmen at a firing point on Templar House high-rise flats on the New Lodge Road area shot dead Gunner Curtis, the first British soldier to be killed by the IRA since 1920. By the end of the year the total was to rise to forty-three. The event served to mark the escalation of the conflict from a matter of riots, raids, arrests and burnings to an IRA campaign. The first wave of bombing came in April 1971 as the police were secretly preparing the lists of republican suspects to be lifted in the August internment swoops. The thirty-seven explosions that month were another definite signal that the Provisionals, now financed by the newly-founded Noraid, were starting to arm and train their men for the sustained violence which they imagined could very soon make Northern Ireland ungovernable.

The issue, they believed, would now be resolved with military hardware, not by the political manoeuvring of the IRA they had left behind. 'There is one hell of a difference between what you are buying and the heavy gear', Provisional Chief of Staff Sean MacStiofain wrote to his Noraid contact in September 1971, adding: 'the position is this, we must have the heavy stuff to win. We are not going to be beaten but at the same time just a few of those would make all the difference.'

This was the very thing that unionist die-hards had been predicting, even longing for, for years. It later emerged that some loyalists, including a number of politicians, were so disconcerted by the unfamiliar tactics of the Civil Rights Movement that they set out to provoke the sort of political shakedown associated with an IRA campaign by organising the bombing of electricity and water installations.[3]

All the same, the genuine article came as a surprise. In loyalist Portadown, a settled town uneasily wedded to next-door Lurgan in the new city of Craigavon, the capture of three would-be IRA bombers in the early hours of Thursday 22 April was big news and a considerable feather in the cap of the arresting officer, Inspector James Martin. Now, fifteen years further into the campaign, the whole incident, born of frustration at incessant attacks on Portadown's Catholic 'Tunnel' area and taking place before Provisional IRA training had passed the rudimentary stage, has a strangely naive feel to it.

The three Provos, two bricklayers and a process worker moving a bomb in their works van, were quickly run to ground in a dramatic early morning car chase through the town. A troop of British soldiers actually formed a human chain across the main road, counting on the bombers to surrender rather than knock them down. In the driving seat IRA Volunteer Malachy Leonard slowed as if to stop but, perhaps on second thoughts, decided to make a run for it. No shots were fired but one soldier did manage to break the windscreen as Leonard roared through, scattering two members of the patrol across the road.

Police and troops continued the chase until their quarry signalled left and cut into the dead end of King Street, where it stopped, its glowing tail lights a dead give-away in the darkened cul de sac. The area was sealed off as Inspector Martin and Constable Ronald Elwood took up the trail on foot. One of the IRA men, Malachi Cullen, was recognised and immediately arrested crouching behind a wall. Further along his two comrades, Malachy Leonard and Brian McCann, were discovered hiding in a yard. McCann, who had a loaded Colt .45 in the yard with him, later told the Inspector he had been very foolish to venture up the entry. 'I knew you weren't armed', the IRA man explained to the RUC officer. In the van police found the manufacturer's wrapping from the explosives stuffed behind the seat. The unexploded bomb (five pounds of gelignite in a paint tin) was discovered lying along the road after Cullen, who was worried that a child might come upon it and be hurt, told the policemen where to look for it. In a search of Leonard's house a manual on bomb making, a list of the registration numbers of policemen's cars and a sketch diagram of a bomb, damningly inscribed '4 volts', 'det' and 'gelly', were stashed together under the wardrobe. In the cupboard beneath the stairs there was a length of Cordtex fuse and a big jar of chlorate and sugar incendiary mix.

The evidence at this stage seemed damaging enough, though it was to be suggested by the defence that some of it was planted. In any case when the accused appeared in the dock after just over a week on remand they were utterly defiant, removing any doubts there may have been in the jury's mind by refusing to recognise the court and remaining silent for most of the trial. Their behaviour was dictated by paragraphs 3 and 4 of General Order 24, as revised by the IRA Army Convention of 1927.

'We are proud of you — keep the flag flying', a teenage girl called as the trio were led away to serve their sentences. At the time some Catholics were fleeing the nationalist quarter of Portadown, the Tunnel and Garvaghy Road areas, to join the exodus to 'refugee camps' south of the border. The loyalist harassment which they feared intensified as the explosions continued in the lead-up to the July marching season. The incident and the more successful Provo operations which took place elsewhere had all the appearance of a serious outburst of violence, confirming in the administration's mind the tragically mistaken notion that internment would be the easiest way to nip the north's discontent in the bud. Before internment was introduced on 9 August the 1971 death toll had been 34. By the end of the year it was 135 and set on a rising trend.

Fourteen years later the outburst showed no sign of abating and loyalist Portadown was once again rocked back on its heels by Brian McCann. This time he was one of two Sinn Féin members to sit on Craigavon Borough council. His colleague was Brendan Curran, a former Provisional IRA explosives expert who was jailed in 1974 after two 150 lb car bombs ripped through the centre of Lurgan, killing RUC officer John Forsythe.

In a sense both men were lucky to be arrested. The intervening years had been ones of dreadful attrition in IRA ranks outside prison and rapid development within it. Their chances of surviving to outrage loyalist opinion by reaching the councils would not have been high had they remained as active IRA volunteers on the streets. When Brian McCann was arrested, just three Provisional IRA men had died violently, all of them in Belfast. By March 1980 the total had risen to 216.[4] In the same period the province's total prison population had increased from around 1,000 to around 2,400.

The prisons no less than the streets were the arena in which the Provisional IRA fought its campaign and many volunteers found that in jail the IRA assumed a more tangible reality than it had in society outside. An early priority was to establish the solidarity of IRA prisoners, to distinguish them from the prison population at large and to establish a command structure within the prison.

For internees the task was an easy one. They were lifted without trial and housed in military-style Nissen huts. In the Long Kesh compounds paramilitary command structures operated in a far purer form than outside the wire. Here confinement was correctly seen as no more than a matter of political convenience on the part of the authorities. For convicts processed by the courts in the normal way and housed in cellular accommodation under prison rules, the situation was far more ambiguous. The clear intention of the authorities was to treat them as criminals who should at worst be punished and at best rehabilitated as useful members of society. The prisoners wanted to preserve their identity as IRA volunteers and to force a recognition of the political motivation for their crimes.

It was to break this system that a campaign for special status was launched and, in 1972, a hunger strike was commenced in which Brian McCann was the youngest participant. The protest was led by veteran IRA men Prionsias McAirt and Billy McKee. An account of this successful strike for political status was drawn up for the information of the Provisional leadership in the run-up to the 1980 hunger strike, which was heavily influenced by its example. It read:

> There were 7 republican political prisoners in Crumlin Road jail when McKee and McAirt went in in June 1971 to A wing.
>
> There was no segregation from ordinary prisoners and 'parades' were held during association in a double cell in A wing. At this time there was one man to a cell. The first outdoor 'parade' was not held until Easter Sunday 1972.
>
> By the time the hunger strike began in mid-June 1972 there were 40 sentenced republican political prisoners. The Sticks[5] (approx 7) decided that they would pursue political status through the courts fighting the issue on 'legal' points. Their OC at that time was Peter Monaghan from Tyrone.
>
> The first group to go on hunger strike consisted of 6 men: Malachy Leonard (Portadown), Boyle (Tyrone), Billy McKee (Belfast), Bobby Campbell (Belfast), Kevin Henry (Newry) and....
>
> By the second week authority was delegated to McAirt because McKee was confined to bed. In the 4th week of the hunger strike an approach was made by the then Governor Major Mullen and deputy Governor Bob McKinley who offered transfer to Long Kesh where the sentenced republican political prisoners would be segregated into

> compounds but wearing prison uniform. The reply was no, there would be no concession on the basic demands of Political Status.
>
> Deputy Governor McKinley returned later to ask if the sentenced republican prisoners were sticking to the name 'Political Status'.
>
> He was told that the name was a matter for the British government as long as the basic demands were met.
>
> By the time the strike ended in late June 1972 over 30 men were on it. Following the strike's conclusion all sentenced republican political prisoners (approx 100) were transferred to A wing. They would receive one parcel and one visit per week. Education facilities were organised by the political prisoners. The lockup time was extended from 7.30 pm to 8.00 pm and eventually to 9.00 pm. This was applicable to the entire jail. Medical and dental facilities at this time were adequate. The sentenced republican political prisoners were eventually transferred to Long Kesh in January 1973 where they were put into compounds 7, 8 and 9.
>
> The conclusion of the hunger strike and the granting of political status came at the commencement of the 1972 truce.

However the fatal simplicity of this account, its equation of the granting of 'status' with the willingness of prisoners to die painfully for it, did not tell the whole story. As in subsequent hunger strikes, there was a political process going on outside the prison walls and the reality is that this political process had at least as much to do with the granting of special category status (the authorities never called it political status) as did the determination of the hunger strikers.

Earlier in the year there had been a major escalation in violence following the 'Bloody Sunday' killing of thirteen people in a Civil Rights march in Derry by the Parachute Regiment on 30 January. The level of IRA activity had soared as new recruits flooded in and anger mounted. As the crisis deepened the Northern Ireland parliament at Stormont was 'suspended' in favour of direct rule by British ministers. The IRA considered it possible that victory was in sight and sought direct negotiations with the administration.[6]

A precondition for these negotiations was the release from internment of Gerry Adams (at 23 already one of the most important men in the Provisional movement) and the granting of special category status to sentenced republican prisoners. The whole thing was made possible by the willingness of the representatives of constitutional nationalism, in the shape of SDLP leaders John Hume and Paddy Devlin, to act as intermediaries shuttling between Britain, IRA leaders (Sean MacStiofain, Seamus Twomey and Daithi O'Conaill) and prison protest leaders Billy McKee and Prionsias McAirt (Frank Card). Adams was eventually released into Devlin's custody, the prisoners' demands were met and an IRA 'bilateral truce' declared following talks in London.

At the time the British believed the ceasefire would signal the end of the IRA campaign (Whitelaw was so pleased he literally hugged Hume) and the IRA briefly felt that they were on the way home, having been recognised by the British both in negotiations and in the prison. However both the British and the Provisionals were later to regret the outcome of the talks, both sides feeling that they had lost out.

The ceasefire was largely the brainchild of the IRA's two main political strategists Daithai O'Conaill and Gerry Adams. It foundered in Belfast where the Brigade Commander, Seamus Twomey, a close ally of Chief of Staff Sean MacStiofain, had always been critical of it. The breaking point was an incident in Lenadoon housing estate where a number of displaced Catholic families had been allocated houses formerly held by Protestants. The loyalist paramilitary UDA, taking this as a setback for their side in the Catholic/Protestant war for territory, assembled in force to stop the move. The UDA's confidence was high because, seeking to avoid confrontation with loyalists at a time when the secret ceasefire agreement allowed the Provisionals to move freely and bear arms, the British Commander of Land Forces, Major General Ford, had held three hours of talks with UDA leader Tommy Herron a few days earlier. In this instance an ugly stand-off developed in which the British army intervened to prevent the families taking possession of their new homes, at one point ramming a furniture lorry.

In IRA Chief of Staff Sean MacStiofain's account, 'The

republican leadership in Belfast knew it could not hold back any longer. It lived up to its responsibility. Weapons put in store during the truce were re-issued, and units moved into position to protect nationalist civilians in Lenadoon and elsewhere. There was no option. If our units had been ordered to stand aside the consequences would have been disastrous. The IRA would have lost the defence initiative and all credibility with the people.'

Hume's assessment was that, by making a row over allocation of a few houses the occasion for breaking its ceasefire, the IRA had shown its inability to negotiate effectively or to build on its gains.

Both versions were true. The Provisional IRA had no choice but to restart its campaign or die. Its policies were sketchy at best. It was not taking part in electoral politics or any other means of struggle. It had been established for the purpose of using physical force and there was simply nothing else that it was equipped to do at this point in its development. This weakness was not lost on the six Provo leaders who had gone to London to negotiate the truce with the British in Chelsea's pleasant Cheyne Walk. Over the coming years Gerry Adams, Martin McGuinness, Ivor Bell, Seamus Twomey, Sean MacStiofain and Daithi O'Conaill were all to wrestle with these issues, each in his own way.

NOTES

1. eg Gerry Adams: 'on mandate, I think, very, very simply, if you are talking about armed struggle, that the very, the presence of armed forces and of a British presence in this country is where people derive their mandate from' (interview with the author, 1983).

2. Particularly useful accounts of this period are contained in *Ulster* (by the Sunday Times Insight Team, Penguin 1972), *Fianna Fáil: the IRA Connection* (Official Sinn Féin Pamphlet, undated) and a series on 'The Arms Crises' in *Magill* (May-July 1980).

3. Gusty Spence, an early leader of the loyalist Ulster Volunteer Force (UVF), has spoken at some length about this murky area. For instance he says 'we had old friends in the Unionist government. I wasn't in charge of the UVF. We would receive orders that there had to be certain incidents not so much to be blamed on the IRA as designed to bring Terence O'Neill down as leader.' (*New Hibernia* July 1985: 'Gusty Spence: Now a Man of Peace').

4. Figures based on *An Phoblacht/Republican News* March 1980, 'Roll of Honour', and are an underestimate due to the IRA practice, in this period, of concealing its casualty level.

5. Members of the Officials. The 'stick' or 'sticky' nickname came from their practice of selling stick-on paper Easter Lilies at their annual parades to commemorate the 1916 rising. The Provisionals, whose lilies were pinned on, were known as 'pinheads' for a time.

6. The following account is indebted to Barry White's *John Hume: Statesman of the Troubles* (Blackstaff 1984), Sean MacStiofain's *Memoirs of a Revolutionary* (Gordon Cremonesi 1975), Tim Pat Coogan's *On the Blanket* (Ward River Press 1980) and a conversation with Paddy Devlin.

1

Hatred to Topple the World

'At eighteen-and-a-half I joined the Provos. My mother wept with pride and fear as I went out to meet and confront the imperial might of an empire with an M1 carbine and enough hate to topple the world. To my surprise, my schoolday friends and neighbours became my comrades in war.'

Bobby Sands: *The Birth of a Republican.*[1]

The ending of the 1972 ceasefire left the British government with the problem of how it was to implement the basic policy it had sustained for the past fifty years, retaining influence in Ireland without allowing the country's politics to impinge on her own. It also exposed what was seen as the IRA's inability to 'turn their chips into money',[2] a flaw with its roots in the very nature of the movement.

Firstly, IRA support came from a small minority of the Catholic population who were themselves a minority in the north which was in turn a minority part of both the political units in which the Provos operated, Ireland and the UK. From this narrow base the IRA could not fight its way to the conference table to negotiate independence like EOKA in Cyprus or one of the third-world liberation movements which it sometimes cited a models. The catch was that even though violence put a low ceiling on support the continued use of violence was the Provisional IRA's defining characteristic.

Internationally the IRA was still heavily dependent on the Noraid network which had been set up in the US and Canada in 1970, its functions set out under General Army Order no. 6. Noraid was a conservative, physical force grouping fronted by Michael Flannery who had been an IRA man since the '20s. Joe Cahill, who had himself rejoined the IRA in 1970 after resigning in 1965 in protest against the rundown of military activity, had promised Noraid to deliver 'a republic without socialist or communist ideas'. With this in mind two Noraid emissaries visited Ireland from 18 to 24 September 1971 to arrange with Cahill,

O'Conaill and MacStiofain for the financing of arms purchases in Europe. In their report they were highly critical of what they saw as the insufficient emphasis on military activity amongst the Provisionals. They were, they wrote,

> Very impressed by the units we met in Belfast and Lurgan. To us they seemed to be doing a great job for the amount of equipment they had. However we got the impression from the people we met there that at the official level not enough was being done for the men doing the fighting. By that I mean they never seem to have money for training or otherwise, they seem to be disturbed by the press statements made at the Dublin level, statements and counter-statements. Their views are shared by us.

The message was to get on with the fighting and forgo any political frills that might confuse the volunteers. With many of the Provo founding fathers, Noraid was pushing at an open door. These were veterans unwilling to question their massive investment of youth and freedom in previous campaigns, fearful of communism polluting their austere Celtic chiliasm. For these old soldiers leaving retirement, like Cinncinnatus returning from his plough to the aid of the republic, the natural reaction to nagging doubt or subtle argument was to 'blatter on regardless' or even, in the Micawberish words of Jimmy Steele, to 'kill someone and let the enemy reorganise us.'

On a tactical level they remembered that southern co-operation had given their organisation its lift-off and in the future they foresaw that something better than a total clamp-down was needed if it was to remain airborne. Despite the Green Book's strictures that 'The leadership of the IRA is the lawful government of the Irish Republic' and 'all other parliaments or assemblies claiming the right to speak for and to pass laws on behalf of the Irish people are illegal assemblies, puppet governments of a foreign power, and willing tools of an occupying force', the practical attitude to the southern authorities was one of 'live and let live'. The south was needed as a launching pad for military operations and a tolerably safe haven for men on the run. Not only was military activity in the south banned under General Army Order no. 8 but political work was confined to support for the northern IRA. The relationship between some of the leadership and their contacts within Garda Special Branch was still more pragmatic, especially when it came to dealing with rival republican groups who might cause trouble in the south, endangering IRA arms dumps and operations along the border.

In theory the breaking point in the pre-split IRA may well have been the decision of first the Army Council and then the Sinn Fein ard fheis (annual conference) to consider participation in the southern parliament. When it came to recruitment the important thing was discontent at the quality and quantity of defence given to the Catholic ghettos against the loyalist backlash of 1969 and the early '70s, and the efforts of the authorities to find a military and security solution to the unrest.

The generation which was to fill the prisons and the republican plots in the coming decade, and some of whom were to make up the next wave of republican leadership, had for their formative experiences internment, pogrom, bombing and interrogation. Their considered reflection was carried out in prison and, if they were to make an impact on the movement, freedom brought them straight back into the hurly-burly of day-to-day conflict with the state. They were badly housed and frequently in the second or third generation of unemployment or broken employment. They came from tight-knit communities where the dole queues held 25 per cent or 30 per cent of the working population. In Catholic areas of west Belfast it would rise to 40 per cent by 1978.[3] They were the raw ingredients of social unrest for any society.

In Ulster (where family memories stretched back to internment, imprisonment, discrimination and harassment over several generations), the IRA was the ready-made conduit for the accumulated ill-feeling of the community. By the ending of the ceasefire in 1972 many young men had themselves been lifted and beaten by the police: Bloody Sunday or the loyalist invasion of the Lower Falls or the experience of being forced out of a mixed area, or workplace harassment or the violent death of a friend or relative were the landmarks of many lives. This suffering was put down to the British presence and the irreformable functions of a sectarian state to which force was the only response.

Many were already veterans. The future hunger striker Pat McGeown was born in 1956. He had been on the barricades of the Falls Road at the age of ten and a member of the IRA's junior wing, Fianna Eireann, at thirteen. At fifteen he had seen his first dead body, that of fellow Fianna boy Gerard McAuley (15) who was shot dead as loyalists attacked the Catholic Clonard Street area. Pat's father Joseph at first thought that young McAuley's body was his son's because they had both been similarly dressed.

From this background Pat McGeown was soon involved in the Belfast City centre bombing campaign and was briefly imprisoned in the Republic for explosives offences before his fifteenth year was out. At sixteen he was interned, and shortly after his release in 1975 was again imprisoned for his part in the bombing of the Europa hotel, not to be freed, after one escape attempt, a hunger strike and several years on the blanket, until 1985. A quiet, slightly built and intelligent man, he describes his path into the IRA as follows:

> You had an influx of British troops onto the streets. You also had the pogroms in 1969, and therefore you had a very violent situation. Probably one of the deciding factors would have been constant harassment of British troops at that time on the streets. It generally created an atmosphere of violence and the desire to fight back and not to accept that type of state.
>
> ... Any nationalist youth at that period could have taken the same decision and most of them did. Then you had the sort of large scale street disturbances which in themselves were probably an indication of just how strong that type of feeling was.
>
> ... If you're talking about the complexity of the problem that probably took maybe ten or fifteen years to actually work out. Initially it's responsive, as most outbursts like that are in any country ... It was a feeling that something needed to be done, and probably it would be true to say there was a protest, rather than actually a desire to solve a problem, because you weren't consciously aware of what the problem was.
>
> ... The environment to some degree produces you and

produces your attitudes. In the case of people who are involved in the IRA, obviously that type of repressive environment that they lived under pushed them further into the movement, or pushed them further in their desire to fight back.[4]

For others the landmarks were different. Gerry Adams recalls the Divis Street riots, sparked by hard-line loyalist leader Ian Paisley's desire to remove an Irish flag from a republican election headquarters; for Martin McGuinness it was Bloody Sunday; Bobby Sands was intimidated out of first his job and then his home and wrote 'it is repression that creates the revolutionary spirit of freedom'.

The impulse to action reached beyond the shores of Northern Ireland. Brendan McFarlane returned to his native Ardoyne in 1970, dropping out of the North Wales St Vincent de Paul seminary where he was training for the mission-field, to join the IRA. Brighton bomber Pat Magee left his parents in England to live in the dismal medium rise barracks of Unity Flats when the troubles broke in 1969. In England there was heavy and successful pressure from within the Irish community for mainland bombings to bring the conflict home to Britain. In Dublin the stream of refugees from the beleaguered Catholic ghettos of the north heightened feeling to the point where a mob burned down the British embassy.

The backdrop was the biggest forced movement of population anywhere in Europe since World War II, intimidation between the two communities and steady pressure from the security forces on areas where they believed the IRA to be strong. Beyond this, inner-city decay drove urban populations to the new suburban ghettos and ate into stable inner-city communities.

Provo volunteers were plentiful. Young, untrained, and without a stake in society, they were motivated by bitterness and ready for anything. As Pat McGeown explained, 'you didn't volunteer for a specific job. It's responsive and you do what needs to be done . . . It would involve a certain amount of technical training, but the will to be involved would be something which initially you volunteer as . . . You don't need to go outside your own area, you don't need to go outside a house to make a bomb. It's a fairly straightforward technical sort of subject.'

The encyclopedias in the public library, Dupont's commercial *Blaster's Handbook* and even the Ladybird children's physics primer *Bulbs, Batteries and Magnets,* were plundered for information on explosives and circuitry. Outside the self-contained border areas around South Armagh most of the donkey work of preparing bombs was carried out by young volunteers without experience of previous campaigns, youngsters sketchily trained in back rooms by people who knew little more than themselves. In this period the lethal expertise which was to make the IRA Europe's most effective terrorist force was bought in the blood of its most enthusiastic members.

The first major accident occurred on May 28 1972 when four volunteers of the Lower Falls D Company, the Dogs as they called themselves, and two civilians were blown to bits as a bomb being prepared for the city centre exploded prematurely. Three of the IRA men (Martin Engelen, Joseph Fitzsimmons and Jackie McIlhone) were under twenty-one and the incident sent a genuine wave of revulsion through the area.

As the year wore on the toll of atrocities from both the IRA and the loyalists mounted. Two days after the ceasefire broke (11 July) a Catholic widow in North Belfast's religiously mixed Oldpark area was raped by the masked gunmen who shot her handicapped son. A day later a Catholic member of the locally raised Ulster Defence Regiment of the British army was tortured, branded, stabbed and shot dead by loyalists in East Belfast. Here were further stark reminders that Catholics on the interface were still caught like fish in a bowl for the loyalist murder gangs and that toeing the state line was not necessarily any protection.

The IRA was itself gearing up for an even more ferocious campaign which opened the loyalist marching season with the murder of eight soldiers and a policeman. On 21 July came the Bloody Friday bombing of Belfast city centre when television pictures of the scattered remains of the nine casualties being bundled into plastic bags by stunned policemen were beamed worldwide. In that single month a total of thirty-six people, nineteen Catholics and seventeen Protestants, were murdered across the province.

The crimes were often planned behind the barricades of the republican and loyalist 'no-go areas'. On 31 July the British army's Operation Motorman moved in force to dismantle them, sending tanks and armoured cars into the small streets of Bogside and Belfast in preparation for the first of many political initiatives designed to fill the constitutional vacuum created by the fall of Stormont. As Motorman rolled on three bombs ripped apart the tiny south Derry village of Claudy, killing nine people, one of them a nine-year-old girl.

The political initiative that emerged aimed to isolate the IRA and split the unionists. Instead it brought loyalism to the fore as the main unconstitutional force in the province. Eager to copper-fasten the co-operation of the south in the expensive[5] and unpopular business of securing the border and to build up a wedge of moderate, middle-class unionists and nationalists to isolate the extremists in both camps, the British government proposed a power-sharing administration with an 'Irish Dimension.'

Hammered out at meetings in Munich, Belfast, London and Sunningdale, the proposal was for the Catholic SDLP to share cabinet power with the Unionists. The Republic would have its say through an Anglo-Irish Conference. Elections were to be conducted by single-transferable vote, a system designed to blur the existing sectarian monoliths by allowing a vote by preference. It was calculated that hardline Unionists led by the posturing figures of William Craig and Dr Ian Paisley, who had bought his degree in America, could be isolated as the pragmatic Brian Faulkner built a consensus for change in the Protestant community. The IRA, having refused to be enticed into politics, could be dealt with by security means, showing Unionist doubters that something was being done and leaving the field clear for the SDLP to secure its lead in the nationalist camp. A border referendum would even remove the constitutional issue from the coming elections.

This beguiling strategy came closest to success with the nationalists. Even before the power-sharing executive was in existence Jack Lynch's southern government took a tougher line on militant republicanism. In Dublin emergency laws were used to close down the Sinn Fein offices in Kevin Street and a premises used as a billet for men on the run in Blessington Street. In the coming months leading Sinn Fein member Maire Drumm was jailed for a speech she had made in Dundalk and Chief of Staff Sean Mac Stiofain got six months for IRA membership. Other aspects of security co-operation, notably the exchange of intelligence, followed apace.

In the border poll a massive 57 per cent of the northern electorate (591,820) people) voted to remain in the UK whilst only 6,463 voted to leave it. Despite its face-saving advice to boycott the poll, the result underlined the inadequacy of the IRA's base as a would-be army of national liberation. Its isolation was confirmed when, in the council elections of May 1973, the SDLP was established as the largest Catholic political entity in the history of the state.

The loyalist nut proved harder to crack. The unionist monolith did indeed split but the rebels carried far more weight than expected. Craig was elected chairman of a group commanding the support of 43 of the 52 Unionist constituency parties and was feted as 'the leader' at a series of fascist type 'Vanguard' political rallies across the province. He warned that unionist resistance could go 'as far as killing'. In one of the most successful terrorist operations of the troubles, loyalist car bombs in Dublin killed two and injured eighty as the Dail debated the controversial anti-terrorist Offences Against the State Act in December 1972. The bill, which looked shaky, passed by a massive seventy votes to twenty-eight as the news of the carnage emerged and, the next week, the loyalists followed up with a car bomb in the border town of Cavan which killed two.

In the North, too, the loyalist murder gangs were active. Unlike the IRA, who concentrated for the most part on uniformed members of the British forces, they had no easily identifiable target. As their discipline and military intelligence was insufficient to act against the Provisionals, their traditional target was the ordinary Catholic community or, in the case of Senator Paddy Wilson who was murdered in June 1973, its political representatives. The numbers killed by the various groups, mainly the outlawed Ulster Volunteer Force and the Ulster Freedom Fighters (a *nom de guerre* for the legal Ulster Defence Association), were 25 in the years up to 1972, 103 in 1972, 80 in

1973, 94 in 1975 and 11 in 1978. In almost every case the number was lower than the kill count of the republicans[6] but the random nature of the loyalist violence and the torture and mutilation with which it was frequently associated struck a special terror into the heart of the Catholic community. The IRA was often the beneficiary of this fear.

The campaign of death was only one component of the loyalist resistance. After attending talks with southern Prime Minister Liam Cosgrave in January 1974 the head of the northern power-sharing executive, Brian Faulkner, was forced to resign as leader of the Unionist Party, handing over the mantle to his harder-line agriculture minister Harry West. In the Westminster elections the next month the breakaway UUUC, which included West's Unionist Party, swept the boards, taking every Northern Ireland seat except West Belfast which was held by the SDLP's Gerry Fitt. In the same election Labour defeated the Conservatives in Britain. The vacillating figure of Merlyn Rees replaced Francis Pym as Secretary of State amidst an atmosphere of increasing funk at the prospect of massive loyalist resistance. Attempts by Cosgrave to calm loyalists with Dail assurances that he accepted that Northern Ireland was in fact part of the UK were ignored. Instead in May a new loyalist body, the Ulster Workers Council, called a strike which brought down the power-sharing executive.

Openly backed by paramilitary muscle, accompanied by UVF bombs which killed thirty-one in the south and a string of sectarian assassinations in the north, the UWC stoppage represented a remarkable and uneasy fusion of paramilitary, political and industrial power which severely dented the authority of both the trade union movement and the state. At the end of it unionist grandees who had encouraged the whole process by nods and winks were able to distance themselves from the outrages of the rougher elements and reap the doubtful political rewards. 'The question you should ask them is how they are always able to walk off and leave everyone in the shit' was the comment of UDA leader John McMichael.[7] In the last analysis the stoppage rested on control of the power stations which were unconnected to either the British or Irish electricity grids and where the workforce were prepared to remove vital components if the army moved in to ensure the supply.

It left behind it a renewed political vacuum in which the coming man of the SDLP, John Hume, retreated to ground once occupied by the old Nationalist Party, saying there was no use in talking to the British authorities as the Secretary of State, Rees, had lost all credibility. After it, the UUUC got ten of the Northern Ireland seats. A weakened Fitt held West Belfast and militant nationalism, in the shape of former IRA man Frank Maguire, made a gain in the key marginal of Fermanagh-South Tyrone.

The search was on for a breathing space. Another ceasefire with an IRA weakened by security successes would be just the thing to give the constitutional convention which was hastily announced a chance of success and the government some semblance of authority. In security terms the years 1972-5 were ones of steady success against a politically isolated IRA, with the British army moving over to be replaced as the 'cutting edge' of the state policy by a revamped RUC.

At an early stage it was realised that the IRA's healthy state after the internment swoops had exposed a massive failure of intelligence. Little information of any kind was available on the loyalist paramilitaries and what there was on the IRA was unreliable. Worse, the IRA had been forewarned of the swoops by a serving paratrooper, Peter McMullan, who was related to two strong republican families, the Loughrans and the Enrights. The army and secret service set about taking the RUC in hand and building up dossiers on the IRA's new recruits, hard intelligence which would not rely on the accumulated suspicions of the '50s but on observation and interrogation of the working-class population.

This process was politically disastrous but in purely military terms it enabled the security forces to keep track of their opponents in a way which had not before been possible. The changes were set in motion at a meeting between senior MI5 and MI6 officers and their RUC counterparts in April 1971. The effects surfaced from early 1972 when a senior Ministry of Defence civilian was sent to Northern Ireland to review intelligence needs and a senior policy officer was installed in the army's Thiepval barracks headquarters. There he liaised with the military and Craig Smellie's secret service contingent who had been sent in to beef up the intelligence establishment which had consisted of two men: a captain and a sergeant.

Army-police conferences were held at all levels of command throughout the coming years and, in 1972 alone, there were a total of eight Special Branch bull sessions in New Scotland Yard attended by an Assistant Chief Constable, a chief Superintendent, a Superintendent, two Detective Sergeants and a Detective Constable. A system of Inter Service Intelligence Committees was also established to ensure that the lessons learned in colonial trouble-spots like Kenya, Malaya, Cyprus and Aden could be put to use.

The hard information was initially built up by the army and the secret service. The special forces SAS, under the command of Captain Julian Ball, had, at its own insistence, been active since 1969, but was officially described as a 'Survey Troop' of the Royal Engineers until its presence was officially announced by Prime Minister Harold Wilson on 7 January 1976. In urban areas it operated Military Reconnaissance Forces based on the lines of the 'counter' or 'pseudo' gangs used against the Mau-Mau in Kenya. These groups of up to ten 'turned' IRA prisoners fulfilled a variety of tasks, from driving around republican areas fingering their former comrades to engaging in gun battles with the real IRA.[8]

Probably the most celebrated MRF operation was the bogus Four Square Laundry which literally took in the dirty washing of republican West Belfast, gathering low-level intelligence on the rounds and analysing clothes for forensic traces. The scam was blown by a 'turned' IRA man to his former comrades who riddled the Four Square van as it passed through Twinbrook in an operation which gave local IRA leader Bobby Sands his nickname 'Sass'.

The SAS also filled many of the top posts in military intelligence and operated undercover south of the border in competition to MI6, who officially have overall control of intelligence gathering in the Republic. There they kidnapped a number of republicans, the last of whom was future hunger striker Sean McKenna in 1976, and dumped them across the border for arrest by the RUC. There is at least one well attested case of the actual murder of an IRA man, John Francis Green, the OC of the 2nd Battalion of the North Armagh Brigade on 19 January 1975, in the Republic. The undercover SAS soldier responsible, Captain Robert Nairac, was himself later murdered by the IRA and was posthumously awarded the George Cross in 1979. However the informer who betrayed Green's hideout to the British, veteran republican George Poyntz, lived on to chair the Co. Monaghan Sinn Féin cumann (branch) named after Green despite having worked for the British for twenty years.

Other 'dirty tricks' included the doctoring of IRA explosives to cause 'own goals' in which IRA members or sympathisers would be killed when bombs exploded prematurely.

'In-depth interrogation', amounting to 'inhuman and degrading treatment', was initially taught to army and RUC officers in the English intelligence centre at Maresfield in Sussex for use on suspects in Northern Ireland. It featured the so-called 'five techniques' of hooding, deprivation of sleep, restricted diet, sensory deprivation and forcing the subject to stand against a wall supported by his fingers; it was capable of bringing about a mental and physical breakdown, especially when combined with beating or blows from an unseen source. By 1974 the RUC was participating in army interrogation using these and other stringent techniques in Palace Barracks Holywood. Later they became totally a police preserve and were conducted in Omagh, Gough Barracks in Armagh and Castlereagh holding centre in East Belfast.[9]

Hand in hand with these methods, most of which came scandalously to light in a report by Amnesty International and the findings of the European Court of Human Rights, went the relatively pedestrian but arguably more effective business of low level intelligence gathering. Based on the recommendations of the civilian MOD scientist each squaddie was tied into the intelligence apparatus, reporting back after every patrol on movements and new faces in his area and trained to spot suspects from photographic 'bingo cards' which were regularly updated from computer files by intelligence personnel. Contacts with local people were cultivated through 'civil representatives' who were empowered to settle small claims for damage to property arising from the troubles. The objective was to recruit 'an informant' of however low a level 'in every street'.

The raw data was refined by a system of mass screening of the population, pulling in new faces and suspected 'players' for a few hours, house searches[10] and vehicle check points. Intelligence gathered in this way could be used as the basis of three- and seven-day detention orders enabling prolonged 'in depth' interrogation at one of the holding centres, which in turn could result in internment orders. Intelligence records were filed by date of birth and car registration number. By its very nature the computer record system required frequent accesses to keep it clean and squaddies were encouraged to ring up and check out any local people they met through it. As a more accurate picture of IRA organisation and movements was built up the way was being prepared for Ulsterisation, a handover to the increasingly streamlined RUC and a replacement of internment with conviction in the courts.

The final stage of what the Provisionals were to dub the 'H-Block Conveyer Belt' was set in place by the Diplock report of 1972.[11] Designed to overcome the intimidation of witnesses (one, Sidney Agnew, had actually been shot dead in October 1971, 20 minutes after he agreed to testify against an IRA man who had hi-jacked and burned a bus) and jurors. The report's main recommendations were the replacement of the jury with trial by a single judge sitting alone for 'scheduled offences' and increased scope to admit confessions obtained in the holding centres.

Under the 'Judges' Rules' safeguards, it had to be established that a confession was 'voluntary in the sense that it had not been obtained by fear of prejudice or hope of advantage, exercised or held out by a person in authority or by oppression.' Lord Diplock effectively diluted this test to a requirement that statements had been given without the use or threat of physical violence. When, in the NI (Emergency Provisions) Act of 1973, Diplock's recommendations reached the statute book this section was further watered down to a simple requirement that the accused had not been subjected to torture or inhuman or degrading treatment. This new legislation came on stream in tandcm with the beginnings of police primacy as the police liaison officer was moved out of Thiepval barracks to RUC headquarters in Knock in 1974.

Despite the collapse of the power sharing executive and the bitterness built up by the years of interrogation, screening and house searches, the authorities were confident that they had a system which was capable of producing intelligence, turning it into evidence acceptable to the courts and putting the IRA behind bars in quantity. All that remained was to remove their political legitimacy and to end the campaign which was at this time, with a series of devastating bombs in London and the Midlands, threatening the security of Britain itself. The first part of this objective was put in train in the Gardiner Report which was to remove special category status.

It was at this stage that five Protestant churchmen[12] entered the picture to hold an extraordinary series of secret meetings with the IRA leadership, the first of which was in Smyth's Village Hotel in Feakle, Co. Clare.

As in the previous truce the main figure pushing the negotiations was Daithi O'Conaill, the best political brain of the older generation of Provo leaders. His high profile opposition to Mac Stiofain (at one time he and Ruadhri O'Bradaigh had considered assassinating 'Mad Jack') and an internal court of inquiry following a highly publicised arms buying expedition to the continent in the company of society girl turned IRA woman Maria Maguire had prevented him from becoming Chief of Staff for some time. But by now he had his head. MacStiofain had dropped out of the IRA the previous January after being busted to the ranks when he abandoned a hunger strike. O'Conaill also had powerful allies in the shape of Ruadhri O'Bradaigh, the Sinn Féin President, and the influential Sinn Féin Vice-President Maire Drumm in whose home the Feakle process had been set in motion through a meeting with Canon William Arlow.

Besides O'Conaill and O'Bradaigh the Provisional negotiators included Belfast Organiser Seamus Loughran, Billy McKee and three recent jailbreakers, Kevin Mallon, Seamus Twomey and J. B. O'Hagan from Lurgan.

Twomey, who had been a close ally of MacStiofain and Chief of Staff since Joe Cahill's arrest with the *Claudia* arms shipment the previous March until his imprisonment, was the only one of the delegation firmly opposed to the idea of a ceasefire. The archetypal 'IRA godfather' of the popular press, he had been Belfast OC during the first ceasefire and was the man blamed for its breakdown by the British.

Mallon was a veteran Tyrone republican with a record going

back to the killing of RUC Sergeant Ovens in 1958. He had made two jailbreaks in as many years. At the time he was the subject of a major manhunt in Britain on suspicion of running the ongoing mainland bombing campaign, which was one of the main factors pressurising the British to talk to the IRA in the first place. But despite his fearsome reputation and formidable record, Mallon was a man of considerable political *nous*. He was prepared to give O'Conaill's line a chance, seeing the need to broaden the Provos' political base more clearly than most IRA men of his generation.

In the event the Feakle talks broke up early when the IRA negotiators, all of them on the run, were tipped off about an impending Garda Special Branch raid on the hotel. Arlow, who had made the contacts with the British authorities and the republicans, felt betrayed. 'I am very critical of the Irish government because they knew what was afoot at Feakle and yet they sent in the security men to interrupt what was a peace conference. If the peace conference had continued I think something well worth while would have come out of it, much more important than what we did get out of it.'[13]

However the churchmen did succeed in putting proposals to the Provisionals which had been drawn up in co-operation with the permanent secretary to the Northern Ireland Office, Sir Frank Cooper. They also set in motion a process which led to a second ceasefire, achieving the British objective of winning a respite from the mainland bombing and giving the republicans the breathing space they needed to regroup.

NOTES

1. First published in *Republican News*, 16 December 1978. The article is intended as a representative life story of a blanket man rather than a scrupulous autobiography. It differs in several specifics from Sands' own life story.

2. J. Whale, 'Modern Guerrilla Movements', in *Community Forum III*. Quoted in P. Buckland's *A History of Northern Ireland*, Gill and Macmillan 1981.

3. Belfast Housing Survey, Northern Ireland Housing Executive 1978.

4. I am indebted for the transcript of this interview, part of which was broadcast in 1986, to Television South and for further background to Pat McGeown.

5. The extra costs associated with the Northern troubles between 1969 and 1976 was £IR126 million, and set on a steeply rising trend. Source 'The Cost of Violence arising from the Northern Ireland Crises since 1969', a document produced for the New Ireland Forum of 1984.

6. The equivalent figures are 118, 255, 128, 98, 102 and 142, do.

7. Interview with the author.

8. On at least one occasion two MRF squads fired on each other in West Belfast's built up Springfield Road, cf *Who Dares Wins* by Tony Geraghty, Fontana 1980. A series of three articles by Duncan Campbell, published by *New Statesman* under the title 'The Dirty War' from 4 May to 18 May 1984 is also a valuable source on British special forces' undercover activities, particularly in Co. Armagh, in the '70s. According to them, Campbell Smellie left his posting as Secret Service controller in Lisburn to become MI6 head of station in Athens in 1975. *Britain's Military Strategy in Ireland: The Kitson Experiment* by Roger Fallgot (Zed/Brandon 1983) is another interesting, if paranoid, source on British Intelligence methods in Northern Ireland whilst Desmond Hamill's *Pig in the Middle* (Methuen 1985) is a more sympathetic account of the British army's role.

9. The definitive account is Peter Taylor's *Beating the Terrorists?*, Penguin 1980.

10. Figures for these were released showing a peak in 1974. They were: 1970: 3,107; 1971: 17,262; 1972: 36,617; 1973: 74,556; 1974: 74,914; 1975: 30,002; 1976: 34,919; after which they tailed off to 4,045 in 1982 (W. D. Flackes *Northern Ireland a Political Directory*, Ariel Books 1983).

11. Full title *Report of the Commission to consider legal procedures to deal with terrorist activities in Northern Ireland* (Cmnd 5185, Dec 1972) HMSO.

12. There were Dr Arthur Butler, Church of Ireland Bishop of Down and Connor; Dr Jack Weir, Clerk of the Presbyterian General Assembly; Rev. Eric Gallagher, former president of the Methodist Church in Ireland; Rev. Ralph Baxter and Rev. William Arlow, respectively secretary and assistant secretary of the (Protestant) Irish Council of Churches; Dr Harold Morton, secretary of the British Council of Churches; Right Rev. Arthur McArthur, moderator of the English United Reformed Church and Stanley Worrall, headmaster of Methodist College Belfast and chairman of the New Ulster Movement.

13. Interview with the author, August 1986.

2

Under Army Organisers at all Levels

'The most important aspect of any organisation, party, group or army is security. Security binds all people within the organisation together in confidence like a chain. So the most important thing is security, that means YOU DON'T TALK IN PUBLIC OR IN PRIVATE PLACES. YOU DON'T TELL YOUR FAMILY, FRIENDS, GIRLFRIENDS OR WORKMATES THAT YOU ARE A MEMBER OF THE IRA. DON'T EXPRESS VIEWS ABOUT MILITARY MATTERS. IN OTHER WORDS YOU SAY NOTHING to any person. Don't be seen in public marches, demonstrations or protests. Don't be seen in the company of known republicans, don't frequent known republican haunts'

The Green Book (IRA Training Manual)

The light burned bright was day now night
Or was night turned to day?
Forty hours, I'd sweated showers
In panic stricken fray.
This waiting game was greatest strain
And though I knew their ploy,
It did not ease nor did appease
But helped more to destroy.

Bobby Sands (*The Crime of Castlereagh*)

In retrospect the 1975 truce negotiations can be seen as the moment at which the O'Conaill/O'Bradaigh axis reached the peak of its influence.

Gerry Adams, who was to be the chief beneficiary of its slow demise, had been re-interned and made no public judgment for a decade. 'When the struggle was limited to armed struggle', he said, 'the prolongation of the truce meant that there was no struggle at all. There was nothing but confusion, frustration and demoralisation, arising directly from what I call spectator politics.'[1]

The comments, pointing up the narrowness of the Provisionals' base and the poverty of their politics, were of a piece with the barrage of criticism which he launched from his vantage point in cage 11 of Long Kesh through a series of articles in *Republican News* written under the house name 'Brownie'.

Preaching a 'complete fusing of military and political strategy',[2] 'Brownie' advocated a tight and secret IRA both directing and shielded by a socially involved movement from which it would in the end be indistinguishable:

> If we have only a local Unit in an area, the Brit wins by isolating or removing that unit from the people. If that Unit is part of an aggressive Republican or people's structure (Local People's Councils), the Brit must remove everyone connected, from schoolchildren to customers in the co-ops, from paper sellers to street committees, before he can defeat us. Immersed in that structure, as part of the Alternative, Republicanism can't be isolated and will never be defeated.

The IRA and its political fringe would not only tear apart the fabric of the existing administration and its social order; it would also build up its own alternative structures. If the ideas showed a familiarity with Guevara and Marighela's theories of guerilla bases, where the armed foci acted as rallying points for popular resistance, they also harked back to the first Dáil of January 1919, when Irish MPs elected to the British House of Commons constituted themselves as an Irish parliament and precipitated the War of Independence. Adams threw various ideas in the air, considering at one point a series of nationalist community councils which would pledge allegiance to a republican Dáil Uladh (Ulster Parliament),[3] creating the new society within the bowels of the old.

The whole strategy assumed a prolonged war in which support would be gradually built up, a far cry from the imminent 'year of victory' which was predicted annually by the leadership at that time. Although, at this early stage he presented his ideas as an extension of established policy, talking of 'making abstentionism work', the logic of the position was to exploit existing governmental structures in order to exhaust them. In the words of Guevara's *Guerrila Warfare*, which circulated in Long Kesh in a then current Penguin edition, 'People must see clearly the futility of maintaining a fight for social goals within the framework of civil debate.' The Provisionals were not only to create political vacuums but also to fill them, denying the SDLP a platform and gradually creating the support necessary to push through their policies after, or even before, a British withdrawal.

The truce showed that the movement still lacked the political weight and depth to exploit the opportunities created by the bombing campaign in Britain and the loyalist rebellion.

Canon Arlow, the pivotal churchman in the Feakle process, was in no doubt that the bombings were one of the major factors leading Merlyn Rees to talk to the republicans. Around 100 IRA explosions had occurred in Britain since 1973 and although several suspected units had been arrested, the signs were that the IRA had the capacity to continue the campaign. Shortly before the Feakle meeting O'Conaill himself had gone on television to threaten renewed attacks in Britain[4] and a few days later twenty-one were killed and 162 injured in the Birmingham pub bombings for which the IRA initially denied responsibility. As in the earlier Guildford coach atrocity the authorities arrested the wrong people, leaving the real Birmingham bomb team and the Guildford unit headed by Harry Duggan still at large. They were painfully aware that the threat still remained and, according to Arlow, the senior British officials with whom he discussed the ceasefire feared further bombs in the London underground, a threat which in fact materialised in April 1976.

The bombings became a source of pressure on the Provisionals no less than the British. The Birmingham detonations at the Mulberry Bush and Tavern in the Town were apparently an attempt by a loosely organised local IRA formation to close down the city's Rotunda shopping complex and the tax office. It went wrong due to the vagueness of the IRA telephone warning to a local paper and the failure of the police to evacuate the areas named in it.[5] However the atrocity was widely perceived as an indiscriminate attack on civilians, coming just four days after O'Conaill's televised threats to 'strike at economic, military and political targets'. It did much to undermine the already flagging IRA support. The Provisionals were therefore negotiating from a position of weakness, squeezed towards a ceasefire both by the security apparatus and their own supporters.

Arlow felt that in the post-Feakle talks the British negotiators, usually civil servants James Allan and Michael Oatley, adopted a devious and patronising attitude to the republicans whom they met (usually Jimmy and Maire Drumm and Frank Card) but were in the end outmanoeuvred by both the Provisionals and the UDA leaders who were eventually drawn into the talks. In fact Allan was a senior MI6 functionary and was, with MI5's Dennis Payne and NIO secretary John Bourn, one of the chief architects of 'Ulsterisation'.

Certainly the concessions on offer were substantial enough to have given the Provisionals a real political foothold and the grounds to claim a victory had they been at a stage where they could exploit it. There was a steady release of internees, promises were being made, and kept, that they would all be out by Christmas 1975. The Price sisters (who had bombed the Old Bailey and Scotland Yard in 1973) were transferred to Northern Ireland prisons after a long and ineffective campaign which had, a year earlier, claimed the life of hunger striker Michael Gaughan. More importantly a network of 'incident centres' were set up to monitor the truce and to avoid a repetition of the Lenadoon incident. Each of the centres was manned by Sinn Féin but paid for and equipped with telexes and hotlines to the Northern Ireland Office by the British. Senior members of the IRA were given effective immunity from arrest provided they were not caught in the commission of a crime. Assurances were also given of continued negotiation, troop withdrawal if the truce held, and a voice for the Provisionals in any political settlement, from which a total British withdrawal was not excluded.

The centres allowed the Provisionals to build up street credibility, giving them virtual control of their own areas and space in which to build support for further military advances. The talk of withdrawal was probably no more than a formal statement of the ongoing policy of Ulsterisation and of the fact that if violence subsided British troops would not be on the streets, yet this was the point on which the IRA chose to stick. According to Arlow, 'O'Conaill asked for it in writing, thinking that perhaps he himself could appear at Stormont and be handed a kind of agreement. I think when they realized that that wasn't on that was the beginning of the end.'[6]

As Adams was to imply, the truce failed because the Provisionals could not yet function without violence, and in fact the period of the truce and ceasefire was a particularly violent one. In South Armagh, for instance, little changed. The Newry incident centre closed a few days after opening and the local IRA, sometimes using the pseudonym South Armagh Republican Action Force, quickly became involved in sectarian tit-for-tat warfare with the UVF and UDA who took the opportunity provided by the truce to launch indiscriminate attacks on the Catholic population. The most notorious incident involving the SARAF came some months after the breakdown of the ceasefire in January 1976. In it five Protestant workmen were taken out of a minibus and shot dead while their single Catholic workmate was sent running down the street at Whitecross. During the ceasefire the South Armagh Provos committed several lesser atrocities, including the sectarian murder of three Protestants at Kileen and the attempted bombing of a pub in Bessbrook.

Even in Belfast the IRA remained active by reacting to the loyalist paramilitaries (who were frightened by the truce and wanted to break it) and, particularly from Ardoyne, waged a sectarian war in which civilians were the main targets. When the Bayardo Bar on the Loyalist Shankill Road was bombed in August 1976, the fleeing patrons were machine gunned as they ran for cover and five people died. Brendan McFarlane, given 25 years for his part in the crime, was later[7] to defend it as a political action on the grounds that the Bayardo was allegedly frequented by members of the UVF. A few months earlier, in April, another IRA bomb in the Mountainview Tavern had claimed similar casualties.

Parallel atrocities were carried out by the loyalists in a conscious attempt to break down the Provo-British accord and precipitate tougher security policies. On 21 July, for instance, a UVF unit which included a serving UDR sergeant, set up a bogus UDR roadblock at which they stopped a minibus carrying the Dublin based Miami Showband and planted a bomb which exploded prematurely, killing three band members and two of the eleven UVF men to die in action that year. These and a host of smaller incidents made the ceasefire period and its aftermath one of the most intense bursts of violence in the entire troubles, a period of indiscriminate but efficient murder in which an average of twenty-six people died violently each month, although the number of bombings and shootings in 1975 was the lowest in four years.

An additional source of conflict was provided by the presence of rival republican organisations. In 1974 the Officials split once more when their former Operations Officer Seamus Costello was expelled from the movement for 'factional activity' and went on to found the rival Irish Republican Socialist Party and People's Liberation Army (later Irish National Liberation Army). His organisation combined far-left rhetoric with a commitment to violence. It created an alternative focus for IRA men who, like Dominic McGlinchey in Co. Derry, were discontented with either the ceasefire or the politics of the movement as well as further reducing the IRA leadership's ability to control the level of violence. The Officials were also strongly challenging what they termed the 'Royal Ulster Provisionals' in their incident centre based community policing role. As Ruadhri O'Bradaigh was to put it on 4 November, 'Like communists all over the world, the Official IRA has tried to gain control of the streets.'

Part of that effort was a determined attempt to strangle the breakaway INLA at birth in a feud which claimed several lives, including that of the Official's very able Belfast Commander Billy McMillan. The Provisionals took advantage of the interregnum following the death of McMillan to unleash their frustrated volunteers on the rival group. They attacked in force on the night of 29 October 1975, swooping on the homes of supposed Official supporters, killing one and wounding 14. The next day the swoops continued and a six-year-old girl, Eileen Kelly, was shot dead in her hallway by Provisionals looking for her father. By the end of hostilities in November the Provos had killed eight supporters of the Officials and suffered two casualties themselves, one the manager of their incident centre on North Belfast's New Lodge Road and one the chairman of the Falls Taxi Association. Another Provisional IRA member, Andersonstown Sinn Féin organiser Paul Best, died in February 1976 whilst undergoing surgery for the removal of bullets.

The 'feud' or 'pogrom' ended with the Provisionals' declaration of a ceasefire following their second fatality on 13 November, just twenty-four hours after the British government announced that the incident centres would be closed. The pace of sectarian killings was also reduced as the Provisionals switched their military effort back onto the British and paramilitaries on all sides adjusted to this return to the status quo.

In fact the ceasefire had become a hollow affair and its official ending by the British followed a renewed bombing and assassination campaign in London by Duggan's unit, most of whose members were captured after a 'siege' in Balcombe Street near Regent's Park. The resumption of the 'mainland' campaign and the capture of what looked like all of those responsible, removed the British incentive to continue the ceasefire and was taken as evidence of the IRA's continuing inability to deliver peace.

The involvement of the Provisionals in the proxy sectarian war with the UDA and UVF and the attacks on the Officials made it impossible to reduce troop numbers as they wished as well as underlining their need to keep fighting in order to survive. The British forces were well aware of this latter point and were prepared to turn a blind eye as long as the violence could be kept to inter-republican feuding, at one point allowing a Provisional kidnap team to proceed on its way with an Official republican captive.[8]

Although the total effect of this activity against non-British forces and of the ceasefire generally was negative for the Provisionals, sewing bitterness and distrust in their home areas, it was not entirely so. The Incident Centres had given the organisation a taste for community politics and policing which was to be reflected in the future growth of advice centre activity. The associated policing activity and the attacks on loyalists and the Officials had all combined to increase Provisional control of their own areas, if not their popularity within them.

The shakiness of IRA support was illustrated in another tailback of the ceasefire period, the 'Peace Movement' which grew up after the tragic death of three children, Joanne, Andrew and John Maguire. The children, aged 8, 6, and 2, were crushed against iron railings in Andersonstown's Finaghy Road North by a hijacked Ford Cortina with a dead IRA volunteer behind the wheel. The dead man was Danny 'Dosser' Lennon, a nineteen-year-old ex-internee who was at one time regarded as Andersonstown's most wanted man. He and a companion, John Chillingworth, were moving a gun after an unsuccessful snipe at troops in nearby Glasmullan Camp. The weapon, which was faulty, was already stripped when army landrovers opened fire on them, killing the young IRA volunteer and sending the car careering into Anne Maguire and her four children. The incident was a particularly gruesome one even by Ulster standards, and in its aftermath the children's aunt Mairead Corrigan, her friend Betty Williams and *Irish Press* journalist Ciaran McKeown launched a peace movement which caught the popular mood of war weariness and attracted world wide support.

Despite the role of the British army in opening fire in a built-up area much of the emotion released was directed against the IRA campaign. Massive marches and rallies for peace were staged along the loyalist Shankill and nationalist Falls roads as well as at centres throughout the province. However the Peace People proved unable to devise a practical programme to sustain their movement once the initial enthusiasm had run its course or to weather the widespread public cynicism which followed the decision of Williams and Corrigan to keep the proceeds of the 1976 Nobel Peace Prize. Nevertheless the movement had served as reminder to the IRA that a potential opposition from within their own areas could arise at any time to swamp them and that that opposition would find an answering chord in loyalist areas as well as in the world at large. The Northern Ireland state might not, after all, be irreformable. A pool of goodwill existed for non-military solutions even if there was no consensus on what those solutions might be. Moreover, people in nationalist areas were clearly not prepared to play the role of passive supporters of the IRA in hope of better times to come.

Like the truce itself the episode had underscored the need for a fundamental military and political restructuring if the IRA was to survive long-term as a significant force in Irish politics.

In fact the IRA had, like the British, already used the truce period to begin a process which was to continue over the next several years.

On the international level two released prisoners, Joe Cahill and Paul Kavanagh,[9] were to play an important part in the attempt to widen the IRA's international resources, reducing dependence on the Noraid network and the parallel Irish organisations in Britain.

Kavanagh was sent for training to the Low Countries where a floating unit had acted as a backup to the British bombing campaign since the early '70s. He commuted regularly to Ireland. He later acted as the quartermaster for the mainland unit, helping to develop the existing network for the movement of weapons and men between the US, the continent and Britain, using Schipol airport and the ferry ports.

Cahill also travelled internationally, re-visiting Libya, where the resident Provo envoy Eddie O'Donnell had been running into problems since a visit by the loyalist UDA. Although O'Donnell and a number of other republicans from his native Monaghan had instigated the visit in 1974 in an ambitious attempt to draw the UDA, with their policy for an independent Ulster, into opposition to Britain, the end result had been to make Qathafi aware of the variety of opinions in Ireland and to reduce aid to the IRA in favour of official Libyan/Irish trade links. Following Cahill's June holiday in Tripoli, O'Donnell visited Belfast in September under the cover of a Libyan diplomat on a trade mission. There seems to have been a brief rapprochement with Qathafi and the growth of links to Al Fatah, the dominant PLO faction which had been out of favour with Qathafi since its participation in USA sponsored peace moves in the Middle East.

Following the April 1976 bombing of the London Ideal Home Exhibition in which eighty were injured, Qathafi's government, which had earlier assured a high-level Irish government delegation that 'no financial assistance should be given to men in Ireland to use violence in an attempt to unite the country', announced through the daily *Al Fajir Jadid* that 'we have sent bombs to the Irish revolutionaries so that Britain will pay the price for its past deeds'. A few weeks later Qathafi himself told the London *Daily Telegraph* that although he supported the independence of Ireland it was not possible to send weapons. In 1978 Yassar Arafat officially severed links with the IRA in anticipation of Irish government recognition of the PLO.

In the interim, however, the IRA did receive weapons from the Arab world and a number of IRA men were trained near Baddawi refugee camp in the Lebanon. Prior to Cahill's trip the

IRA armoury had consisted mainly of antiquated Thompson sub-machine guns, World War II M1 .30 Garand rifles, British made Lee Enfields in the border area, 'spitting dummy' US special forces 'grease guns' and Japanese made AR180 armalites. The reopening of links with the Middle East, where the Provos' heaviest artillery (a batch of RPG7 rocket launchers) had been acquired in 1973, created a source of supply for even more up-to-date weapons which fortuitously bore fruit shortly after the Mounties cracked a major Canadian IRA supply line in June 1975. In the period up to June 1977 a large number of Chinese SK series armalites were successfully landed at Dundalk to supplement the high quality M742 Remington Woodmaster sporting rifles which were beginning to trickle in in ones and twos from the rejigged US networks. However the vast potential of the Middle East was demonstrated in a massive seizure of weapons aboard the *MV Towerstream* on 3 December 1977.

The consignment had been supplied by Fatah in Lebanon and had been shipped on from Limassol in Cyprus, an island where the PLO and the IRA both had strong links, only to be intercepted at Antwerp by Belgian police acting on an Israeli tip-off. It amounted to six tons of ordnance, including Bren guns, Kalashnikov AK series rifles, submachine guns, 428 lbs of TNT, 400 lbs of plastic explosives, mortars, 26 RPG7 rocket launchers and ammunition of all types. It was enough to have supplied the IRA for several years, at a stroke giving them the 'heavy gear' they had lacked from the outset, extending their mortaring range from 1,200 metres to 3,000 metres and solving the problems for the manufacture of explosives posed by the outlawing of benzine as a constituent of fertiliser in the Republic and the removal from the market of a variety of commercial bleach in the north. Its seizure was less than crippling only because the IRA had simultaneously acquired a number of stolen US National Guard M60 sub-machine guns from organised crime sources and had, in October 1977, developed a new explosive mix, ANFO, which could be made up by 'cooking' Ammonium Nitrate based fertiliser and mixing the resulting solids with diesel oil and metal filings.

More serious than the actual loss of the weapons, estimated at £400,000, was the loss of credibility on the international arms market, where the IRA were henceforth expected to pay a premium price on supplies, and the loss of Seamus Twomey and Seamus McCollum who had set up the deal from an import agency in Dublin. When Twomey was arrested at Royal Terrace Dun Laoghaire, Gardai found in his home a re-organisation document ranging over the whole spectrum of IRA and Sinn Féin activity, reflecting the increasingly dominant analysis of the younger northerners of whom Gerry Adams was the leading figure.

Adams had been released from Cage 11 in Long Kesh, of which he was OC, in 1976, his imprisonment lengthened beyond the ending of internment by an eighteen month sentence for attempting to escape with Brendan 'Darkie' Hughes and Owen Coogan. His release coincided with the re-arrest of O'Conaill, who had already been transferred to political duties as the truce lurched into irrelevance, in the Republic and his jailing on IRA membership charges. Adams was soon given an opportunity to formalise the ideas developed in jail when he was put in charge of a commission with a brief to report to the republican movement's General Headquarters Staff on the future organisation of the movement. It was a copy of this commission's report which was captured by the Gardai in Twomey's flat.

Ideas associated with the commission had already been mooted at the June 1977 Bodenstown commemoration by Jimmy Drumm. The timing of the oration and the choice of Drumm to deliver it were calculated to give the new ideas maximum weight with traditional republicans. Bodenstown cemetery holds the remains of Irish republicanism's founding father, the eighteenth-century monarchist turned Jacobin Theobald Wolfe Tone. The annual gathering at Tone's graveside is a reunion of the republican faithful at which the movement's basic tenets would be re-affirmed in bad times and good. The instigator of the links with the Feakle clergy, Drumm was a popular and affable figure, as well as a symbol of continuity widely respected for his honesty and reliability. He had served more time in jail than any living republican, a circumstance which led his wife, the near legendary Maire Drumm who had been shot dead by loyalists as she lay in her hospital bed a year earlier, to tell chat show host Gay Byrne that the British prison system had relieved her of all worry about contraception. A confidant of old line leaders like Billy McKee and Frank Card he carried credentials of orthodoxy which were rightly considered unimpeachable by older republicans. In a word Drumm was 'sound' and his introduction of new concepts was likely to be taken as a seasoned recognition of the exigencies of the times. It was for this reason that he was chosen to administer the bitter pill, warning that 'the British government is not withdrawing from the six counties', that 'the isolation of socialist republicans around the armed struggle is dangerous' and stating roundly that 'We find that a successful war of liberation cannot be fought exclusively on the backs of the oppressed in the six counties, nor around the physical presence of the British army. Hatred and resentment of the army cannot sustain the war'. The republican movement, he implied, would move beyond the simplicities of force into political and community involvement and the word 'socialist' would no longer be taboo.

The reorganisation document[10] went further, putting into practice Adams' ideas on the fusion of political and military activity. The problem it addressed was the continuing isolation of the movement through its fall off in support, its failure to make a political impact and the inroads being made by the RUC interrogators.

Since 1976 the new three- and seven-day detention orders and the interrogation methods at Castlereagh and Gough barracks had cracked hundreds of IRA men, helping to push the north's prison population to 2,878 as Drumm spoke and reducing the loss of life due to terrorist activity between 1976 and 1977 from 221 to 55. The effects of the breaking of the volunteers were widespread because the IRA's existing brigade and battalion structure meant that an active member could know a great deal about the chain of command and identity of those responsible for operations in his own area. Despite the dearly bought experience and improved equipment of the IRA the problems of internal security and the shortcomings of the secret army's open structures were bringing it to its knees. Perhaps more seriously, the fear of betrayal through the Castlereagh confession machine was crippling morale in the ranks. As the IRA itself pointed out,[11] 'The old system also came close to identifying those responsible for different operations, for if a car was hijacked in, say, Turf Lodge, and used in a bombing expedition or such like, the British knew that the unit which carried out the expedition was one based in Turf Lodge. Then all they had to do was arrest all the known or suspected activists in that area, torture them, and eventually they would get a confession from at least one implicating the others.'

The solutions proposed in the document included a return to strict internal discipline, with the automatic suspension of any new volunteer found associating with known activists and the revamping of the education structure to allow the 'indoctrinating of the volunteers with the psychological strength to resist interrogation'. In practice this meant the isolation of the basic interrogation methods used by the British and the RUC and their description to volunteers together with reminders that while interrogation was limited to seven days, imprisonment was open ended and the punishment for informing was death. The beating handed out by interrogators, volunteers were reminded, was probably no worse than they might get in a dance hall. Silence was the best possible policy and the orders of interrogators to stand up or sit down should be resisted. In practice the same interrogation methods were adopted for use on suspected informers.

More wide-ranging changes were proposed in the IRA's structures. Its existing organisation was loosely based on that of the British army. There were three battalions in the Belfast Brigade area covering respectively Upper Falls, Lower Falls and the rest of the city. Another brigade existed in Derry City and there were units of organisation in Newry, North Antrim, North Armagh, South Armagh, South Fermanagh, North Fermanagh, South Down, Tyrone and West Fermanagh. The reorganisation left these old structures intact but reduced their significance to that of a 'civil and military administration' responsible for community policing and back-up work. The real cutting edge of the IRA was to be a series of four- to five-man cells organised by specialisation (e.g. intelligence, sniping, execution, explosives, robberies) and controlled by an OC co-ordinator on the brigade staff. Sinn Féin was to be an even more open form of organisation than the civil and military administration but would be placed 'under army organisers at all levels' and radicalised 'under army direction'. The role of Sinn Féin would be to gain 'the respect of the people which in turn leads to increased support for the cell' and to 'infiltrate other organisations to win support for, and sympathy to, the movement.'

The reorganisation did not go in all respects according to this blueprint. Some of the country areas, particularly South Armagh, went their own way, pointing out that the old arrangements worked well locally. A new structure, the Northern Ireland Command (NIC) was eventually created to co-ordinate the cells and the reorganisation first took place in Belfast where it temporarily paralysed IRA activity. Inevitably the close family and community ties in the areas where the IRA drew its support meant that absolute security was impossible and that news of who was involved in operations was often more widely known than the IRA wished. However the reorganisation did bring the IRA closer to the ideal of absolute security and severely limited the damage which even a well-placed informer could cause. By November 1978 a British Intelligence report[12] conceded that 'we know little of the detailed workings of the hierarchy in Dublin. In particular we have scant knowledge of how the logistic system works, nor do we know the extent to which older, apparently retired, republican leaders influence the movement.'

There can be little doubt that the reorganisation saved the day for the IRA, allowing it to survive for the long war which had replaced the 'year of victory' in republican thinking. Internally it strengthened the hand of those who had mapped out the new direction, giving them the weight to push through their policies in other areas and to take control. The shake up associated with the reorganisation also created endless opportunities for replacing old faces or shifting them sideways on grounds of security while the central control of arms and the slimmed down nature of the organisation made it possible successfully to 'box off' potential dissidents, making a split impracticable.

By the time the reorganisation had made its mark around mid

1978, the IRA was in good shape militarily. The Castlereagh machine still took its toll but the new structures and training had performed an effective damage limitation exercise. A pool of seasoned and experienced volunteers, those who had survived the mill of the early years, existed and there was no problem about recruiting in sufficient numbers for its slimmed down structures. Arms supply, while far from perfect, was diverse and sufficient to meet the needs of the campaign. The explosive problem had been solved by the discovery of ANFO and effective and little-known networks existed on the continent which produced occasional supplies of commercial gelignite, usually the Frangex Eversoft manufactured by Irish Industrial Explosives in Co. Meath.

Most of the technical innovations used in the IRA campaign up until 1986 had been made by this stage. The making of detonators from mercury fulminate had been perfected in response to an international system of crimp marking commercial detonators and a tightening up of supplies. Mortaring had advanced to the point where the IRA current Mk 9 shell, made from brewery gas canisters, was admitted by the British[13] to be as good as their own standard issue Howitzer shells. Pre-packed and easy to operate devices known to the British as 'Timing and Power Units' or TPUs and to republicans as 'box timers' had simplified bomb construction, reducing the possibility of human error.

Long delay timers, similar to those used in domestic video-recorders, had been acquired in Canada and used to plant three 'sleeper' bombs at Coleraine timed to go off during a Royal Jubilee visit there by Queen Elizabeth in August 1977. Radio controlled bombs based on McGregor 27 series equipment, normally used for the control of model aircraft, had also been used in the border areas since 1972 and the innovation of pulse coding the firing message to prevent premature detonation by British army 'sweeper' radio devices had by now been introduced. They were used to most spectacular effect in the murder of Lord Mountbatten, his grandson Nicholas and the Dowager Lady Brabourne and boatman Paul Maxwell aboard their pleasure cruiser off Co. Sligo on 27 August 1979. Indeed, the range of technical choice in bomb detonation devices available to the Provos far exceeded their operational needs. By 1979 the last real technical innovation, the adoption of a communal heating failsafe device known as the 'mercury tilt switch' as a movement activated detonating mechanism, had been made by the INLA who used it to assassinate Conservative Northern Ireland spokesman Airey Neave in the House of Commons car park.

Blast incendiaries had reached a state of the art stage by 1976 and the simple devices were used to great effect in a brief campaign towards the end of 1977, during a firemen's strike. Besides they provided two further grisly highlights of the campaign in the period up to 1980. The first came in a Saturday morning bomb blitz of the town centre of Ballymena on 9 October 1977. The incendiaries, which were made of sugar and flammable liquid, were planted in audio cassettes and duffle bags in boutiques and shops throughout the shopping area and at one stage eight fires raged in the centre of the mainly Protestant town, killing one woman. The IRA team who planted the devices came mainly from Bellaghy, Clady, Magherafelt and Portglenone and some of them suffered fearful injuries themselves when one of a further four devices went off in their Toyota car before they could be planted. The driver of the car was the future hunger striker Tom McIlwee who lost his right eye and in whose pocket the list of targets had been found. His front seat passenger was his brother Benedict, another future blanketman, and in the back seat Colm Scullion lost several toes while Sean McPeake suffered injuries that led to the amputation of his leg.

Blast incendiaries yet again hit the headlines when the IRA firebombed the La Mon House Hotel outside Belfast during a dog breeders meeting in February 1978. In what was said to be a premature detonation the napalm effect of the devices reduced many of the dozen casualties to charred remains identifiable only by dental records.

The campaign was settling into a lower gear for a longer haul than had previously been envisaged. Each pound of explosives was now causing an estimated £1,000 in damage and the number of people charged with terrorist type offences fell rapidly from the 1977 high of 1,380 to a low of 550 in 1980[14] thanks to the pressure on the Castlereagh system provided by Amnesty International and the March 1979 Bennett report on police procedures as well as the IRA's own improvements in its security. However the post reorganisation mood of military realism and effectiveness was not reflected at the political level.

The long war strategy demanded an imaginative leap from the O'Conaill/O'Bradaigh vision of a victorious IRA pushing the British into a corner and negotiating with them an orderly withdrawal. In the context of such a victory push, too much internal politicking was a dangerous thing and the granting of any kind of recognition to existing institutions of government was a surrender of principle which would serve to give them credibility. Once it was accepted that speedy military victory was not in sight, different tactics became appropriate in order to win support and make the best use of a situation which was likely to persist for some years.

These issues came up at the 1978 Sinn Féin ard fheis in which the younger northern leadership began to reap the political rewards of securing the future of the military campaign. Adams himself was appointed Vice-President when O'Conaill moved sideways to become joint general secretary. The international left, in the shape of Michael Pablo, the leader of the Trotskyist Fourth International, was introduced by foreign affairs director Richard Behal, one of the most radical of the old line leadership. Heated debates took place between the rising Belfast triumvirate of Gerry Adams, Danny Morrison and Tom Hartley on the one side and more traditionally minded delegates on the other.

The position of the northerners, increasingly described as 'the left', was not yet secure and on one significant issue, that of talks with grass roots loyalist organisations, they suffered a significant defeat at the hands of O'Conaill. The idea, tried before in O'Donnell's Libyan initiative and presaged by O'Conaill's welcome of the Ulster Workers Council strike, was of a piece with the traditional view of the IRA as the government of Ireland without further need for mandate and ready to negotiate from present strength with all interested parties. The position of the 'left', hammered out in the hard school of the Belfast ghettos, was that loyalism must be smashed and was neatly summed up by Hartley in the words, 'loyalism stands for the division of the Irish people, republicanism stands for the unity of the Irish people.' However the political push for a Sinn Féin which would extend its base rather than simply holding itself in readiness for negotiations in anticipation of an IRA victory was advanced by the passage of a motion which endorsed the contesting of local council elections in the south.

What might loosely be termed the 'Adams faction' was gambling that the political inertia of the North, intensified by the running sore of the IRA campaign, would remain until the conditions arose for a political advance.[15] In the meantime the IRA could claim a victory by virtue of its continued existence in the face of massive odds.

In this the new emerging leadership found an unlikely ally in the form of tough talking, pipe-smoking secretary of state Roy Mason who came to the province to succeed Rees in September 1975. Like the most traditionalist elements of the republican movement, Mason saw the Northern Ireland problem almost entirely in military terms. Apparently more at home with soldiers and businessmen than politicians, he concentrated on toughening security policies and attempting to make the government more popular by attracting inward investment like the De Lorean car company which for a time provided several thousand jobs in the West Belfast nationalist overspill estate of Twinbrook. A pugnacious performer given to appearing publicly in safari suits, he was much given to publicly throwing down the gauntlet to the IRA by predicting their imminent demise. He steered well clear of political initiatives throughout his three years in the province.

During his term there were a steady stream of plastic bullet deaths and other security force excesses to fuel nationalist resentment and his constant predictions that the IRA was 'reeling' or finished allowed the Provos to claim considerable kudos by continuing to function at all.

But at this stage the new policies of the Provisionals were still in waiting. Minor advances were made at the 1979 ard fheis with the addition of a 'social dimension' to the Eire Nua document but any kind of entry into politics was likely to be a long haul. And in the background another issue was emerging, one that was at the time thought likely to divert the main thrust of republican development into a side issue, that of the political status of IRA prisoners. The prisoners had, by 1979, heightened their protest to the point that they were refusing to wear prison uniform or slop out, staying naked in their cells 24 hours a day and rubbing their excrement up the walls. Yet their plight was attracting scant public support and the internal republican pressure to make it the organisation's main priority was widely perceived at army council level as a threat to the movement's survival.

NOTES

1. Bobby Sands Memorial Lecture, 5 May 1985.

2. 'The Republic A Reality' in *Republican News*, 29 November 1975.

3. Dail Uladh was one of the regional assemblies proposed under the Eire Nua (New Ireland) document first issued by Provisional Sinn Féin in 1971 and updated in 1972 and 1973. Later characterised by the Adams faction as a 'sop to loyalism', it provided for a federal Ireland in which each of the four historic Irish provinces of Ulster, Munster, Leinster and Connacht would have a regional parliament with some degree of autonomy. Dail Uladh would include in its jurisdiction not only the six counties included in the Northern Ireland state but also the historic Ulster counties of Donegal, Cavan and Monaghan which are at present in the Republic. Dail Uladh would thus have offered Ulster Protestants some degree of control over local affairs but with a reduced majority and with overall supervision from Dublin rather than Westminster. Eire Nua underlined the first generation of Provisional leadership's emphasis on constitutional 'fixes' and on decentralisation as well as their sensitivity to any suggestion of socialism epitomised by Seamus Twomey's legendary comment that 'At heart I am a socialist. I have been involved in setting up trades unions and so forth. But at the same time, I am a right winger.' To quote from Eire Nua itself, 'In the drafting of this programme our aim has been to outline a social system that would strike a balance between Western capitalism, with its poor and hungry amid plenty, on the right and Eastern Soviet state capitalism (or any of its variations) with its denial of human rights, on the left.' In fact Eire Nua was quite an influential document whose main provisions were rehashed by John Hume in 1978, when he pointed out that federalism had strong echoes of the US constitution.

4. 'Weekend World', 17 November 1974.

5. cf. Chris Mullin *Error of Judgement* (Chatto and Windus).

6. In fact he had already been handed the substance of what he wanted in an offer, transmitted at Feakle, that HM government would issue a statement in which it would reaffirm 'that it has no political or territorial interests in Ireland beyond its obligations to the citizens of Northern Ireland', guaranteeing 'to all its people a full participation in the life of the community, whatever the relationship of the Province to the EEC, the United Kingdom or the Republic of Ireland' and that 'contingent upon the maintenance of a declared ceasefire and upon effective policing, HM government will relieve the army as

quickly as possible of its internal security duties.' The IRA delegation turned the proposal down as a basis for peace.

7. In April 1986, in a Dutch court, when he was fighting an application from Britain that he be returned to Ireland to complete his sentence.

8. I am indebted for this anecdote to the hostage, Tommy Flanagan, who escaped from his captors on foot shortly after their car was stopped by a British army patrol.

9. Cahill was released from jail in the south in January 1975 following a heart attack. He had been serving five years for his part in an attempt, in 1973, to smuggle arms from Libya aboard the *MV Claudia*. Kavanagh, a veteran of the early '70s' Belfast bombing campaign, was released in 1976 after serving three years of a five-year sentence for an arms offence.

10. See Appendix 4.

11. IRA interview in *Magill*, August 1978.

12. The so-called 'Document 37' on 'Future Terrorist Trends' drawn up by Brigadier Jim Glover on 2 November 1978, captured by the IRA, leaked by them to the Press Association and published in full as an appendix to Sean Cronin's *Irish Nationalism* (Academy Press 1980).

13. See Lt Col. Derrick Patrick's *Fetch Felix: The Fight Against the Ulster Bombers 1976-77* (Hamish Hamilton 1981).

14. RUC *Chief Constable's Annual Report* 1985.

15. Adams told Geoff Bell of the British based *Socialist Challenge*: 'since 1975 the British government has been intensifying its efforts to split the republican movement from its base of support. The last eighteen months have shown that they have failed. The republican movement and Sinn Féin have survived and remain strong. This situation could continue for the foreseeable future unless the British people mobilise behind the demand for disengagement. Until that is done I believe we will have a continuation of the last ten years.'

3

Men Behind the Wire

> 'We are of the opinion that we are a microcosm of outside society and we perhaps believe that society can benefit, especially the political element, if they give attention to what is happening here and the relationship prevailing.'
>
> Statement by Republican and Loyalist prisoners, 1974[1]

Maire and Jimmy Drumm, two of the republicans who put most effort into the Feakle process, represented the Provisionals at a number of meetings with Northern Ireland Office officials. During the ceasefire they were given a preview of the new, enlightened, prison regime which was proposed as part of the rapprochement with the IRA.

The most hopeful sign was that standard remission was to be raised from 30% to 50%, something unheard of elsewhere in the UK or Ireland. The administration, concerned lest convicts stagnate 'like cabbages' in the bleak surroundings of the compounds, planned to extend educational and training facilities. As the new wings were completed the dreary Nissen huts at the Maze would become a thing of the past, but where they remained there would be a TV and cooker in every hut. The administration would recognise the prisoners' OCs, and would allow them weekly meetings with their UDA and UVF counterparts. A prisoners' welfare unit in Central Belfast's Rosemary Street would be funded to the tune of £40,000, and there would be another £10,000 in government aid to help with the cost of such facilities as the 'Long Kesh minibuses' which took prisoners' families to visit them.

Mrs Drumm nodded her way approvingly past the gift horses. The civil servants appeared surprised when she turned and warned them they were asking for trouble. Running ahead of the official account despite the troublesome cataracts in her eyes, she had extracted from the small print something that the functionaries dismissed as a minor and uncontentious detail. Prisoners in the new cellular accommodation of the H-Blocks would be required to wear prison uniform, the very point, Mrs Drumm insisted, 'that Billy McKee and the rest of them went on hunger strike for.' She went on: 'You think we are going for that? Let me tell you something: you can keep your 50 per cent, you can keep your engineering classes, because we will not accept that and we'll be on the streets, and I'll be at the head of them.'[2]

As she foresaw, the uniform provision signaled the ending of special category status. Confirmation came in a government statement on 5 November that, in line with the recommendations of the Gardiner Report, political status would not be available for crimes committed after 1 March 1976.[3] Increased remission was the glittering prize at the end of a 'criminalisation' process which would attempt to pour the IRA through Castlereagh and the Diplock courts into the normal penal system. Weeks later, on 5 April, Peter Dillon, the first of eighteen prison officers to be murdered as part of the IRA's response, died. His death sparked the suspicion from the authorities that the loyalists, equally angry at the threatened loss of inmate control in the jails, were prepared to give the IRA the names and addresses of prison officers.[4]

Maire Drumm did not survive to fulfil her prediction of leading massive street demonstrations against the changes but on 16 September, a month before her murder, the first firm evidence of the prisoners' rejection of the deal was evident. It was then that the first post-1 March offender, Ciaran Nugent, who had been sentenced two days earlier for hi-jacking, asked his surprised guards for a prison uniform only to remove it again during a visit by his mother. This time he told them 'if you want me to wear prison gear you will have to nail it to my back'. The refusal to get kitted out or to do any prison work was treated as a breach of rules to be handled by the normal disciplinary procedures, starting with the withdrawal of privileges.

As a result Nugent and those who came after him went without any clothes at all and, since they were not dressed, were not allowed to leave their cells for association with other prisoners. Visits were reduced from four a month to one, for which a blue denim prison uniform left lying in the cell must be worn, and letters were limited to one in and one out each month, with an additional letter each way for prisoners who refused, or did not have, visits. The protesters were also periodically subjected to three-day stretches on the disciplinary 'number one diet', which consisted of black tea, dry bread, potatoes and soup.

In practice it meant that the protesting prisoners, usually amounting to about half the Catholics and sometimes a number of the Protestants convicted in the Diplock courts, remained in their cells without a radio for twenty-four hours a day wrapped in a blanket, leaving only to wash, use the toilet or collect food and with only religious magazines and a bible to read. A day's remission was lost for each day spent in this state.

All the ingredients for the coming years of protest were already potentially present in these unpromising surroundings. The blanket itself became the symbol of the protest while the attempts of the prisoners to increase their contact with the outside would through smuggled communications or concealed crystal radio sets provided the impetus for the body searches and beatings which did so much to harden their resistance. The slops and the food were the only remaining elements in the protesting prisoners' environment; they too were to be incorporated as the dirty protest and, finally the hunger strike, unfolded.

Nevertheless it was possible for any prisoner at any time to ring the bell beside his cell door and to inform the authorities that he wanted to conform. He would then shorten his sentence by up to half as well as qualifying for facilities which were as good or better than those in most high security prisons in the world. He would have a radio in his cell, four visits a month, the opportunity to receive a weekly food parcel from the outside, the option of wearing his own clothes at some times in the day, access to a full modern gymnasium and playing pitches, access to the block library, a few pounds a week wages which could be spent in the prison shop and even the possibility of leave to visit his home for special occasions towards the end of his sentence. This regime was chosen by at least half the republican prisoners at most points in the protest and at times the blanketmen themselves discussed the prospect of ending their protest both for their own good and that of the movement.[5] The reasons why this softer option did not prevail with all prisoners are to be found in the potent traditions of protest with which the more dedicated IRA men sustained themselves through their imprisonment.

The first republican prison protesters, members of the Fenian

Brotherhood jailed from 1865 onwards following an abortive attempt at a rising, were closely attuned to the romantic movement and their ideology was heavily couched in the nineteenth-century idealism which remains as a tapering strand of Sinn Féin thinking until the present day. It was the Fenian leaders who made individual sacrifice and the use of force principles, rather than tactics, in republican thinking.

Swinging from conservatism to radicalism, often training in the very armies who were putting down the European revolution which at other times inspired them,[6] the Fenians showed a capability for individual sacrifice which, the former Fenian John Devoy wrote, 'is why the movement which missed the chance to show heroism in the battlefield and had no military victories to its account has exercised such a profound influence on the Irish people.' The sacrifices were largely made in the prisons of Britain and Australia. Many died or went insane after being kept in conditions of sensory deprivation or starved. The dominant image of the period was O'Donovan Rossa who was held with his hands shackled behind his back and forced to lap his food from the prison floor like a dog. The suffering of the Fenians brought out huge crowds in demonstrations in Ireland and became an international issue, bringing the prisoners far more support than their failed campaign ever enjoyed.

The pattern was to become a familiar one as a succession of republican prisoners in the '80s, the '20s and every decade since put their lives on the line to defy the governments who confined them as criminals. The suffering and fortitude of prisoners became, in the twentieth century, an inspiration for the blood sacrifice advocated by Patrick Pearse and carried into potent political reality in the 1916 Rising in which the leaders, giving their lives in an apparently hopeless and unpopular cause, became, in their deaths before a British firing squad, the inspiration for a national uprising. The ideal of blood sacrifice fed back into the prison system and from the 1920s we have prisoners giving their lives on hunger strike, at first for release and later for a degree of control over the conditions of confinement. Their actions were almost always accompanied by profound political consequences.

This rich tradition and experience of prison protest meant

that by the time the Provisionals' campaign had produced its first prisoners a great many ground rules and options had already been created for imprisoned republicans. Most fundamentally an IRA member entering jail loses any previous rank but remains a volunteer, taking his orders from the organisation, regarding the regime that holds him as without legitimacy and making whatever contribution he can to the overall campaign in which he remains engaged. Where the aims of modern penal systems are couched in terms of rehabilitation of the offenders and the creation of useful members of society, the aims of republican prisoners are to maintain their organizational and personal integrity within the prison. If the idea of imprisonment itself is seen as an unavoidable moment in the revolutionary career the idea of rehabilitation or of repaying a debt to society is an immediate focus for resistance. As Bobby Sands put it:

> I am now in H-Block, where I refuse to change to suit the people who oppress, torture or imprison me, and who wish to dehumanise me. Like the lark I need no changing. It is my political ideology and my principles that my captors wish to change. They have suppressed my body and attacked my dignity. If I were an ordinary prisoner they would pay little, if any, attention to me, knowing that I would conform to their institutional whims.[7]

In real life imprisonment is often an occasion for self-doubt and not all, or even many, republican prisoners are individually motivated to lenthen their sentences in isolated conflict with the administration. If it is to hope for a reasonable return to active involvement of its imprisoned members, the IRA must ensure that jailed volunteers have the full practical solidarity of the organisation as well as the historic example of past generations. This is achieved in a number of ways. Green Cross and Cumann Cabrach funds are used to help families through weekly payments and extra assistance at times of special expense. An equally important part is played by prison related protests outside the bars and IRA activity (like the shooting of warders) in support of the prisoners as well as the constant round of protests for the prisoners to take up in order to maintain morale and to ensure that the IRA organisation in the prison has the maximum possible control of its own members. Prisoners are a part of the overall campaign, regularly consulted and encouraged to make a contribution both by acting as a sounding board for issues which arise on the outside and by devising new weapons where the opportunity arises.

The Provisional IRA's first experience of imprisonment came after the 9 August internment swoops in 1971. The rules governing confinement, if not the physical conditions in the compounds, during internment provided the IRA with a model for the prison regime as a whole. Prisoners were segregated according to their paramilitary allegiance in Nissen huts grouped in wire cages within compounds hastily constructed at the disused airfield of Long Kesh near the village of Maze. Here they wore their own clothes, drilled, painted political murals on the walls and behaved in most respects like prisoners of war. In each cage the appropriate paramilitary organisation's OC held sway, imposing internal discipline which in one case, that of loyalist internee George Hyde in 1973, extended to murder. OCs also negotiated with the authorities as well as organising educational classes in subjects ranging from history to explosives. Each OC would be allowed periodic meetings with his counterparts in the other terrorist groups which were organised within the prison and there was a lively trade in carved harps, painted hankies, plaques, hand tooled wallets and other items of ornamental propaganda made by the prisoners to be sold or raffled for their benefit.

There was, under internment, little resistance from the prison officers to the idea that they were handling special prisoners as opposed to run of the mill criminals because of the fact that no inmate had been charged or tried for any offence.

This is not to say that internment was a bed of roses. Leaving aside the injustice of indefinite imprisonment on the basis of unproven suspicion, conditions were primitive and many inmates were physically abused either before or after being lifted, as emerged in the 1976 'Hooded Men' case against Britain at the European Court of Human Rights. In cash terms £302,043 had been paid out by the British government in 473 claims by detainees or former detainees seeking redress for false imprisonment, assault and battery and there were 1,193 further claims outstanding by 31 January 1975.[8] Ten internees received prison sentences for trying to escape[9] and one, Hugh Coney, was shot during an escape attempt. Internment was undoubtedly an embittering experience which brought many closer to the fledging paramilitary organisations. One internee, Joe Clarke, recalled the process: 'At the start there were young fellows who didn't know much about politics or about Irish history but as time went on with discussions at the camp people were able to educate themselves in Irish history and politics. They came out far stronger people. More dedicated. They knew what they were fighting for.'[10]

Nevertheless life in what was known as the 'Lazy K' was often enervating. The open-ended sentence and the undeveloped politics of the internees, many of whom had little or no prior involvement with the paramilitaries whose compounds they chose to enter, were the main problems. Pat McGeown, who was interned at the age of sixteen after being arrested near Newry with a bus load of other youths on their way to a training camp and has spent the bulk of his adult life in prison, explains:

> It made life in the prisons so easy that you actually ended up adjusting to prison and ended up seeing life as little more than prison. You had basically everything you wanted and often it was quite easy to forget you were in prison. The prisoner could feel very apathetic towards the world around him. He could sort of drift into a state of isolation where he accepts isolation. It doesn't actually suit a prisoner... Internment ended in 1975 which was in the early years of the struggle. We didn't have people who were highly politicised, that had actually thought about the issues. Internment was taken up with a lot of passing the dish. You never really adapted to any sort of stable routine or pattern, you couldn't start any sort of programme, be it educational or whatever because you always had this in the back of your mind, well tomorrow I might be released.[11]

Conditions for special category prisoners convicted before 1 March 1976 were broadly similar to those of the internees. The difference was provided by the fact that the inmates had definite sentences and, because they included more politically involved men, had a higher level of motivation than the internees. Here increasingly ambitious training and educational programmes could be put into effect and many of the ideas and techniques which were to carry the Provisionals through the reorganisation into long-term viability could be threshed out. The degree of association granted was such that weapons classes, using real and replica guns, took place and escapes could be planned in relative ease and privacy, often round a blackboard drawing of the prison's defences. In the view of the British army, the Maze was 'an advanced training establishment for the IRA bombers and at least two booby-trap switches had been produced by the prisoners there.'[12]

Gerry Adams was struck by the contrast when he became a sentenced prisoner after his attempt to escape from internment. Expecting to spend his days 'learning Irish and reading' he found that the 'republican regime was very severe, parades and drills and all that went with it, to a degree which I for one found excessive' and that although there was a programme of lectures in operation there was 'a lack of consistent political discussion'. The more relaxed regime and more developed education structure he introduced in Cage 11, of which he was OC, became the broad norm for future republican organisation within the prisons. It was at this stage that the ad hoc practice of prisoners discussing and being consulted on current issues was developed and formalised and that the value of prisoners as a group of IRA men with the time to thoroughly thresh out policy was fully realised.

The process of radicalisation within the jail gathered momentum around 1975 and the aftermath of the truce period, when a fundamental reappraisal was forced on the IRA both within and outside the prison. A strong background factor in these discussions was the Vietnam war, which was ending in victory for the Vietnamese after thirty years of armed struggle. The failure of the truce and the long run of the Vietnam conflict combined to persuade prisoners that they should be preparing for a 'long war' in which endurance would bring victory. This went hand in hand with a new evaluation of British intentions, an acceptance, as Pat McGeown put it, that 'the Brits aren't going to solve our problems for us and that the mistake of the truce was that we expected them to solve the problem when all we could do was sit down and talk.'[11] The fact that the Vietcong were a broad popular movement with the government of half the country behind them while the IRA was a minority grouping bent on liberating a nation that did not support them was seen as a problem to be overcome rather than a weakness in the analogy.

In Adams' cage both an Irish speaking Gaeltacht hut and a study hut were set aside and the new education process began with a consideration of the reasons why the inmates (who included Brendan Hughes, Brendan McFarlane, Bobby Sands, Jim Gibney and Danny Lennon) were in prison. From this practical base discussions could work outwards to the nature of republicanism or the effect of various sorts of actions, including the sectarian killings in which the IRA was involved during the truce, and in this way the ideas which were to transform the Provos over the next few years were developed behind the wire.

Part of the impetus for the changeover from this Colditz style regime to the so-called 'H-Block Conveyor Belt' also came from behind the wire when in October 1974 a wave of rioting flared through Long Kesh, Magilligan, Crumlin Road and Armagh prisons. General protest at conditions had been building up over several months amidst threats of a mass hunger strike by both loyalist and republican prisoners working together through an organised camp council. In the short term the riots had been sparked off by a number of changes in procedures, the most important of which was a restriction on the ability of OCs to travel between compounds on camp council business.

The serious trouble, which was in the end confined to republican prisoners, started amongst internees who burnt several huts, injured twenty-three soldiers and fourteen prison officers and suffered numerous injuries themselves. In Armagh the women even took the prison governor Hugh Cunningham and three female members of staff hostage overnight and in all £2 million pounds worth of damage was caused. The situation was resolved when the prison chaplains in Armagh and the UVF OC Gusty Spence in Long Kesh acted as go-betweens. They negotiated a republican surrender in return for a no brutality commitment, which was honoured in Armagh but not in Long Kesh where the British army proceeded to beat the prisoners.

The crisis had helped convince the government of the need to break paramilitary organisation in the prison and to phase out the compound system which confidential assessments at the time acknowledged to be insecure and to require a permanent army presence 'not only to prevent prisoners escaping but also to deter incursions from the outside'.[13] Even if the control the authorities had over life in the prison depended on the goodwill of the OCs or the muscle of the permanent army presence the recidivism rates of compound inmates, many of them with a bellyfull of paramilitary discipline by the time they got out, were lower than in British prisons and the stated objectives of the prisoners sometimes came close to the rehabilitation which republican tradition and the blanketmen so strongly rejected. For instance less than a month before the burning of Long Kesh a joint statement was issued by all prisoners complaining of the standard of food, bedding and educational facilities and stating:

> We see our role in this camp as being to return men to their homes and loved ones without bitterness and readily able to contribute to a society that has suffered so much and it could be in the not too distant future that these men will give a lead which will bring shame to those who contributed and permitted society to become the mess that it is today.
>
> We all make mistakes but we must benefit from our mistakes. Is Long Kesh to be permitted by society to make mistake after mistake?

The new regime was all the easier to introduce because of the universally acknowledged need for new prison accommodation at a time when Northern Ireland was being transformed from one of the most law abiding societies in Europe to one of the most violent. The number of known offences more than doubled between 1969 and 1976 and the number of prison officers rose from 292 to 1,926 in the same period. In the talks with prisoners' OCs following the burning of Long Kesh the changes which were pushing the prison budget over the £30 million mark in 1976 could be presented as meeting the prisoners' own demands for better conditions.

The Provisional OC David Morley and his counterparts from the Official IRA (Adrian Clarke), INLA (Frank Gallagher), the UVF (Gusty Spence) and the UDA (Jim Craig) were shown details of the planned new accommodation and taken on a guided tour of the H-Blocks by Captain Davies, the Inspector of Prisons. They made various requests at the time for prisoners to be allowed to wear their own clothes, for cell doors to be left open, for education and work to be liberally interpreted and for remission to be raised to two-thirds in return for good behaviour; Spence in particular predicted bloodshed if the administration's plans for the running of the blocks went ahead but the OCs' overall impression was not entirely unfavourable. Despite the later propaganda, the single storey H-Blocks represented advanced penal design both in terms of security and facilities. The legs of each H comprised a wing of 25 centrally heated 8 x 12 cells plus a toilet area, dining, recreation and handicraft rooms. The central bar of the H, which included the medical and control rooms, was intended as a secure administrative area and was protected by double steel entrance grills at the four corridors which entered it from the wings. Facilities for conforming prisoners were better than any elsewhere in Ireland or the UK.

As well as being shown the building of the H-Blocks and the proposed premises in Rosemary Street, where it was at one stage thought that Maire Drumm and the UVF prisoners' welfare worker Jim McDonald might share offices, Morley and Craig, who were nearing the end of their sentence, were allowed leave to consult with IRA leaders on negotiations. On one occasion Morley was even supplied with a gun for his own protection and on another he was cleared to leave the UK and visit the Republic.[14]

Merlyn Rees' Westminster speech of 25 March 1976 was also passed to Morley for vetting and criticisms of the IRA were toned down at his insistence. However the full significance of the cellular design of the new H-Blocks and the full importance of the removal of special category status either eluded Morley or, more likely, were discounted in the truce optimism that since British withdrawal and a possible amnesty were in the pipeline the victory on conditions of existing prisoners outweighed the details of future prison architecture.

Two days after the speech had actually been made the penny had well and truly dropped and the anti-truce Belfast Brigade had issued a statement condemning the new arrangements. A fuller statement was produced by the prisoners rejecting the

Rosemary Street offices and an associated resettlement scheme as attempts to 'politicise' the prison issue and adding:

> Volunteers of *Oglaigh na hEireann* have been instructed that they are not to engage in any institutional schemes under the control of the prison administration. They are further instructed that they are not to wear any clothing provided by the prison administration, even if such clothes are of a civilian type. They will respond only to the commands and directives of their superior officers, regardless of the consequences. They are political prisoners and any other imaginary label tagged to them by the British government will make not the slightest difference to that very basic fact... We are prepared to die for the *right* to retain political status. Those who try to take it away must be fully prepared to pay the same price.

As the document was delivered to the prison the IRA was weakened and confused and the authorities hoped it was tottering towards defeat. The statement was taken as little more than a defiant flourish and so history might have seen it had not the determination of the administration to smash all opposition rallied the prisoners behind its sentiments, making it an accurate prediction of the course of events.

NOTES

1. As quoted in *An Phoblacht,* September 1974.
2. I am indebted for this anecdote to Jimmy Drumm.
3. Full title *Report of a Committee to consider, in the light of civil liberties and human rights, measures to deal with terrorism in Northern Ireland* (Cmnd 5847, January 1975). Later the measure was to be toughened to include offences charged after 1 April 1976, whenever committed.
4. Minutes of the Prison Inter Services Intelligence Committee which was chaired by the Director of Prison Ops and included representatives of the RUC Special Branch, HM Prison the Maze, HM Prison Magilligan, HM Prison Belfast, HM Prison Armagh and the Northern Ireland Office's Prison Ops section. The Committee met in Room 330, Dundonald House at various dates between 1976 and 1979.
5. For instance in 1977 the Prison Inter Services Intelligence Committee received a report from the Maze authorities stating that 'the republicans in the H-Blocks are arguing amongst themselves saying that if they could get out in five years instead of ten years they would be of more use to the organisation.'
6. John Devoy fought in the French Foreign Legion, Luby in the French army and numerous Fenians on both sides in the American Civil War as a

means of learning military tactics. John Mitchel, a veteran of the Confederate side in the US Civil War and a staunch defender of slavery, had the cause of his release championed by Karl Marx, was a radical on many issues, but in his vastly influential *Jail Journal* described socialists as 'something worse than wild beasts'.

7. 'The Lark and the Freedom Fighter' first published in *An Phoblacht/Republican News* 3 February 1979, collected in *The Writings of Bobby Sands* (Sinn Féin POW Dept April 1981).

8. *Hansard* 27 April 1975.

9. They were Marshal Mooney, Martin O'Rawe, Ivor Malachy Bell, Owen Coogan, Harry O'Rawe, Tommy Tolan, Gerry Adams, Tom Cahill, Edward Duffy and Gerry Lynch.

10. Joe Clarke was one of the twelve 'Hooded Men' in the Court of Human Rights case mentioned above. The others were Patrick Shivers, Paddy Joe McClean, Michael J. Donnelly, Mickey Montgomery, Kevin Hannaway, Francis McGuigan, Patrick McNally, Brian Turley, Gerrard McKerr, James Auld and the future hunger striker Sean McKenna. Clarke was interned for three years. I am indebted to TV South for transcripts of unbroadcast sections of an interview with him and to Joe Clarke for his own assistance. Other ex-internees have more jaundiced recollections. For instance future *An Phobhlacht* editor Gerry O'Hare told Granada's 'World in Action': 'I was in Long Kesh at the same time as Gerry Adams and myself and others, as he would have done as well, would have broken into small study groups and we would have sent out for books from people like Marx, Lenin, James Connolly, Che Guevara, James Larkin and we would have studied successes and failures of other revolutions. I would say that from around that particular period of time, '73-'74, the leftwing rhetoric that one associates with Gerry Adams and all the rest was born' (The Honourable Member for West Belfast) 12 December 1983.

11. Interview with the author, 31/5/'86.

12. Lt Col. Derrick Patrick in *Fetch Felix*.

13. Documents in the author's possession outlining prison security around 1977. They state 'compounds are not secure and prisoners have ability to break out and take over Phases 5 and 6 at any time. However they should be contained by the perimeter and phase walls.'

14. This section is indebted to the account given by T. P. Coogan in his *On The Blanket* (Ward River Press) and to a conversation with Gusty Spence.

4

In the H-Blocks of Long Kesh

'I said to Hughes, "They were all wrong beating those boys because if you think about it when they are locked up in the cell they have nothing to think about. They need something to hold them together." What they had was hate. The officers played right into their hands. The Northern Ireland Office didn't know any psychology at all. They didn't know the makeup of who they were up against; the beatings they got just stiffened them as nothing else could. I can tell you that for a fact. I told Brendan Hughes that what they should have done was killed them with kindness and he said that he had ordered a few fights, or caused disturbances himself on several occasions to keep the hate going, to keep them together,'

Pat McCusker, former H-Block Prison Officer[1]

'To deal with the hunger strike and the political consequences on the outside alone is to me like dealing with crucifixion without the agony in the garden.'

Brendan Hughes[2]

As Maire Drumm foresaw, it was a mistake for the authorities to make the wearing of prison uniform an issue. Women prisoners in Armagh could already wear their own clothes as could conforming male prisoners during visits and association periods; it would have been a simple matter to have extended the right to wear approved clothing to all. Failing that, refusal to wear uniform at specified times could, like refusal to work, have been punished by loss of remission or privileges.

Initially, however, depriving the prisoners of clothes was seen as a promising way to slap down any potential protest. Nugent's decision to follow IRA policy onto the blanket was not a common one and most convicted republicans chose to conform to prison rules. Later in the year some women prisoners in Armagh (starting with Brenda Murray, Eileen Morgan, Rosin Rouse and the future hunger striker Mairead Farrell), who were allowed to wear their own clothes, began a no work protest showing, as the authorities pointed out, that the underlying issue was one of control, revolving around the desire of the IRA to maintain its own organisational structures within the prison.

However the women's protest was partly in support of the blanketmen and without the emotive image of naked prisoners to keep it going it did comparatively little to disrupt the life of the jail or to attract outside sympathy. By 29 December 1976 things in Armagh were still fairly low key. The Prison Inter Service Intelligence Committee was told: 'Prison fairly quiet. There are now four females refusing to conform with prison rules. Two of these females do not have the support of their family regarding their action. Special category prisoners are still not showing any support for post 1 March offenders.' For the committee, the most worrying development in the prison was that 'male [prison] officers are starting to sway in favour of the return of special category status as they think the government will let them down at the last minute'.

In fact sensitive handling of the situation by Governor Hugh Cunningham and his successor Ernest Whittington did much to sap the Armagh protest. The numbers of protesting prisoners there only reached far into double figures in response to the heavier hand of George Scott who opened his term of office in 1978 with a vigorous attempt not only to break the protest but to force the dwindling company of existing special category prisoners to relinquish their status. At Easter 1978 Scott tried splitting up the protesting prisoners and mixing them with loyalists and ODCs (Ordinary Decent Criminals) for a period. He eventually abandoned this strategy but in the meantime increased the number of disciplinary charges against both conforming and non-conforming prisoners. On 7-8 May 1978 protests by remand prisoners were met by a baton charge of male prison officers, hardening feeling both within and outside the prison as well as increasing the rate of recruitment for the protest.

Even in the Maze matters other than the blanket protest took up most of the PSIC's time at the end of 1976. The threat, they believed, came from 'Shankill Butcher' gang leader Lenny Murphy who had taken command of both UDA and UVF inmates and was planning to cause aggro with IRA prisoners in an effort to force the administration to segregate the two factions.

By early 1977 around 600 people had been convicted in the

Diplock courts since the ending of special category status, about 70 per cent of them solely on the basis of confessions given in Castlereagh[3] and a second prison officer, Hamilton, had been murdered. Public disquiet at the ease with which supposedly hardened terrorists could be induced to sign away their liberty in the interrogation centres was growing and was fueled on 9 March by the screening of a BBC interview with Fermanagh teacher Bernard O'Connor who had been severely beaten in Castlereagh in an attempt to get him to sign statements admitting to being a local IRA godfather.

Attention, even in terms of republican agitation, was away from the blanketmen and their number was rising only modestly. A cameo picture is given by Billy 'Twister' McQuistan who was moved to Long Kesh in March when he became OC of the UDA's Young Prisoners in H2. Despite coming straight from Crumlin Road Prison where he had been involved in daily hand-to-hand fighting with republican prisoners (who were trying to force the authorities to segregate them from the loyalists) McQuistan was appalled at the treatment of the scattering of blanketmen he found spread along the same wings as loyalist conforming prisoners:

> I was in for what I saw as a fight against republicanism but at the same time it was hard for me to take, seeing these men getting beat about and it happened on a regular basis. They would shout out if I was brushing my cell out 'Here mate throw us a fag in' and I would give them a cigarette; although I hated everything about republicanism the way they were being treated made me have sympathy towards them. I also understood their plight, I thought that what they were fighting for was right, they wanted to be political prisoners . . . The other republican prisoners weren't on the blanket, they were mixing along with us and were getting on although when I say we were mixing, we weren't sitting at the same tables, but were sitting in the same canteen, they were sitting in half the canteen and we were sitting in the other, but there was dialogue between us.'[4]

Sympathy for the blanketmen encouraged the loyalists to co-operate with the majority population of conforming republican prisoners, keeping violence to a minimum and prompting a number of joint approaches to the authorities on the provision of snooker tables and other recreational facilities which were still absent from the half completed H-Blocks. In 1978 there was even an abortive five-month loyalist blanket protest involving some fifty prisoners which ended only after the UDA on the outside issued three separate orders for the prisoners to stop emulating the republican protest. Later McQuistan himself went on hunger strike for segregation in 1983.

The early beatings were, prison staff have claimed, in response to a directive to break the blanket protest before it got a grip in the new prison, keeping the attractions of conforming and the disadvantages of protest constantly before the prisoners. As McQuistan's account shows, the effect was often the opposite, not only strengthening the determination of most of the original blanketmen but building sympathy and admiration for them amongst other prisoners. If the harsh treatment did induce a few men to conform the traffic was not all one way. Some, like Hugh Nellis from Derry, who had left the protest returned to it. Not only were overall numbers on the blanket on a rising trend but the protest was set to escalate.

By the spring of 1977, when the numbers were around the seventy mark, the protesting IRA men were gathered into the most recently built H5 in stage two of the prison, the first of what the prison officers called the 'streaker blocks'. Many prisoners initially took the move as a victory and an effective granting of their demand for segregation. Rumour, the *Sceal* as it was called, had it that other concessions amounting to a return to special category status would soon follow.

Instead the move was followed by two important developments for the lengthening of the protest; the introduction of new rules and the transfer of a number of older prisoners from the compounds to the H-Blocks.

Perhaps the most important of these transferees were Brendan 'Darkie' Hughes, the so-called 'Gypsy OC', and, later, Brendan 'Bic' McFarlane. Hughes, in particular, is a charismatic and astute man, widely respected by both the prison officers and the other prisoners. Originally jailed for fourteen years in 1974 on arms and explosive charges, he lost status and was sentenced to an additional five years because of a fight between warders and prisoners in the compounds which, a prison officer testified at his trial, he had been trying to break up. Shortly after arriving in the Blocks in January 1978 Hughes and four others sentenced with him withdrew appeals against conviction in what looked like a conscious decision to stay involved in the blanket protest. Hughes now took charge of the protest, his transfer coinciding with a sharp rise in the number of blanketmen from 208 in December 1977 to 299 in April 1978. Bic McFarlane, another experienced and intelligent leader, was transferred with Larry Marley and Pat McGeown following an attempt to get over the wire in makeshift prison officers' uniforms in March 1978. Also in early 1978 one of the most influential INLA prisoners, John Nixon, who for a time became overall OC of all republicans in the blocks, was sentenced and joined the protest. Bobby Sands was sentenced in September 1977 when the number of blanketmen was around 160.

The addition of the experienced prison leaders tended to give a direction and perspective to the protest. Their presence helped ensure that the younger blanket men would neither crack under the increasing pressure from the warders nor embark on the early hunger strike some had argued for ever since nine young offenders won a transfer to the blanket blocks after a hunger strike lasting only four days in early 1977. On a day-to-day level the old hands brought with them a knowledge of the layout and organisation of the rest of the prison as well as the contacts necessary to build up a communications network stretching through the lower security compounds and conforming wings where there were no internal searches before visits. Many of the most sensitive communications and reports from the OCs to the IRA on the outside were now sent via the prison's essential services vehicles to the young prisoners' areas where visits were less closely supervised than in the H-Blocks.

By early 1978 prison staff, four of whose number had by now been shot dead, noticed a fall in the number of blanketmen 'Squeaky Booting', as putting on the heavy prison issue boots to leave the protest was known to the prisoners. The administration's response was to place further restrictions on the protesters.

In the first year of the protest it had been customary to leave a number of objects in the prison cell including a blue denim uniform, the bed, religious magazines, a bible, a chair and table, three army blankets, a towel, a child's po and a locker. Prisoners were also allowed to leave the cells to wash and collect food wearing a towel. All these objects and circumstances provided some comfort to the prisoner and many of them were incorporated in the protest. Their gradual removal reduced the options of the prisoners for protest, moving the idea of a hunger strike slowly up their agenda of possibilities.

When the furniture was present it was wrecked in response to unpopular actions by the warders and sometimes used to attack prison officers. Beds had a number of uses. Their mattresses and frames were used to conceal contraband while the springs could serve as aerials for crystal sets, levers for hooking open the rectangular 'judas' spy flaps from the gaps at the top of the ill-fitting H-Block cell doors or tools to poke open the small holes between the pre-fabricated slabs of the cell walls to allow passage of communications.

The despised denim prison uniforms were, like the blankets, plundered for thread used to swing tobacco and communications between cells. Buttons from the uniforms were also attached to lines of thread and punted, shove halfpenny style, across the corridors so that small packages of contraband could be hauled from one cell to another.

The hard toilet paper itself was used as writing paper or, glued together with mashed potatoes, as wrapping for contraband and for roll-up cigarettes. Entire letters, reports to the movement on the outside or poems by creative prisoners like Bobby Sands could be fitted onto sheets of toilet paper, inscribed in tiny block capitals or copperplate with smuggled ballpen refills.

Visits to the bathroom or toilet were used to stock up on toilet rolls, to pass communications, to lift discarded cigarette butts from the corridors between the toes of the prisoners' bare feet and to steal cigarettes or other goods from the guard room. Visits from relatives or friends were, for those prisoners prepared to put on a uniform to take them, the occasion for passing toilet roll communications wrapped in clingfilm from mouth to mouth during kisses, or for passing tobacco, biro tubes, clingfilm, paper and other items to be swallowed or smuggled internally.

Andersonstown man John Bernard McMullan was apparently the first blanketman to conceal contraband up his rectum. According to Seamus Boyle:

> Towards the end of a visit, if Jackie had not managed to put tobacco up his back passage unobserved by the warders, then he would just put it up anyway whilst the warders looked on in amazement at the wriggling prisoner before them. Jackie reckons 'once it's up they can't get it anyway'; his attitude is 'damn them'.[5]

Trips to mass or confession were used in a similar way and priests would often fill their upper pockets with biros or biro tubes which the prisoners would then take as they walked past and conceal internally.[6] So expert did prisoners become at this initially distasteful practice that small cigarette lighters, both swallowed and inserted in the anus, were amongst the articles recovered in searches and radio parts were amongst those missed.

Many of the problems caused for the authorities by the ingenuity of the prisoners could have been solved by a relaxation of conditions. Communications could have been all but eliminated by the simple substitution of soft toilet rolls for the standard prison issue. It must also be questioned whether the authorities were, even in their own terms, well advised to go to the lengths they did to deny the prisoners tobacco, non-religious papers, writing materials, letters or even radios. Certainly these petty restrictions presented the blanketmen with a clearer and more feasible target for resistance than the main punishments of loss of remission and association or even periods on the boards.

However, it was the policy of the prison administration to apply more rather than less pressure and to challenge the prisoners on each individual point. The smuggling of contraband was answered with demands that prisoners squat over a mirror before and after visits or moves outside their cells. Where this was refused there were, until October 1978, forcible body searches in which, as one blanketman put it, 'you are thrown onto the table like a chicken and pulled apart like a fish'. These degrading internal searches, in which tobacco or letters were sometimes retrieved with tongs, were occasions for conflict and beatings.

Another minor battlefield which soon assumed major importance arose over the arrangements for washing. After November 1976 prisoners were forbidden to take 'prison property' blankets out of their cells to collect food, wash or go to the toilet, a problem which they answered by wrapping their larger bath towel around themselves and carrying a smaller hand towel with which to dry themselves. After a few months they were forbidden the second towel on the grounds that prison regulations allowed only one. Prisoners continuing the protest were now forced to go naked to collect food and were also naked when they took off the towel to dry themselves. They claimed that they were being jeered and humiliated by the orderlies, warders and prisoners on the mixed wings and refused to leave their cells to wash.

The response of the authorities was to refuse to allow them to leave the cells to go to the toilet unless they first put on a uniform and asked a prison officer, addressing him as 'Sir'. Again the prisoners refused, preferring to use the small plastic potties in their cells but requesting buckets to slop out into. The buckets were refused.

At this stage the protest confined them to the cells twenty-four hours a day and furniture had been removed to prevent it being wrecked or used to assault the staff. The prisoners had also destroyed the paint work and removed silicon filler from the windows to dull the lights, both of which they claimed were designed to cause them blinding headaches. A new routine had been established by which trollies wheeled by mainly loyalist blanket orderlies, who were given increased remission in return for their unpleasant duties, appeared each day at around 7.30 am, 12.25 pm and 4.30 pm. As the breakfast trollies came round the prisoners were at first allowed to leave the cells to 'slop out' but finding that they missed breakfast, they started refusing to do so. The task then fell to the orderlies with the result that the slops were sometimes splashed around the cells or onto the food.

In answer to this problem the prisoners started disposing of the slops themselves. At first they poured urine and hurled packages of faeces wrapped in paper torn from bibles and religious magazines through the outside windows into the exercise yard. When the windows were blocked they poured or shoved the waste, under the bottoms of the doors and into the corridors. However during cell searches, which became increasingly frequent, orderlies knocked the chamber pots and packets of excrement over the mattresses lying on the floor, which were now the only furnishings the prisoners had not destroyed. At this stage, towards the end of 1978, the blanketmen responded by smearing their excrement over the walls and stuffing it into the observation slots in the cell doors with pieces of foam torn from the mattress. Urine was simply poured under the doors. The 'Dirty Protest' was now in full swing.

The grotesque conditions created struck prisoners and outsiders differently. Prison Officer Pat McCusker, who was initially attached to the prison hospital, had occasion to visit the blocks during 1978 and was eventually transferred there in 1979 when there were 370 dirty protesters. His first impressions were as follows:

> The doctor and I had to put on our wellies to go down to it. I was after my dinner and I boked my guts up. The stink and the stench — there was piddle under the doors and when they opened one of their doors, I'm not exaggerating now, you couldn't see the paint on the door for the shite that was on it.

For prisoners the conditions were on a gradually escalating scale of the bizarre. The increasingly perverse and violent conditions presented an element of challenge and variety in the grim monotony of months or years on the blanket. The future hunger striker Liam McCloskey who entered the protest in December 1977 after being arrested with Kevin Lynch and Harry Mullan, two fellow members of a fledgling Dungiven based INLA unit, recalls:

> With the beginning of the no-wash protest during March 1977 things became more interesting with a developing protest to keep the boredom at bay. As the no-wash protest increased so did the level of violence within the block as prison staff became frustrated with the conditions under which they had to work. Added to this was the opinion of the wing OC ['Cleeky' Clarke from Ardoyne] that there

wasn't enough beatings taking place for propaganda and if we could build up a good propaganda campaign the protest would be over all the sooner. He told us to give the warders abuse when they were in the yard or corridor.[7]

In the initial stages the escalating dirty protest and the series of challenges which it threw out were seen as an almost hopeful sign, both a relief to the monotony and a means of bringing the protest issue to a head. This hiatus of desperate optimism waned as the dirty protest itself settled into a still more sordid and punishing routine with no apparent end in sight. Support outside the prison, as the leading blanketmen were well aware, was not rising as dramatically as had been hoped and the efforts of the authorities to crack the protest became more wearing with the passage of time.

Some minor restrictions applied to the blanketmen that did not apply elsewhere in the prison and did not follow directly from their freakish form of protest. Conforming prisoners were allowed to wear their own clothes on visits but the blanketmen were not and the blue denim uniforms were, early in 1978, removed from their cells and placed in a separate cell at the end of the block to which they had to go to collect them for visits. In an effort to stop communications the number of pieces of toilet paper allowed to a prisoner was reduced to three per day, sometimes less, and religious magazines were removed to prevent prisoners 'misusing them' to save toilet paper.

A constant war was fought over cell windows which were first smashed by the prisoners in August 1978 in response to the decision of the authorities to disinfect the poorly ventilated cells with bleach and ammonia. The windows were left open through the early winter until, with the heating often off and the prisoners freezing, they were replaced by 'unbreakable' perspex windows. These the prisoners burned with 'tinder boxes' made from flints and splinters of glass, preferring to freeze than to choke on the disinfectant fumes. They were left to their fate, through the hardest winter in sixteen years, until corridor windows were eventually replaced in March 1979 with newly developed foot-wide frosted affairs which defeated even the blanketmen's desperate ingenuity. The outside windows remained broken.

Liam McCloskey, whose cellmate was Kevin Lynch, recalls many instances of defiance and their consequences, instances which bring home not only the brutality of life in the blocks but also the grinding pettiness to which warders and prisoners were alike reduced.

> There was no glass in the windows as we had broken them and we were putting excrement on the walls outside the cells. Every morning the orderlies hosed the walls with a high powered hose. Each cell got a certain amount of water with the splashing from the hoses. The orderlies were not too careful where the water went. Almost every morning when they had to hose up after washing the walls I would put excrement out knowing that it was annoying them. Each morning after our cell would get special treatment with the hose leaving it flooded out. We both got fed up with it and talked about doing something about it. We also complained to the wing OC who sent word to the OC of the blocks asking to do something about it and was awaiting permission from him before starting. One morning [Friday 15 September 1978] as I was about to put my usual morning waste out, not knowing that the orderlies were in the yard, one of them came into view and, on impulse, I let fly. He turned his face away just in time and got it on his shoulder, hair and side of face. I got down from the window and waited for the warders.
>
> It wasn't long before I heard the sound of heavy boots tramping up the corridor, the door opened with the PO (Principal Officer) standing there along with ten or twelve warders. Although I had been to the toilet a short time before I felt like going again. I was marched down the corridor expecting fists and boots to land on me at any minute — nothing happened. I was told to put a pair of trousers on, which was the procedure for going to the boards (i.e. punishment block). The PO asked me why I had done it. I was so nervous I could hardly answer. Although the warders were all around me nothing happened. From there I was taken to the centre of the block and examined by the doctor who found nothing physically wrong with me. I was then walked to a corner and told to

face the wall. Not feeling very much like arguing I did it. For the next five to ten minutes I stood there, during which time a lock-up was called. I was told to turn around. When I did so I was hit in the face by an orderly. As I went down what seemed like a sea of fists and boots rained in on me. I was booted and punched from there out through the grills and out the front door to a waiting van. I scrambled into the back of the van thinking that I was getting away from the beating, but no luck. About three of them came in and continued punching and kicking. One managed to get his boot in between my ribs . . .

I did three days on the boards during which time I got a forced wash which entailed being washed with scrubbing brushes. One of the bristles from the brushes entered my ear and opened an old wound that I had since childhood. I was almost deaf at that time with a yellow fluid coming from the ear while the other was blocked with wax. I spent those three days running over Irish in my mind and reading the bible although I wasn't getting much out of it. It was a case of seeing but not able to see, hearing but not able to hear. What Jesus said in those bygone days still applies today to most of us. One act of kindness still sticks in my mind and that was one evening when supper came around I was very hungry and all we got was one round of bread for supper. There was an old warder along with an orderly. He must have seen the hungry look in my eye because he smiled and said 'take what's left on my plate and I'll go and get more.' I grabbed them and went back to my cell . . .

About two or three days after arriving back into the block came the wing move on which my nose was broken, being spreadeagled naked over a table. The procedure at the time was that on the morning of the wing move we were moved one at a time to the other wing. When the door opened the warder would hand one of us a card on which was written our names, date of committal and prisoner type, in our case NCP [non-conformist prisoner]. When I received the card I walked to the centre of the block where ten or twelve warders stood along with the PO. About six of them stood around a table in the middle of the centre.

When I reached the table I was told to remove the towel that was around my waist and leave the card. I was told to bend over the table which I refused to do. Our policy was not to co-operate with degrading searches. No resistance but don't bend. As I stood there four of the warders grabbed me and threw me onto the table. As I was landing a hand came upon my head. It hit the table with a bad crack and I felt a bad pain in my nose. When they had finished looking me over I was allowed to back up. I put my towel back on and walked to my cell in the other wing. When my cell mate Kevin arrived I was standing spitting blood onto the wall. He said he had seen the blood and suspected it was mine. He was angry over what had happened. At the time I was none too pleased either. When the wing move had ended I was taken out to the doctor who, after examining me and taking notes on the ear injury and bruises from the previous incident, sent me to the prison hospital to recuperate. I remained there about a week getting x-rays and taking things easy ...

After the incident with my nose [19 September 1978] the tables were removed but soon after the mirror search began which was no improvement... We usually knew when a wing move was coming with the sound of orderlies moving lockers in which the prison clothes were kept. This mostly was the night before a move. In the morning after breakfast a shout from the PO calling lock-up, then the sound of doors banging, a silence and then a shout of 'SEND THEM ON'. A door opened and someone gave a shout 'AN TAOBH SEO' [this side]. We knew by the voice which side was moving first. We stood there with our ears to the door to hear if it was a rough move or not. Sometimes a few got across without much noise coming from the place where the mirror was (either the bottom of the wing in which we were, the centre or the other wing). If the move was rough the sounds of slaps and thumps soon reached our ears. I can't speak for anyone else but my nerves were tensed up from the moment lock-up was called and grew worse as they would get nearer our cell. When the door would open a name was called out, Lynch or McCloskey. If it was my name I grabbed my possessions which were a bible, a few prayers, and a pair of rosary beads and walked out wearing a towel. My card would be handed to me and I walked towards where a mirror was. Once there I left my possessions on a chair and took the towel off and stood over the mirror with a leg on each side. Usually there were three or four warders standing around, one with a torch and another with a metal detector. One of them said 'bend'. I didn't move. Again this was the procedure with us. I was then kicked behind the knees and at the same time pushed into a squatting position, sometimes punched as well, depending on the mood of the warders and which PO was working that day. While in this position the torch was shone up my anus and sometimes the cheeks would be parted by a hand. On most occasions this was not done. When I stood up again the metal detector was run over my body. With the search over I put the towel back on, collected my things and went over to the other wing. When the move ended we waited for blankets and mattresses to arrive. Sometimes they came within an hour and sometimes it took hours. Again it depended on who was moving them and the mood they were in. Once on a move a warder ran two of his fingers around my anus and then searched the inside of my mouth with them. I was disgusted with him.

The hosings described by McCloskey were carried out at pressures of 160 lbs per square inch and ceased towards the end of 1978. They were replaced by an industrial steam cleaning process carried out following infestations of white maggots, lice and scabies in the course of 1978, and the fears that an epidemic of some sort might break out among the protesters. During wing shifts, every 10 days after the steam cleaners were introduced, the prisoners would move any contraband they had with them and this provided the rationale for the frequent searches.

In contrast to the cells the prisoners' bodies themselves were reasonably clean because of the rubbing action of the blanket but their hair and beards were filthy and they had what one relative described as 'a ghastly greeney white pallor.'[8] Nails were kept short by rubbing on the floors.

The response of the authorities to this problem, which like the entire dirty protest could have been defused by allowing each prisoner more than one towel when he left his cell, was forced washings and haircuts, also starting in late 1978. As McCloskey recalls the details:

> One Sunday evening the OC in the wing and two other men were taken out to the class office where the PO of the block was. When they were taken in he began to go into a rage saying that if anything happened his men, if so much as a hand was laid on them he would order the batons to be used. I don't know all that was said that night but the OC knew what he was talking about and shouted to H5 telling them what had happened and giving his own opinion that things would be rough. I didn't know what he was talking about and thought perhaps the PO is drunk. The next morning about an hour after breakfast I heard what seemed like a lot of heavy boots coming down the wing and thought, what's this? A door opened and almost immediately the sound of thuds, slaps and shouting, and moans and groans. It was Martin Hurson on the receiving end. He was dragged out of the cell to the doctor's surgery where he was certified as having lice and afterwards force washed by which time he was in a mess. He spent three weeks in the prison hospital recovering from the assault. That morning five men were treated in similar manner.

In fact Hurson, whose stretcher was kicked as he was carried out of the wing, had injuries to his kidneys which were to prove crucial to the course of his hunger strike in 1981. However subsequent forced washings were not so traumatic and, after the final replacement of the cell windows in March 1979, there was even a slight easing of the situation when number one diet was discontinued and disciplinary hearings before the governor for the formal removal of remission and privileges were reduced from one a fortnight to one a month. Both these improvements followed the, ultimately fruitless, decision of four protesting prisoners to take a case to the European Court of Human Rights at Strasbourg.[9]

The major epidemic outbreak predicted from the early days of the dirty protest never materialised and indeed the prisoners proved to have more than normal resistance to diseases like 'flu.[10] However disorders such as diarrhoea, bleeding gums, rashes, ulcers and nausea were common and some prisoners were weak and underweight. The thinness was partly, as Bobby Sands succintly puts it in *The Torture Mill*, because 'to eat and sit where you've just shit!/is not so bloody sweet!' and partly because of the inadequacy of the food. Blanketmen believed that the orderlies sometimes urinated, spat or put scouring powder in the food and prison staff have confirmed that milk intended for the blanketmen was sometimes poured down the sink. Besides this the food was cold and unappetising because of the time it took to get round from the kitchens to the cells and was, in consequence, often thrown to rot in the corners or through the windows by the prisoners.

As might be imagined human relations between staff and prisoners were worse than poor. By 1980 a total of eighteen prison officers had been murdered by the IRA in an effort to exert pressure on the NIO to return political status. Although the killings were openly cheered and celebrated by the prisoners the threat of death had little deterrent effect on the officers, who tended to believe that their own behaviour in the prison would not greatly affect their chance of being killed one way or the other. With the exception of the assassination in September 1979 of Crumlin Road's Deputy Governor Albert Myles, who was taken to have thrown down the gauntlet to the IRA by telling remand prisoners who had gone on the blanket there that he would be the man to break them, most of the murders looked like random or opportunity affairs bearing scant relation to the actions of the victims within the jail. This fatalistic attitude was confirmed when, in April 1979, a woman warder from relatively peaceful Armagh, Agnes Wallach, was cut to pieces in a burst of INLA machine-gun fire as she drove home. If anything the slaughter of their colleagues and the occasional threats by visitors and prisoners encouraged some officers to redouble their efforts to break a protest which they saw as the root of their problems.

The threat of murder was combined with the depressing and unfulfilling conditions of the H-Blocks and the stress of working daily with some of the most dangerous men in Northern Ireland, men who had in some cases committed or attempted multiple murder, who were daily showing a fearful fixity of purpose, who were clearly well motivated to kill their jailers and who had every sign of believing their most violent crimes to be moral acts. These circumstances, coupled with the constricted social life enforced by the daily threat of attack, meant that prison officers were isolated, frequently turning to drink and sometimes becoming unstable, which in its turn exacerbated the problems on the wings.

Mental health was equally hard to preserve for prisoners living in this hellish and unpromising environment. Group loyalty, religious devotion, political fervour, the struggle to make their case heard on the outside, the use of the Irish language and the constant battle with the authorities seem to be the main means by which sanity was maintained. The first of these, the powerful bond built on years of shared hardship, was probably the most important for most prisoners for, despite their periods on the boards and virtual confinement to their cells in the later stages, the blanketmen did have a good deal of contact with each other. This was achieved in the chinks in the prison system, the points in the day when supervision was absent, as well as the fissures in the structure of the prison itself. Small plastered-over holes existed in the walls where cranes had gripped the massive precast sections of the H-Block walls. These were opened and resealed as a means of passing messages. Like prisoners everywhere the blanketmen also used the heating pipes as a means of communication.

The main opportunity for talk came during the lockups which were approximately from 12.30 pm to 2.00 pm while staff had lunch, from 4.00 until 5.30 pm while staff had dinner and from 8.30 pm until 7.30 am. During these periods the wings were locked and staff would not be present. At these times the prisoners would stand at the door and shout to each other. The normal staff procedure for the long evening lockup, as described by Pat McCusker, was:

> A PO was supposed to be between the two wings. One on A and B and one on C and D. When the day staff had gone we would sit there and rule out the book and then we would fuck away off into the canteen and have a game of cards or a sleep. Conscientious officers.

Aware of the routine, prisoners on most blocks used the short lockups for Irish classes or writing 'comms' and the early period of the overnight lockup for communal prayers in Gaelic. It was estimated that curiosity amongst the predominantly Protestant prison staff would be killed off by a few decades of the rosary in Irish. After this political lectures and serious discussion could begin in reasonable safety. These times would also be the occasion for playing bingo and hearing the *sceal,* a cover-all term for news of any kind from the views of the OC on the course of the campaign, through recent IRA activity to current TV shows enjoyed by new arrivals. Also during lockups poetry and prose were recited, especially by Bobby Sands. On a good night news could be simply roared by *scorchers* (from the Irish *scair,* to share or *scairt,* a shout) the 100 or so feet from one H-Block to the other.

The standard of political discussion amongst republicans in the blocks was, by all accounts, in advance of that on the outside. The Sinn Féin Prisoner of War Department, increasingly dominated by the Adams faction, would regularly use the prisoners as a think tank or sounding board for new ideas. The education programme was, until late 1980, co-ordinated by Pat McGeown and, in general, blanketmen were, like him, part of the younger and more radical stratum. They thought of themselves as socialists as well as republicans and talked of replacing the 'reactionary nationalist outlook' of the past with 'a deeper left-wing outlook' but never seriously questioned the republican sacred cow of the necessity to use force to unite the country. The politics they developed were closely in accord with those which came to the fore in the re-organisation and were now being propounded by such men as Tom Hartley, Gerry Adams, Joe Austin and Danny Morrison. Although the use or primacy of force never came into question the concept of a long war and parallel political initiatives were well accepted by most. After release the blanket men were encouraged to involve themselves in community groups, trades unions and cultural bodies which they would try to swing round to the movement's objectives, as well as continuing with the armed struggle. This was seen as a necessary part of the long war because it was felt that people could not realistically be expected to support armed struggle for twenty or thirty years if the movement carrying it out did not attempt to meet their immediate needs. Besides, with final victory postponed until they were old men, involvement on several fronts would give the movement interim victories, both building confidence in its ability to deliver, training it for a peacetime role and showing the limitations of the existing state institutions. Many of these ideas were considerably in advance of what could openly be said in most Sinn Féin cumainn at the time.

The blanketmen's education programme also stressed that the revolution would not stop in the north; after the state there had been destroyed the southern state would also be toppled by means of a strategy which would include violence. A good deal of thought was also given to the shape of a 'Britless Ireland' which was seen as independent of the major power blocks, trading with the third world and relying on its own natural resources including wind and water power for electricity. Underlying these ideas, which are based on the recollection of more than one blanketman, was the belief that, as Pat McGeown put it in explaining his reasons for wishing to escape from prison, 'in the end, when you came down to it, those discussions, those debates, those politics were sound but they were not the cutting edge of the struggle. The cutting edge of the struggle was armed struggle and therefore the place to be was effectively involved in that armed struggle'.[11]

The politics and jail security merged easily in the learning of Irish in lessons roared through the doors and carefully inscribed on the walls with stubs of pencils for later study. Two classes a day ran in many blocks, beginners in the morning and more advanced in the afternoon. As well as reaffirming their Irish identity, the language met the demands of secrecy and for this reason the prison officers were encouraged to learn it, though those that did found that the prison 'jailic' was sufficiently different from the official version to defeat eavesdropping. Officers who were suspected of learning Irish found that a variety of blood-curdling threats were hurled at them by smiling prisoners testing for a reaction.

As in any situation of stress many blanketmen turned to religion for comfort. As well as the nightly communal rosaries several prisoners kept the cold and boredom at bay by pacing their cells praying. The bible was also read, if only because it was the only literature officially available. Most attended mass, if not out of piety then for the *sceal* and the opportunity to meet outside the cells. Not surprisingly many prisoners came to see their plight in religious terms and images; Bobby Sands, for instance, returns frequently in his writings to the image of the blanketmen as Christlike or sacrificial figures who 'wear this crown of thorns' in 'Calvary or Dachau'.[12]

These religious notions melded easily with the traditions of sacrifice handed down from the Fenians and refined by Pearse in his oration at the graveside of the Fenian hero O'Donovan Rossa where he said that: 'Life springs from death and from the graves of patriot men spring living nations.' The sentiments find an ironic echo in Sands' mocking reflection of the death of a prison officer at the hands of the IRA:

> The grave is deep the grave is cold
> A murky red clay tomb,
> While underneath the body rots,
> Above the primrose bloom,
> So do not cringe and do not whinge
> For each will be there soon.[13]

Throughout his poetry, the best of it stylistically reminiscent of Wilde's 'Ballad of Reading Jail', the predominant images are of butchery, the crypt, hell and sacrifice, with death as the sole and inevitable release. H-Block itself is repeatedly seen as a tomb in which the inmates are already dead meat, tortured by 'black friends' in the shape of the 'screws' and destined for a reward in heaven. In his prose, too, he constantly returns to the theme that once in H-Block he is already lost to life, has in fact 'forgotten what it is like to live', in an underworld where physical death is only a matter of time. His most powerful prose image is that of a caged lark, explicitly identified with both himself and a string of former hunger strikers, which starves to death rather than sing in captivity.

Against this it could be argued that Sands was the blanketmen's PRO and his writing was practical propaganda, perhaps intended more to awake sympathy and anger in the outside world than to express his own inner psyche. His communications and the memories of fellow prisoners often reveal a more cheerful and cheering disposition. However, it is impossible to believe that there could be a complete disjuncture between what is written and felt about a situation; that the gloomy, hopeless and determined world of his published writings do not reveal a side of the author's mind, even if it was not the one which was always uppermost. The prison writings are powerful work that appear the credible product of a sensitive young man who daily faced such depressive conditions; especially credible when one remembers the early tragedies of Bobby Sands' life and the fact that he had by this time few enough threads to pick up in the outside world — unemployment and a broken marriage in Poleglass.

These writings were also, as Danny Morrison put it, 'the raw literature of the H-Block prison protest which hundreds of naked men stood up against their cell doors (in the late of the night when the screws had left the wings) to listen to and applaud'.[14] They were recited at length to the protesters, offering an interpretation of their sordid and mortified existence in terms of easily recognised moral categories, as were a number of other works which Sands had committed to memory. The longest of these was Leon Uris' *Trinity,* a sentimental modern American bestseller of some 890 pages built around Irish republicanism. Bobby Sands was capable of reciting *Trinity,* more or less in its entirety, to the listening blanketmen over a period of days.

The familiar sub-ascetic themes of blood sacrifice and victory in death are very powerfully stated by the novel's romantic heroes Long Dan Sweeney and Conor Larkin, both of whom are abused in captivity and consciously give their lives against hopeless odds. Shortly before his death Larkin tells his girlfriend, 'All we can hope for is a glorious defeat. A defeat that may somehow stir the ashes of our people into a series of more glorious defeats. Every man in the brotherhood must defy, scream, kick, die hard, bloody, shake consciences. You see the true job of the brotherhood is not to expand to win but to sharpen its teeth to die hard.' In its climactic final act ninety pages later the body of the dead Larkin and his old Fenian companion are, like that of O'Donovan Rossa in history, accorded a funeral oration by an IRB leader who 'lashed the millennium of tyranny in exquisite rage. And over the land long dead stirrings were heard at last.'[15] Art had imitated life, and life art, fairly closely. The funeral oratory, both in the pulp epic and the history books, planted the

those in the North who, like the Drumms, supported them. Naturally there were differences in attitude. The Northerners were more pragmatic, more sectarian and more interested in the strength of the IRA than in venerable *piseogs* about legitimacy; consequently they were far less inclined to seek salvation in constitutional fixes or deals with outside forces. The debate would eventually be seen in terms of ideology and age as the younger men got a grip on the organisation, bringing in a new generation of ex-prisoners and young hopefuls and developing a political strategy to supersede that of the truce makers.

At an early stage the dangers inherent in the blanket protest became clear to most republican leaders. The British had made it a matter of central principle and it would not be easily resolved. Yet the prisoners' honour was, from their first statement on the issue, so deeply invested in their ability to resist that only substantial concessions could save them from a severe humiliation which was bound to reflect on the IRA as a whole. At the same time the dangers of moving the issue too far up the movement's list of priorities were clear: there were other pressing problems many of which were, like the procedures in Castlereagh, more promising in propaganda terms. At a time when the Provisionals were being squeezed on many fronts there was a danger that the whole organisation would get bogged down in a side issue and that the military campaign, which was already under reorganisation, would suffer.

In any case no solution presented itself. Since early 1977 there had been intermittent pressure from some prisoners to be allowed to go on hunger strike but this was resisted by the leadership on both sides of the wire. Hunger striking was seen as a tactic which had brought very mixed results. Historically a number of hunger strikers had died on protest[3] and all experience showed that, except in the context of truce negotiations, hunger striking had not been a notably successful tactic in modern times. Both MacStiofain and O'Conaill were forced to abandon hunger strikes without having their demands met in 1976 and 1977 and the aftermath of the most recent case of a hunger strike death, that of Frank Stagg in 1976, had degenerated into a morbid tug-of-war for the dead man's body, yielding no lasting benefits to either the movement or the prisoners.

Stagg had died on 12 February 1976 after 60 days on hunger strike in Wakefield prison. It was immediately clear that although the death had engaged a great deal of public sympathy (it was preceded by mass demonstrations and followed by widespread rioting) there were serious divisions within the Stagg family and at the huge West Belfast rally to mark his death Maire Drumm had to deny publicly that the IRA had wanted him to die. Two of the hunger striker's brothers, George and Joe, followed the republican line by accusing the British of murder and by supporting the wave of demonstrations, but other family members did not. Another brother, Emmet, publicly blamed the IRA and a sister, Veronica Philips, joined him to 'disown all talk of bombing campaigns or violence in Ireland and Britain.' Frank Stagg's widow Bridie and his mother, who were both present when he expired, blamed the IRA at least as much as the British for their bereavement and asked that there should be no paramilitary funeral.

Both Bridie and Emmet Stagg were pressurised as a result of their stance. In the case of Emmet, a socialist who had been active in both the Irish Communist Party and the Irish Labour Party (he is now a Labour TD), shots were fired through his window and it was necessary for his home to be protected by armed Gardai for months after his brother's death.

The situation lurched further into the grotesque when the emaciated four-stone body of the hunger striker was returned home. It had to be diverted to Shannon when it was realised that Joe Cahill and Ruadhri O'Bradaigh were maintaining a macabre vigil in Dublin airport to try and grab it for burial in the republican plot at Leigue cemetery in Ballina, Co. Mayo. When, instead, the Gardai and some family members buried it privately under a concrete shield elsewhere in the cemetery the IRA held their own ceremony at which O'Bradaigh vowed to the 1,000 strong crowd that the body would be re-interred in the republican plot. As a result a twenty-four-hour police guard was placed on the concreted grave but, when the police left in November, the IRA dug under the cement, hauled out the corpse and transferred it to the republican plot where they fired a single shot over it as a mark of respect.

The early blanket protest unfolded against this ghoulish backdrop. It was partly due to the example of the Stagg family, partly to avoid becoming ensnared by the issue to the exclusion of all else and partly to broaden the campaign out that the Provisionals decided to allow the relatives to make the running on the H-Block issue.

Historically the IRA had strong misgivings about working with anyone outside its direct control. Born of military elitism, this suspicion extended to all who were not 'sound', who did not give full support to the armed struggle and to the authority of the IRA as the legitimate government of Ireland.[4] In practice this dogmatism was fed by political insecurity and fear that they might be subverted or led astray if they treated politically more sophisticated allies on a basis of equality.

An earlier attempt to co-operate with what was described as the anti-imperialist left had come to grief in 1972 when the briefly flourishing Political Hostages Release Committee broke up in a welter of disagreement over the legitimacy of IRA violence. In February 1976 there were renewed overtures from People's Democracy, the thirty-five-day hunger strike of whose leaders Michael Farrell and Tony Canavan had inspired the PHRC and which was now closely linked to the Paris-based Trotskyist Fourth International and the British International Marxist Group, for a joint front of some sort on the removal of political status. The Provo side strung them along, reviving painful memories of the last days of the PHRC when a statement had been issued saying that, 'Sinn Féin will not allow itself to be used to support the meandering politics of PD nor will it allow pseudo revolutionaries to bathe in the glory of Ireland's recent dead.'

Relatives were, by virtue of their close links to the prisoners, reckoned to be a safer bet so in April 1977, with the IRA's encouragement, the Relative's Action Campaign was set up to provide external support for the prisoners' struggle against criminalisation. However, as the RAC developed a life of its own the old difficulties were to re-surface.

Initially the RAC was confined to Belfast and provided a useful vehicle to counterpoint the suffering of prisoners to the Peace People's criticisms of the IRA. It successfully linked the political status campaign to the emerging evidence of police brutality against IRA suspects and disquiet at the operation of the no-jury Diplock courts. This was an important function at a time when the revamped IRA's campaign was becoming increasingly unpopular both in Ireland and internationally. The first effects of half digested left-wing ideology, the murder of leading foreign businessmen like Courtaulds executive Geoffrey Agate (for which future hunger striker Raymond McCartney was jailed) and the proxy bombing of commercial premises, were losing the terror campaign support at home and abroad. In the south the July murder of British Ambassador Christopher Ewart-Biggs was an unwelcome spillover of the northern violence which increased support for the peace campaign. A string of murders by the floating unit in the Low Countries, starting with Sir Richard Sykes, who had actually investigated the Biggs assassination for the British secret service and including the assassination of a Belgian businessman in mistake for British EEC Commissioner Christopher Tugendhat, helped further undermine the H-Block effort abroad.

Despite the debilitating influence of the Peace People, and the mood of popular revulsion and weariness which they captured, the humanitarian approach of the RAC was able to bring fairly large crowds of people onto the streets of Belfast when the first prisoner to lose status, Kieran Nugent, was sentenced on 14 September 1976. Over the next couple of years RAC activists' constant willingness to interrupt meetings of almost any group with the question 'How about the men on the blanket?' contributed enormously to public awareness of the issue, grinding its imagery into the language of local protest: for years any complaint about housing standards was likely to be backed up by the claim that conditions were 'as bad as the H-Blocks'. The initiative also inspired a number of other groups such as the Trades Union Campaign Against Repression (TUCAR) and the Student Campaign Against Repression (SCAR) who, although very small, were prepared to raise republican grievances at every opportunity in a wide variety of forums.

By late 1977 the relatives had also started to make an impact internationally with a two-week tour of Europe in late September and early October in which five mothers of blanketmen staged demonstrations in Paris, Brussels, Amsterdam, the Hague and Geneva and to meet a number of international bodies including the International Committee of the Red Cross, the United Nations Commission on Human Rights, Amnesty International, the International Commission of Jurists and the European Council of Churches. The form of the demonstrations, first tried by Mrs Mary Nellis eleven months earlier in front of Derry's St Eugene's Cathedral and soon to become common, was to parade in blankets carrying posters highlighting the prison issue.

As this campaign gathered momentum the Provisionals began to encourage the growth of H-Block Committees in country areas. The first were in Co. Tyrone where a string of non-party activists had worked for years to raise money for local prisoners and their dependants without causing any ripples for Sinn Féin.

Soon a more formidable figure was to enter the frame in the person of Bernadette Devlin McAliskey. A powerful orator and personality with the ability to work hard and motivate others, McAliskey joined forces with the Coalisland H-Block Committee shortly after it was formed early in 1977. Although never actually a member of the Northern Ireland Civil Rights Association she had hit the headlines in the early civil rights struggle after gravitating towards PD as a psychology student in Queen's University. Her place in the history books was secured when she became, at the age of twenty-two, the youngest ever woman MP in a 1969 landslide victory against the Unionist in Mid-Ulster. A gifted self-publicist she was lionised by the British popular press as 'the mini-skirted MP' until she outraged tabloid sensibilities by first being imprisoned for incitement to riot in Derry, then having a child whose father she refused to name and finally assaulting Home Secretary Reginald Maudling in the House of Commons in protest at his statement on the Bloody Sunday shootings. Described by her detractors as a 'political nomad' she had already drifted away from PD towards first the SDLP and then Official Sinn Féin before taking the plunge and joining the newly founded IRSP in 1974. After a disagreement with IRSP founder Seamus Costello — she shared his engagingly direct manner but not his militarism — she fomented a split to form her own Independent Socialist Party which she later abandoned to retire into private life in rural Tyrone.

Under her influence, the Coalisland RAC set about organising a broadly based delegate conference for January 1978. The guest list spanned the entire nationalist spectrum from Sinn Féin to the SDLP as well as PD, the smaller ultra-left factions, the Communist Party, NICRA, the Association for Legal Justice (ALJ) and a string of community organisations like the Association of Local Advice Centres. The ground rules assumed that organisations present should not attack each other and that the qualification for attendance was concern for the plight of the prisoners, not necessarily support for the IRA.

Sinn Féin were immediately hostile, fearing that the talented but erratic McAliskey would end up by taking the prison issue from them. They wanted the SDLP to be excluded altogether and while they demanded the right to criticise other groups they insisted that no criticism of the 'armed struggle' should be allowed. A warning was delivered that they would walk out if things did not go as they suggested and in the end they declined to send delegates, but unsuccessfully attempted to swamp the meeting with a contingent of around fifty observers.

They had prepared a paranoid and insecure statement, saying nothing about prisoners apart from the fact that Sinn Féin spoke for them. Instead it lambasted nationalists who criticised IRA activity as 'domestic cockroaches', 'traitors' and 'collaborators'. They believed, it said, that the naiveté of the conference organisers towards such people meant that 'far from exposing hypocrisy in them you will allow them room to manoeuvre, give them breathing space, as it were, to get BACK TO THE BARRICADES'. This was a mistake because:

> Repression condemned on moral grounds isn't good enough. For while it brings sections of the population into opposition it rarely brings them into Resistance. Also if analysed outside of its historical context it leads people to wrongly conclude that any act of resistance, like the killing of an English soldier, causes house raids, arrests and torture by the hated forces of the state.[5]

By this exacting standard only active members of the IRA or their close collaborators were really qualified to support the prisoners and no broad movement was possible.

A more diffuse approach was advanced by tiny PD who lectured the Provisionals that 'Sinn Féin in particular must learn that the Provos' military struggle is only one tactic in the overall struggle against imperialism and there are many in the north who do not support that tactic but are strongly opposed to British Imperialism and its day to day manifestation like torture victimisation of prisoners etc. The support of these people is vital to success.'[6]

The eventual motion to emerge reflected PD's views rather than the Provos'. It was very wide ranging, calling for British withdrawal, repeal of emergency legislation, an end to torture, withdrawal of troops, the disarming of the RUC and UDR and, last on the list, the granting of prisoner of war status to political prisoners pending their unconditional release. Trades unions, governments and the people of the thirty-two counties of Ireland were 'called on' to pursue the hopeless melange of short- and long-term demands in a long list of ways.

In a further compromise motion, it was decided to hold another conference a month later at which all those who had been involved in 'physical activity, i.e. pickets, protest etc.' could be represented.

Sinn Féin had been taken by surprise at the attendance, about 800, at Coalisland and disturbed at the way in which McAliskey and the smaller left-wing groups were taking control of the issue, demanding to be treated as equals and offering criticisms of the IRA. Doubts were raised in their minds about the usefulness of the entire RAC project with its increasingly independent existence. These were fueled by an open row at the follow-up 12 February conference in Andersonstown when veteran Communist Party and NICRA stalwart Betty Sinclair told delegates that an end to violence alone would 'create the conditions of peace which will enable us to empty all the jails'. She appealed to the IRA, then in the midst of a commercial fire-bombing campaign which was to culminate in the La Mon massacre a few days later, to lay down their arms.

During 1978, when a prominent new northern Chief of Staff was still putting his seal on the IRA, and much of 1979 the lack of a way out of the prisoners' dilemma and the competition of other problems meant that it was often not high on their list of priorities for action. In a major interview in August 1978 (with

Vincent Browne of *Magill*) an IRA army council representative failed to mention the H-Block situation and in *Republican News'* three-page review of 1979 the prisoners got just one economic column inch of copy: 'And with the H-Block struggle three years old that was another thing for republicans not to be happy about.'

During the period the IRA's main tactics on the prison issue were to keep on shooting prison officers, making it clear after the September 1979 murder of Albert Myles that 'prison warders are only targets because of the H-Blocks', and to hope that constantly raising the issue in the right quarters would resolve the situation. The Castlereagh experience gave hope that if the facts were made available human rights pressure and journalistic enquiry would eventually force the state to produce a solution. After the initial torture allegations against the RUC were aired publicly by BBC's interview with Bernard O'Connor, Amnesty International had taken up the issue, finding in June 1978 that 'maltreatment had taken place with sufficient frequency to warrant a public enquiry'. This report and the case of Brian Maguire, who was found hanged from a ventilation grille twelve feet from the floor during detention in Castlereagh, raised the complaints to a level where they could no longer be brushed off with assertions that, as RUC Chief Constable Sir Kenneth Newman put it, suspects 'were injuring themselves as part of an IRA propaganda campaign'.[7] Over the next year the pressure mounted as police doctors came forward with evidence of brutal treatment of prisoners under interrogation until finally the state rid itself of the embarrassment by cleaning up interrogation techniques following the Bennett Report in early 1979.

The IRA waited to see if the H-Block issue would develop in the same way, whilst making sure that it was not hijacked as a platform by the unpredictable or self seeking. In Belfast SF held its own demonstrations and pickets, for which it insisted that no statutory notice should be given to the RUC. In August 1978 they provoked a showdown with PD by directing the RACs to attend a Sinn Féin blanket protest instead of holding one of their own. PD predictably put themselves forward as champions of the autonomy of the RACs, and exposed Sinn Féin's high-handed tactics in their paper *Unfree Citizen*. As a result they were immediately expelled from the RACs for breach of confidentiality.

At the same time the RAC-based approach produced promising results in the early part of 1978. Statements of concern flooded in from such diverse quarters as Dr Deeney of the official prison board of governors, the Irish Association of Democratic Lawyers, Una O'Higgins O'Malley of Fine Gael, Official Unionist MP for North Belfast John Carson who visited the H-Blocks in April, Peace People leader Ciaran McKeown and Lord Longford. Novel forms of protests were adopted including the hurling of horse shit at MPs from the visitors' gallery at the British House of Commons, and thousands were brought onto the Falls Road in a march to the GAA pitch at Casement Park.

The Roman Catholic church was also becoming involved. A number of priests including Fr Raymond Murray, the chaplain of Armagh prison, Fr Brian Brady of St Joseph's teacher training college, Fr Alec Reid of the Redemptorist community at Clonard and Fr Denis Faul, the tireless Dungannon based campaigner and chronicler of human rights abuses, had for some time been warning of the dangerous situation in the H-Blocks. Faul and Murray in particular had been taking an active but independent role and had travelled widely to speak on the issue. Behind the scenes the new tough-minded Archbishop of Armagh, Tomas O'Fiach, had visited the prison and made strong private representations to Secretary of State Roy Mason. By late April the issue was being editorialised in the province's Catholic daily the *Irish News* and on 9 June two major figures in the Catholic hierarchy made public interventions. They were Bishop Edward Daly of Derry, who called for a solution to the conditions of 'indescribable filth' after a pastoral visit to the H-Blocks, and the papal nuncio in Dublin, Dr Gaetano Alibrandi, who granted an audience to relatives of blanketmen and spoke of the pope's concern at the situation. There was no hint of support for the political status demand but the church was helping to move the prisons beyond the fringes of public awareness.

Archbishop O'Fiach went further. A native of the republican village of Crossmaglen, where the British army's dustbins have to be lifted by helicopter, he concealed neither his strong nationalist sentiments nor his misgivings about some IRA methods. In early July he took the opportunity of the funeral of a Crossmaglen man killed by the IRA as an informer to put his marker down, saying that he regarded such 'slaughter of a fellow Irishman' as murder, a crime and nothing to do with patriotism. Later in the month he made a second visit to Long Kesh and issued a detailed statement which came close enough to backing political status for Sinn Féin to call it 'a clear pointer to all those who up to now have failed to take a clear stand on political status.'

Saying that he had been unable to speak in two of the cells for fear of vomiting he described the condition of the 300 blanket-men as like to that of the 'hundreds of homeless people living in the sewer pipes of Calcutta' and stated:

> The authorities refuse to admit that these prisoners are in a different category from the ordinary, yet everything about their trial and family background indicates that they are different. They were sentenced by special courts without juries. The vast majority were convicted on allegedly voluntary confessions obtained in circumstances which are now placed under grave suspicion by the recent report of Amnesty International. Many are very youthful and come from families which have never been in trouble with the law, though they lived in areas which suffered discrimination in housing and jobs. How can one explain the jump in the prison population of Northern Ireland from 500 to 3,000 unless a new type of prisoner had emerged?

In a sustained polemic he predicted that the prisoners would 'prefer to face death rather than be classed as criminals' and described their use of the Irish language as 'an indication of the triumph of the human spirit over adverse material conditions', urging both an investigation of their treatment and a substantial return of the privileges denied to protesters under prison rules. He would, he said, be making a report to the Vatican.

The statement carried the issue around the world and offered hope to prisoners that their protest might in the end get results, perhaps without any deaths on hunger strike. The Northern Ireland Office, which wanted to keep the situation out of the public eye, were enraged and the Catholic establishment, which wished to sit on the fence, were left queasy and incredulous at the strength of the clergyman's language. Typical of the Catholic consensus view was the *Irish News*, motto *pro fide et patria*, which editorialised once more on the issue, defending the Archbishop's right to speak but warning, 'On the face of it this is not the time to bring up this lingering issue. To do so is to be labelled a Provisional sympathiser or to act as their propagandist.' The paper went on to suggest that Archbishop O'Fiach, who had criticised neither the protest nor the IRA in his statement, had really said that the blanketmen were themselves responsible for their conditions and that he regarded their action as criminal.

The NIO's reply summed itself up in its opening lines:

> These criminals are totally responsible for the situation in which they find themselves. It is they who have been smearing excreta on the walls and pouring their urine through the doors.

O'Fiach's retort was to warn grimly that, however Roy Mason might deplore the dirty protest, it was better than a hunger strike. In fact at the end of August the Provisionals had, with some difficulty, dissuaded the prisoners from putting their plans for one into action.

The Protestant churches were drawn in, if only to condemn the Archbishop, the British press was forced to react, in one way or another, and politicians at home and abroad began expressing opinions on it. The NIO's primary objective of keeping discussion of H-Blocks confined to the republican fringe was now torpedoed and on that fringe the Archbishop's statement was a morale booster. After the expulsion, fights, confusion and demoralisation which at times seemed terminal, it now seemed that the prisoners might indeed become a major issue. If anything this increased Sinn Féin's suspicion of McAliskey and PD and their reluctance to get more deeply involved with them, though there was mounting pressure from within the prison to take some action. As Joe Austin saw it 'the situation was one that was almost taking place outside the republican movement between the prisoners and the RAC'.

By the end of 1978 the NIO's efforts to put the lid back on the publicity had collapsed. Four prisoners initiated a complaint to the European Commission of Human Rights through NICRA activist and civil rights lawyer Frank Keenan. O'Fiach plugged away on the media, there were a few large marches and 'respectable' bodies like the Catholic peace organisation Pax Christi expressed concern as did some trades councils. However the major payoff came from the campaign of lobbying journalists and politicians carried on by prisoners and their relatives. In October this bore fruit in the Jack Anderson column, supplied by United Features Syndicate to 800 US newspapers including the *Washington Post*. The column's representative had been refused admission to the Maze but had interviewed Rita Mullan, a North Belfast woman working for the New York based Irish National Caucus, who had helped arrange a highly successful speaking tour of the US for Father Raymond Murray and six prisoners' relatives.

The column called for strong US action against the present British administration in Ulster which it compared to 'Oliver Cromwell's iron-fisted rule' and 'the most barbarous regimes of communist commissars or tinhorn Latin America dictators'. Implicit in the article was the mistaken belief that there was a single 'H-Block or hell block' in which conditions of filth and degradation were deliberately imposed, as they were in the 'tiger cages' used in South Vietnam to break prisoners under interrogation. This very confusion exposed the weaknesses of the NIO's policy of keeping journalists out of the prison, which was abandoned as a result. Follow-up lobbying by the well-informed Irish National Caucus and its associated Ad Hoc Congressional Committee on Irish Affairs, which included the future US Ambassador to Dublin Margaret Heckler amongst its members, helped ensure that the issue never died down in the US, providing a constant source of irritation for British diplomacy there.

Not only was the British Ambassador Peter Jay forced to issue a detailed apology for Britain's role in Ireland but the restrictions on entering H3, H4, H5 and H6 were relaxed to allow an all-party group of MPs into the jail in January 1979 and a representative press delegation in March. The basic facts about H-Blocks were now well and truly out in the open, though a solution seemed as far away as ever.

Two elections, to Westminster in May and the first direct elections to the European parliament in June, provided possible opportunities to push the issue further through prisoners' candidates. Taking part in the Westminster poll meant recognising a British parliament, still anathema to orthodox Provos, and created the practical problem that an intervention might be seen as splitting the Catholic vote. In the EEC poll, where Northern Ireland was a single constituency electing three members, the sin of vote-splitting was avoided by the single-transferrable vote system and the loyalties of the province's notoriously conservative voters might be more fluid. It seemed to present the ideal opportunity for an unofficial H-Block referendum — and the perfect re-entry to mainstream politics for Bernadette McAliskey. Her offer to stand was supported by some relatives and individual prisoners and even by parts of Sinn Féin and the IRA. However the 1978 Sinn Féin ard fheis had voted to boycott the European parliament, like all others, and in any case the Provisional organisation was vehemently opposed to the McAliskey iniative, feeling that it confirmed their worst fears about the possible hi-jacking of the campaign. It was one issue on which the urban northerners, who were already planning the long-term entry of Sinn Féin into politics and were not about to be turned into a support group for someone else, and the most dyed-in-the-wool traditionalists, who were abstentionist as a matter of principle, could unite. The authority of the IRA Army Council as the legitimate government of Ireland was even hauled in at one meeting, in an unsuccessful attempt to quash support for her bid.

When Bernadette went ahead in any case the strength of organised Sinn Féin was thrown against her, with the younger radicals taking a particularly hard line and occasionally assaulting her supporters. The whole episode was extremely damaging to the internal cohesion of the H-Block campaign, in some cases dividing households. In Andersonstown, for instance, Mary McDermott, a member of the Ulster executive of Sinn Féin and a regular visitor to the prison, frequently had the task of taking a Sinn Féin loud speaker van up and down the Falls calling for a boycott whilst her daughter, the leading civil rights lawyer Eilish McDermott, campaigned on the same route for Bernadette McAliskey.

When the votes were in McAliskey had secured 33,969 first preference votes or 5.9 per cent of the poll which, while nowhere close to a seat or to forcing the state to do something about the prison issue, was a respectable enough vote for a single-issue candidate. The casualties were the Relatives Action Committees, morale amongst the prisoners and to a lesser extent Sinn Féin which, with whatever justice, was felt by some of its own supporters to have campaigned against the blanketmen.

At Bodenstown the next month Gerry Adams gave the oration, taking the opportunity to return to his familiar themes of 'building an agitational struggle in the 26 counties, an economic resistance movement, linking up republicans with other sections of the working class'. He added 'it needs to be done now because to date our most glaring weakness lies in our failure to develop revolutionary politics and to build an alternative to so-called constitutional politics'. The popularity of the H-Blocks in the election, the eagerness of others to take the issue over and the clearing of the ground in the RACs all suggested the prisons issue as the one on which to start those agitations and alliances on terms that would be favourable to Sinn Féin.

But more pressing than these outside considerations was the situation within the prisons where, after a brief surge, morale was at an all-time low. The blanketmen's leaders saw the possibility of several years (seven was one estimate) of dirty protest stretching before them and the idea of a hunger strike to resolve the issue once and for all was gaining ground rapidly. The pressure peaked in June and July when the OCs actually agreed to a hunger strike and sent their plans to the outside leadership. As Pat McGeown recalls:

> It was suspended for two reasons. Firstly was the formation of the National H-Block Committee. People outside said 'Look, give us a chance to sort it out before you actually go on hunger strike. We think we can broaden it out to a campaign on the H-Block issue rather than another "The H-Block Prisoners are IRA prisoners" campaign.' That was obviously acceptable to us in that we realised the campaign would have to be broadened anyway; republicans couldn't necessarily sway the British government in an argument but if you could recruit your liberal and your

> left and even your Fianna Failer and your SDLP type of politician then perhaps you could get a shift in that it then became a political crisis.

Such arguments were a long way from Sinn Féin's determination at Coalisland the previous year to keep the 'domestic cockroaches' off the barricades at any costs, and the change represented a developing debate in Provisional ranks. Just as the unrelenting and seemingly hopeless pressure of the protest had forced Britain to open the H-Blocks to public scrutiny so it had forced the Provisionals to move it up their list of priorities and reassess their tactics. Whatever their fears of sinking with it or being absorbed by it the issue was now one that they had to resolve. If possible they wished to avoid the crunch situation of a hunger strike in which prisoners would die and defeat was more likely than victory.

Before the Sinn Féin initiative became public a number of significant events occurred.

The Westminster election brought no change to the overall sectarian balance of power in Northern Ireland though Ian Paisley's Democratic Unionist Party gained ground at the expense of the more respectable Official Unionists, sending Peter Robinson, Johnny McQuade and Paisley himself to parliament. In Britain James Callaghan's minority Labour administration was replaced by the Conservatives under the self-styled 'conviction politician' Margaret Thatcher. A heroine of the new right and a believer in 'facing down' problems rather than fudging them, Mrs Thatcher broke decisively with the consensus politics of the past several UK governments to embrace confrontation as a means of overcoming difficulty. Her antipathy to armed republicanism, which had been responsible for the death of her close associate Airey Neave in an INLA car bomb, was particularly strong.

Initially, however, she was an unknown quantity in Ireland, as was her new Secretary of State for Northern Ireland Humphrey Atkins, a low profile and mild mannered former Chief Whip whom the Falls Road graffitti artists immediately dubbed 'Humphrey Who?' Power had also changed hands in the Catholic church where, following the death of John Paul I, the traditionalist Polish Cardinal Karl Wojtyla was elected pope. One of his first acts as pontiff was to fill the year old vacancy for the primacy of all Ireland by making Archbishop O'Fiach a cardinal. A short time later it became known that Ireland was to have its first ever papal visit in the autumn. The Polish church's role as a rallying point for opposition to the state, and the selection of the eminent but outspoken O'Fiach as primate, led to some hopes that John Paul II might take the opportunity of his visit to express the Vatican's concern on the H-Block issue.

O'Fiach suggested his own cathedral city of Armagh in the North as the venue for the main event of the tour. This had actually been agreed when on 27 August, the very day that the cardinal left Northern Ireland for Rome to finalise arrangements, the IRA effectively pulled the plug on the plan with two dramatic operations. They were the early morning radio bombing of Lord Mountbatten's boat in Sligo, killing the peer and three others, and the bomb and gun attack which took the lives of eighteen soldiers at Narrow Water in South Co. Down. Two days later the Vatican announced that, as a result of the violence, Drogheda in Co. Louth would replace Armagh on the papal itinerary.

Any remaining hopes that the pope would intervene on the side of the prisoners, or even draw attention to their plight, was dashed by his speech at Drogheda. Instead, it contained an exhortation to politicians and governments to prove the men of violence wrong by guaranteeing social justice and a considerably more strongly worded appeal to the IRA to end their campaign:

> I wish to speak to all men and women engaged in violence. I appeal to you in language of passionate pleading, on my knees I beg you, to turn away from the paths of violence to return to the ways of justice. I, too, believe in justice and seek justice, but violence only delays the day of justice. Further violence in Ireland will only drag down to ruin the land you claim to love and the values you claim to cherish.

Sinn Féin made the best of the situation, blaming the British for the violence and saying that they would like to meet the pontiff to explain this more fully to him. However there was no concealing the fact that once again the demands of the military campaign were not those of the political mobilisation. The events of 27 August had not only affected the papal visit but had also temporarily undermined the RAC case around the world. In this atmosphere security talks opened between Mrs Thatcher and the Taoiseach Jack Lynch, and RUC numbers were increased by 1,000 following a flying visit to the north by Thatcher.

Despite the setback the Provisionals pushed ahead with plans for a restructured National H-Block Armagh Committee, to be established at a conference in the Green Briar restaurant and dance hall in Andersonstown on 21 October 1979.

The Green Briar conference was held during another of McAliskey's trips to America, but otherwise it held much the same groups as the earlier Coalisland meeting. On this occasion, however, the Provos had control of affairs. Their line had been well threshed out with the prisoners in advance and Kieran Nugent, one of several blanketmen to have been released by this stage, opened the meeting with an account of life in H-Block. Now the issues were narrowed down from the complete republican manifesto included in the RAC's aims[8] to the single issue 'Smash H-Block' and a limited set of five demands which the prisoners believed would give them the substance of political status by allowing them to maintain their own command structures within the prison. At the same time it was thought that they would be sufficiently reasonable to enable the building of a more broadly based campaign, especially when backed by the mass emotional appeal of the prisoners and their families. The demands, in their original form as proposed by Gerry Adams in the main Sinn Féin motion to the conference, were:

1. To be exempt from wearing prison clothes.
2. To be exempt from prison work.
3. To have freedom of association with fellow political prisoners.
4. The right to organise educational and recreational facilities, to have one weekly visit, to receive and send

out one letter per week and to receive one parcel per week.
5. Entitlement to full remission of sentence.

As time went on, the reference to political status would be dropped, but the demands remained the bricks with which the campaign would from now on be built. Bobby Sands was also urging that the issue should be used to get the movement into politics by means of standing blanketmen as candidates and then getting substitutes 'who must be red minded or at least nationalistic'[9] to stand in for prisoners who were elected; eventually these proxy prisoners might form an alternative assembly of some sort which would seek recognition abroad in the same way as the PLO. Adams went on to demand a 'national and international thrust to the smash H-Block campaign which has been lacking' and in an abrupt reversal of the 'domestic cockroaches' approach, he told delegates that so long as people supported the fight for political status, even if they did not support the political views of the prisoners, they were welcome in the RAC campaign. 'What we want is these people on the streets no matter what their reason for supporting us may be', he announced. Arrangements were made to lobby the SDLP, and Peace People leader Ciaran McKeown was applauded for supporting the five demands, even after he asked those present to inform the police about any IRA arms dumps they might know of.[10]

McKeown's intervention, in which he called for 'emergency status' to reflect the emergency legislation under which the prisoners were tried and held, led to a row in the Peace People and contributed to a split in the organisation. Already the H-Block Committee was displaying the ability to polarise non-republican organisations around itself and to become the crunch issue for them.

All Sinn Féin's proposals were passed at the meeting and they emerged the dominant force on the 17-strong committee which was chaired by Dublin priest Father Piaras O'Duill.[11] The committee agreed, though the decision was eventually set aside, to leave local organisation in the north to the RACs and to concentrate on setting up local committees of its own in the south. A conference to push forward this work was set in train for 21 December in Dublin's Mansion House.

In tandem with these initiatives Sinn Féin sought its own private meeting with O'Fiach by first getting prisoners to write to him asking for help and then by making the arrangements through two West Belfast priests, Des Wilson and Alec Reid. Fathers Faul and Murray, both of whom had been very active on the prisoners' issue and had good relations with the cardinal, were apparantly avoided because Sinn Féin was wary of their independent influence amongst relatives. Faul, in particular, had been almost ceaselessly active on the issue.

The first meeting with the cardinal was shortly before the Mansion House conference. At it the Provo side told the priests that the prisoners were close to a hunger strike and asked the primate to use his influence for a resolution. O'Fiach reminded them of the pope's speech at Drogheda, saying that a decrease in violence would create a better atmosphere for progress. He agreed to meet them again on 1 February and in the interim wrote to Atkins, underlining the urgency of the situation.

Between the two meetings the prisoners, discontented with the progress of the National H-Block Committee which had caused them to hold off until now, again threatened a hunger strike and were again dissuaded, this time to give the cardinal a chance. During the period, on 18 January, a PO Fox became the seventh prison officer to be murdered since September and an IRA volunteer, twenty-six year old Kevin 'Dee' Delaney, died with two civilians when the bomb he was transporting on the Belfast train detonated prematurely at Dunmurry. Both deaths were mentioned. The Provisionals complained that four West Belfast churches had turned Delaney's body away. The clergy put a specific demand to them, that they should stop killing prison officers as a sign of good faith in the cardinal's attempts to resolve the crisis in other ways. This was agreed, and no other warders were killed by the IRA, though one was fired on and wounded in East Belfast on 10 June when O'Fiach's negotiations appeared bogged down.

The privacy of negotiations with the cardinal underlined the still uneasy relations with the other groups and individuals on the National H-Block Committee. This was partly due to the series of strongly argued internal debates going on within Sinn

Féin and the IRA about the movement's future tactics which were in turn influenced by the developing Anglo-Irish contacts between Charles Haughey and Margaret Thatcher.

Haughey, who had fallen from political favour in 1970 when he was accused and acquitted of running guns for the north, had become Taoiseach when his predecessor Jack Lynch retired as leader of the ruling Fianna Fáil party in December 1979. Haughey inherited a party which was bitterly divided by the leadership battle and polarised around his own personality. He was consequently eager to produce solid achievements which would enable him to go to the country and strengthen his hand. In terms of domestic policy a building boom was financed by increased overseas borrowing. On the north, despite his hardline verbal republican image, he began an assiduous political courtship of Margaret Thatcher in the apparent belief that she might be the woman to make a radical break with past British policy there. He was encouraged in this view by her *volte face* on Rhodesia, where, under the influence of foreign secretary Lord Carrington, she was in the process of dumping Ian Smith's all-white regime and encouraging the formation of the independent state of Zimbabwe, ruled by the black majority. There was hope of Carrington taking a fresh view on the north too. Haughey's tack over the coming year was to ridicule the efforts of Humphrey Atkins to create an internal political solution in the north through a devolved administration but to keep Thatcher sweet for more talks if the initiative failed. One of his first acts as Taoiseach was a swingeing attack on the IRA and the use of force.

This new atmosphere in Anglo-Irish affairs led the Provisionals to fear a security clampdown, and made them aware of their lack of influence in the Republic. There was renewed emphasis on the south as an area of expansion. New policies had begun to appear in the formation of a Sinn Féin's Women's Committee and an Economic Resistance Campaign (to co-ordinate work in the trades unions) under Phil Flynn, who later became General Secretary of the Republic's Local Government and Public Services Union. It was at this stage that the urban northerners finally secured a four to three majority on the Army Council and were in a position to encourage new blood in the south. The depth of ill feeling, and the bluntness permissible in internal debate, can be judged by the comments of Sean Crowe, the Sinn Féin National Youth spokesman, when he criticised the age of ard comhairle members and the absence of a coherent social and economic policy:

> The people fighting the war in the north are the young people and the people lying in the H-Blocks and other prisons are the young people. We are determined that young people will play an equally major role in the rest of the movement.[12]

Similar disputes erupted in the letters pages of *Republican News* as the last distinctive policy plank of the O'Bradaigh/O'Conaill axis, federalism, came under attack. All this meant that when Sinn Féin reacted to an idea at the National H-Block Committee what they said often reflected a compromise reached after close internal debate, and that their approach often appeared erratic or dictatorial. Despite, or because of, the discussions and factional activity at many levels in their organisation they were resolved to present a common front to outsiders.

At the same time the attitudes expressed by Sinn Féin leaders like Adams on the National Committee were not always those of local cumainn on the ground. In February, for instance, it was considered to be a 'political problem' to ask youngsters not to stone the local RUC barracks at a march which brought nearly ten thousand people of all ages onto the street in Coalisland. The issue of 'filing' for marches was another cause of contention, with traditional Sinn Féin members arguing that to do so was to collaborate with the RUC and other H-Block supporters maintaining that filing was necessary to get large crowds on the demonstrations. Both Bernadette McAliskey and Finbar O'Doherty from Derry were at times hauled over the coals for giving the police notice and, in March, at Newry the entire Sinn Féin contingent stamped out of a meeting over the issue.[13]

There was still uncertainty about both the appropriateness of the prison issue as a major political campaign and of the committee as a means of solving it. In essence the committee was being used as backup and held in reserve in case the O'Fiach negotiations failed. It was not entirely trusted. Throughout the year the Provisionals reserved to themselves the control of communication with the prisoners and the right to give reports on the prisoners' conditions. They had their own H-Block Information Centre and internal committees to deal with the conduct of the agitation and the priority which they were prepared to give the committee and its work varied widely over time. As late as May, for instance, Fr O'Duill complained to Gerry Adams about the lack of coverage of H-Block activity in *An Phoblacht/Republican News*. The balance of forces within the committee in mid year can be shown in the voting for membership of the National H-Block Committee at a second Green Briar Conference held on 15 June. In it Fergus O'Hare of PD, who had consistently argued against 'secret negotiations', easily topped the poll with 303 votes, followed by Fr O'Duill with 244 whilst the three main Sinn Féin runners, Gerry Adams, Jim Gibney and Tom Hartley (the full-time head of Sinn Féin's POW department), tailed somewhat behind with 199, 172 and 147 respectively. Ginny Hamilton, a close associate of O'Conaill, had to be co-opted when she failed to reach the quota for election.

Sinn Féin's behaviour on the National Committee, often infuriating or mystifying to other members, was not without reason. Despite its closely argued internal politics, its growing support amongst some prominent personalities and the fairly large numbers of people out on the streets for some of the marches, it was not, as some may have hoped, a re-run of the civil rights era. IRA prisoners evoked a degree of outright antagonism and widespread indifference in Irish society, and not only because of the gravity of some of their crimes or the viciousness of the ongoing IRA campaign. Their condition was remote to the rest of society which had problems of its own.

Despite PD's enthusiasm, it was not an issue which was going to bring workers out on strike or evoke overwhelming feelings of solidarity in society at large. The by now well-documented accounts of conditions in the Blocks aroused sympathy but this was diluted by the more widespread feeling that the conditions were the responsibility of the prisoners themselves. Even amongst nationalists who had a general sympathy with the prisoners and believed that the government was inflexible there was the feeling that the IRA was on a hook largely of its own making. The effective hard core support for the blanketmen was in the last analysis limited to those people who believed that the IRA was fighting a just war and deserved to be recognised as an army. This was supplemented by the rent a mob of footloose and deprived youngsters who could be mobilised for any large demonstration; the same young people who were being knee-capped by the IRA as part of their 'community policing' policy or shot by the British army as they crashed through road blocks whilst joyriding in stolen cars. Even the prisoners' own relatives were often opposed to the protest, and most IRA members did not feel strongly enough to join it if they were imprisoned.

Although this hard core may have looked like mass influence to people who had spent years in tiny far-left groups and had little political capital to lose, it did not look that way to Sinn Féin and was not so in reality. Conversely Sinn Féin realised that anything less than a massive political mobilisation was not going to create the political crisis necessary to change British policy on such an issue. Prolonged ineffective action would only lead to slow defeat and demoralisation of their supporters. Pushing bodies like the church to take a stand and back door diplomacy, backed if necessary by H-Block activity, was a more promising means of finding a resolution and one that exposed both the movement on the outside and the prisoners to less risk. It was as this process exhausted itself that Sinn Féin appeared to 'come round' to ideas put forward by the smaller groups which they had earlier rejected. As they did so they were forced to put more and more of their human and material resources into the campaign, to the detriment of other projects.

The only possible way of getting enough people aroused to force a change of policy was, the prisoners had suggested, by means of a hunger strike. A hunger strike was a high-risk venture in which men were likely to die without any guarantee of success and if it was to be understood by supporters everything else would have to be seen to be tried first.

NOTES

1. Interviews with the author.
2. It was Twomey who insisted on Adams' and Ivor Bell's presence, as intellectual minders, in the first truce negotiations and who pushed for Adams to head the commission which drew up the reorganisation document.
3. They were Thomas Ashe who died in 1917 after being force fed by the

British authorities of the day; Terence McSwiney, the Lord Mayor of Cork, who also died after seventy-four days without food in 1917; Tony D'Arcy and John McNeela who died on hunger strike for political status in Dublin's Mountjoy jail in 1940; Sean McCaughey who died hunger striking for unconditional release in the Republic's Portlaoise prison in 1946; Michael Gaughan who died on hunger strike in Parkhurst prison on the Isle of Wight demanding political status; and Frank Stagg, who had been on hunger strike with Gaughan but came off after the latter's death, who died in Wakefield Prison in 1976.

4. The principle was enunciated in its most liberal form in *Republican News* columns: 'If, despite education, persons find they disagree with these objectives then they have no place in the republican movement and should be left in a supporting role. No-one should be allowed to influence policy except those whose adherence is whole-hearted and single minded.' For an example of an organisation founded on these principles see the RAC rules in Appendix 5.

5. Quoted in Kevin Kelley's *The Longest War: Northern Ireland and the IRA* (Brandon Books 1982).

6. Quotations from a typescript of the Sinn Féin speech and a PD/MSR conference document in the author's possession. MSR was the Movement for a Socialist Republic, the Irish section of the Fourth International with which PD later merged.

7. Such dismissals reached their state of the art amongst security officers who briefed the *Daily Telegraph* of 31 October 1977 to the effect that 'Investigations indicate that one hardline Provisional was given large whiskeys and a box of king size cigarettes for punching himself in both eyes while in the RUC's Castlereagh Interrogation Centre — and then filing a brutality complaint against the police' whilst in another case 'a man being interviewed by the police took off a shoe and struck himself on the head' (Quoted in Liz Curtis *Ireland: The propaganda war*, Pluto Press 1984).

8. See Appendix 5.

9. See Bobby Sands' 4 August Communication for the state of thinking amongst prisoners after their initial threat of hunger strike had been withdrawn.

10. Quotations from motions and speeches are taken from conference papers. Ciaran McKeown's own account is in *The Passion for Peace* (Blackstaff 1984) and the *Irish News* of 23 October 1979.

11. Besides O'Duill the membership included Gerry Brannigan and Martha McClelland from Sinn Féin, Miriam Daly and Niall Lennoch from the IRSP, Pat Finucane (a lawyer and the brother of blanketman Seamus Finucane), Gordon Hayes (a solicitor from Limerick), Sean Murphy, Joe Stagg (brother of Frank), Fergus O'Hare and Martin MacAnGhoill from PD, Leo Wilson, Maura McCrory, Mary Enwright and Kathleen Gallagher. Bernadette McAliskey and Kathleen Holden were shortly co-opted. In the future there were numerous other co-options, mainly of Sinn Féin members.

12. *Republican News*, 10 May 1980.

13. Instances taken from H-Block minutes. The Newry incident was excised from the minutes but is detailed in a hand-written report to Sinn Féin in the author's possession. The filing issue was finally decided by an understanding

that no republican should be asked to sign the papers and that Frank Maguire, who had already taken the oath of allegiance to enter parliament, would normally allow his name to be used.

6

Like the Seven of 1916

> We want the H-Blocks settled, we don't want to see the warders killed, and the H-Blocks are of no propaganda purpose to us. Our people in the jails are suffering real deprivation and we want that resolved.
>
> IRA Spokesperson, August 1980.[1]

Nineteen-eighty was a year of narrowing options for the protesting prisoners. Grim as conditions were, the prospects of matters being brought to a head by a natural development like the outbreak of disease had receded with time and the advent of steam cleaning. Neither the battle to publicise conditions nor the outside protests had proved decisive. The O'Fiach negotiations and the outcome of the European Commission of Human Rights case remained as hopes, but vague ones because the Provisionals at large were often in the dark about the details of what was happening.

In these circumstances it is not surprising that despite the continuing flow of IRA convicts from the Diplock courts, the overall number of men on the blanket had remained more or less static at around 370 for the best part of a year and had even fallen from 380 to 360 over the December to January period. In its present form the protest was coming apart at the seams. Many prisoners were on the brink of abandoning it or were unwilling to join it in the first place and, sometimes the flip side of the same coin, some were prepared to embark on hunger strike as a way out of the impasse. As this situation unfolded it became clear that, after raising the profile of the H-Block issue, the IRA in freedom and captivity had a great deal riding on the protest and could be permanently damaged by its collapse.

Where the links between jails and the overall aims of the IRA had been highlighted, the projection was now softening to suggest a problem of human rights and prison conditions which Britain could resolve with a little humanity and flexibility. This explains the much more limited demands of the National H-

Block Committee as opposed to the RAC. The introduction of the five demands, abandoning all formal mention of political status and not yet much stressed by the prisoners themselves, not only gave specific content to the protest but, the Provos hoped, created a way round British rejection of special status for IRA prisoners. In Margaret Thatcher the IRA had, however, found an opponent who, like themselves, took readiness to treat as weakness, who had read little Irish history and who did not understand the perverse relationship between suffering and strength in the history of physical force nationalism.

By early February, when the prisoners were dissuaded from embarking on a hunger strike to give O'Fiach room to manoeuvre, the long-running protest showed signs of losing its media novelty. Despite a reassuring build-up in support from prominent figures in Irish society,[2] Joe Stagg, by now a member of the Sinn Féin ard comhairle and director of publicity for the National H-Block Committee, reported[3] that only *Newsline*, organ of the tiny Workers Revolutionary Party, and *Hibernia*, whose editor John Mulcahy sponsored the campaign, had written favourably about the protest. The next real change in the tempo of events, and perhaps the major pressure on the IRA to raise the profile of the prison issue, came just four days later from an unexpected quarter, Armagh women's prison.

In Armagh thirty-three prisoners were protesting but, since they were allowed to wear their own clothes and did not object to being integrated with other Catholic prisoners the only real target for resistance had been the attempts, abandoned in 1978, to integrate them with loyalists. Since then they had refused to do prison work but as they still got up to four and a half hours association a day and were not put 'on the boards' the situation was unlike that in the H-Blocks. Nevertheless there had, since Autumn 1979, been pressure from some inmates to start a dirty protest in solidarity with the blanketmen. On 12 January one prisoner, twenty-year-old Anne-Marie Quinn from Ballymurphy who remained in her cell due to illness, had been involved in a fracas after she refused to let prison staff search her chamber pot. As a result the pot was spilt and, prisoners claimed, a used sanitary towel was thrown at Quinn.

There followed a build-up of disputes over hygiene. Prisoners complained that they weren't given long enough to clean their cells, that there were too few brushes, that the three baths available were not enough for them and that water for washing clothes was too cold. The crunch came, deceptively, with an announcement on 7 February that there would be chicken and apple pie for dinner.

The improved menu was designed to get the prisoners out of their cells to allow a search for black berets, IRA uniforms and a tricolour which had recently been used to stage a parade in the exercise yard commemorating the death of Kevin Delaney in the premature Dunmurry train blast. As the women queued at the hot plates they found that their path back to the cells was blocked by thirty-six male prison officers, mainly 'trade' officers such as carpenters. Governor Scott told them to go to the association rooms as the cells were to be searched. When the republicans and three loyalists tried to return to their cells they clashed with the prison officers, plates of chicken were hurled and seven republican and one loyalist sustained bruises or other injuries. Further violence followed after Provo OC Mairead Farrell told Scott that she and four other senior IRA prisoners[4] would not go to the guard room for disciplinary hearings which in the more relaxed Armagh regime, were usually held in the prisoners' own cells. As a result baton wielding male officers 'trailed' the resisting women, whose cloths were left in disarray by the struggle, before the governor.

The other prisoners who had been involved in the original fight with the male officers were locked in their cells and began emptying chamber pots, which they said were too full to wait until slop out, through the judas flaps in the doors. In a now familiar pattern the authorities blocked up the spy holes, the prisoners smashed them and, when they were re-blocked, spread the contents of the pots over the walls.

After some toilets were again made available, the women continued with the protest, accepting a change of clothes every three months. At times they were also without sanitary towels and smeared their menstrual blood on the walls.

The Armagh no-wash protest lacked the momentum of the H-Blocks protest and might have been ended without any real loss of face or surrender of principles. However the protest was linked to events in the H-Blocks and the women's determination to persist played an important part in raising the temperature of the overall prison struggle. Uniquely, it could unite the feminist left with the Catholic right through its powerful images of outraged Irish womanhood, forced immodesty and bodily violation. The appeal was put in its rawest terms by the influential journalist Nell McCafferty, writing on the plight of a sick prisoner, Pauline McLaughlin:

> Shall we feminists record that she is inflicting the condition on herself in case any question of moral dereliction arises against us? The menstrual blood on the walls of Armagh prison smells to high heaven. Shall we turn our noses up?[5]

This new broadening of the campaign was in marked contrast to the narrowing options that were presenting themselves to the IRA on other fronts.

In the O'Fiach/Atkins negotiations it was correctly suspected that the pace was being dictated by the Prime Minister, Margaret Thatcher. There was a flurry of activity towards the end of February, when Atkins visited the Cardinal's residence. In March O'Fiach spent eleven hours in the Maze visiting both Brendan Hughes and the UVF's Gusty Spence before he again met Atkins with Bishop Edward Daly. This toing and froing was accompanied by letters from Atkins saying that he would not negotiate with the protesting prisoners, but in fact the British government was, as it would continue to do throughout the prison crisis, effectively negotiating through the church, the relatives, the SDLP and anybody else except the Provisionals' chosen representatives.

Atkins had already taken the opportunity of a meeting with a group of relatives and the SDLP to gauge priorities and to make it clear that, whatever else happened, there would be no return to special category status.[6] Following O'Fiach's shuttle diplomacy he offered concessions of which the Provisionals were informed before their official announcement. At the National H-Block Committee of Sunday 23 March 1980:

> A discussion took place on information that Atkins was making a public statement on the H-Blocks on Wednesday

> in Westminster. The informant asked delegates to adhere to confidentiality about the details he gave. Atkins is to announce a series of minor reforms which could be the fore-runner of a major development, but this was dependent on the attitude of the prisoners. After some discussion it was agreed that the Nat Ctte would issue a 'middle of the road' statement following the prisoners' and Sinn Féin's response. The statement should point out the reasonable-ness of the five demands and criticise the BG for intran-sigence. If Atkins' statement amounted to a major break-through but was divisive then an emergency meeting of the ctte was to be held.[7]

Atkins' statement, which wasn't issued until the following Wednesday (26 March), was designed to cover Britain for the forthcoming judgment of the European Commission, as much as to influence local and Anglo-Irish politics. Accompanied by the announcement that political status would be withdrawn for all offences committed before 1 March 1976, the concessions doubled the number of visits available to protesters to two a month, quadrupled letters to one a week and allowed the men to exercise in prison issue sports gear rather than the normal denim uniforms. The concessions were immediately rejected but were followed five days later by the announcement that Marian Price, who was suffering from anorexia nervosa, was to be released.

These measures were accompanied by increasing violence on H-Block marches and a closer relationship between Haughey and Thatcher which resulted in the Taoiseach's acceptance of a unionist veto over any constitutional change in the status of Northern Ireland.[8]

In June the European Commission of Human Rights added to the squeeze, ruling against the prisoners on each and every one of the five demands as well as making it clear that special status was not their right under international law. The Commission found that there was nothing 'inherently degrading or objectionable about the requirement to wear prison uniform': that prison uniform was 'necessary in a democratic society in the interests of public safety and for the prevention of crime' because it made it easier to recognise prisoners in the event of escape or attempted escape; that the legal concept of freedom of association 'does not concern the right of prisoners to enjoy the company of other prisoners'; that the absence of exercise from the protesting prisoners' regime was something 'that they alone must bear responsibility for' since they could exercise in uniform, sports gear or naked and that the disciplinary restrictions on visits and letters were permissible, as was the removal of remission. The Commission concluded: 'the protest campaign was designed and co-ordinated by the prisoners to create the maximum public sympathy and support for their political aims. That such a strategy involved self-inflicted debasement and humiliation to an almost sub-human degree must be taken into account.'

One narrow window of opportunity opened in paragraphs 46 and 64 which expressed 'concern at the inflexible approach of the state authorities which has been concerned more to punish offenders against prison discipline that to explore ways of resolving such a serious deadlock' and stated that 'efforts should be made by the authorities to ensure that the applicants could avail of certain facilities such as taking regular exercise in the open air with some form of clothing (other than prison clothing) and making greater use of the prison facilities under similar conditions'.

For prisoners the damning findings came on top of the 6 February US State Department's annual report to the Senate which had exonerated Britain of any human rights violations in Northern Ireland. Before the Commission's views were officially known the Provisionals announced, at a 26 May internal seminar, that the H-Blocks issue was their top immediate priority, making the head of the Prisoner of War department into a full-time post and deciding to channel resources and time into the Department as a dry run for other specialist committees. Each Comhairle Cuige (Provincial Executive) was to appoint a POW officer and a regular internal news sheet on the prisons was to be produced. This move was followed by an ultimatum from the blanketmen to O'Fiach and the other bishops seeking to negotiate for them that they would take matters into their own hands if significant progress had not been made by the end of the year.

At the same time the IRA campaign was running down,

making 1980 the most peaceful year since the early troubles in 1971. The decrease was partly due to the reduced tempo imposed by the long war strategy and the cumbersome cell structure, partly to the increased priority being given to the prison issue and partly to the security clampdown accompanying the Anglo-Irish process and changes within the RUC.

State intelligence and security was now in the latter stages of Ulsterisation, marked by a steady withdrawal of troops in recognition of 'police primacy', increases in RUC patrols and the growth of specialist police intelligence and paramilitary units. Many of the changes were assisted by an increase in current year security spending to £296.19 million and by former MI5 chief, Sir Maurice Oldfield, the security co-ordinator, who had, by 1980, a new RUC Chief Constable and a new Commander of Land Forces, John Hermon and Lt General Sir Richard Lawson, to deal with. Hermon, a man of strong personal religious beliefs, came from a uniformed police background and set about streamlining the force. Officers regarded as bigots found themselves transferred or shunted sideways, a number of Hermon's associates were moved into RUC HQ in Knock, established Special Branch empires were broken up and the RUC made steady progress in patrolling in Nationalist areas. Hand in hand with this 'professional' approach went a resistance to local political pressure (many Unionist politicians felt Hermon treated them with contempt), a determination that the RUC would control security and the creation of units to take over some tasks previously carried out by troops and special forces.

Oldfield, who cut short his term as security co-ordinator after it was confirmed that he had terminal cancer and was replaced by Sir Richard Brookes in June, advised on the introduction of sophisticated bugging and covert tactics in the RUC. During this period a number of undercover squads were built up who would, it later emerged in court, be told it was their duty to lie to CID about their activities and trained on the basis that 'once you have decided to fire, you shoot to take out your enemy'.[9] These units were often composed of ex-soldiers with scant police training but drew on the experience of the Divisional Mobile

Support Units which had been developed in 1978 to act in a 'fireman' role for riot and civil disorder. They were known as the Special Support Units and backed up an elite special branch unit, Echo Four Alpha, or E4A.

Members of both the SSUs and E4A had their own chain of command stretching to the Chief Constable and were instructed to tell the curious that they were routine patrols. From late 1979 they trained in 'quick fire and aggression', first at the SAS 'killing house' in Hereford and later in the British army's purpose built 'PIRA Town' in Ballykinlar Camp. The training was similar to that given to special forces, concentrating on quick reaction firing against armed and dangerous enemies. Officers would burst into rooms full of dummies and be graded on their ability to 'kill' as many as possible in a set period of time. By early 1980 both these units were deployed, E4A (who worked closely with MI5 and Military Intelligence) primarily in a surveillance and informer handling role and the SSUs or HMSUs[10] acting as Quick Reaction Forces to back them up. These were the units which were to come under scrutiny in John Stalker's report into the RUC's alleged shoot-to-kill policy.

Their secret deployment and period of takeover from similar army units was accompanied by the first disputed killing of a civilian by the RUC since 1976. The victim was sixteen-year old Michael McCartan who was shot when police mistook the paint brush he was using to paint H-Block slogans on a wall for a gun. The introduction of the special units also coincided with the premature detonation of Dee Delaney's bomb on the Dunmurry train and the first successful assassinations of targeted republican or nationalist activists by loyalists since the killing of Maire Drumm.

First to die was John Turnley, a Ballycastle company director and former British army officer who had moved from his Protestant-unionist landowning background first to the SDLP and then the IIP. He was murdered beside his Japanese born wife when loyalists opened fire on his car as he returned from a H-Block meeting. In 1982 Robert McConnell, a UFF[11] man convicted of the crime, told the court he was working for the SAS. He named two officers as his controllers and claimed they gave him a radio bus to plant in a Cushendall pub favoured by Gerry Adams as well as a collection of firearms which included the

Sterling sub-machine gun used to kill Turnley. Detectives said they destroyed notes from an interview with another of the accused, McConnell's brother Eric, because their contents were too sensitive to be shown to any but a few senior officers.

In June Miriam Daly was murdered at Queen's University where she worked as a lecturer. Mrs Daly was a member of the National H-Blocks Committee and had recently resigned from the IRSP, of which she had been chairperson.

On 1 July a police patrol was right on the spot as Terence 'Teddy' O'Neill ran off after kneecapping an eighteen-year-old IRA youth behind Whiterock Leisure Centre. They shot the hooded man dead as he attempted to make off.

In August another IRSP and H-Block activist, this time a leading member of the INLA, made a series of allegations against the police after being released from detention. Ronnie Bunting, like Turnley a nationalist of Protestant and unionist background,[12] was convicted of wasting police time when he made an official complaint to the RUC that his interrogators had threatened him with death. At 3.30 on the morning of 15 October, a short time after the charge was quashed on appeal, khaki clad men sledge-hammered Bunting's door down, ran up to his bedroom and shot him dead. They also murdered Noel Lyttle, another INLA man who had recently been released from Castlereagh and was staying in the house, leaving Bunting's wife Suzanne for dead after shooting her in the mouth. Unusually in such crimes, no hijacked vehicles were used and the raiders appeared well versed both with the layout of the republican Andersonstown area and with the Buntings' sleeping arrangements. Due to the professionalism of the raid and the calmness of those involved Mrs Bunting and local SDLP representative Paddy Devlin believed the killers were associated with the security forces.

This bizarre series of attacks extended into 1981 with an attempt on the life of Bernadette McAliskey and was eventually answered in kind by the Provisionals who battered down the door of Sir James Stronge and his son Norman, two Unionists unassociated with the security forces, and shot them both dead. Before that happened, on 15 November, another H-Block activist, thirty-three-year old Peter Valente, was found shot dead in the Protestant Highfield area. Again loyalists were blamed, but this time the IRA were responsible. Later it emerged that Valente, who was a member of the IRA and had a brother, James, on the blanket, was a police informer whose cover was blown by a member of the 'Bronze Squad', an RUC Reserve unit who worked in co-operation with E4A and the SSUs.[13]

The year also saw intelligence gains for the authorities in the Republic who captured IRA training documents, raided a training camp and finally made their two biggest ever explosives finds, totalling over three tons, in Co. Donegal.

In the latter half of 1980 prison life became a preparation for a hunger strike. Pat McGeown, now OC of H6, estimates that 200 to 300 letters a week were leaving the prison for publicity purposes. Much of this effort was inspired by Bobby Sands, one of whose own communications had brought O'Fiach back to the prison at the beginning of the year, who was Darkie Hughes' right-hand man within the jail. Such was the volume of this material that doubts arose now, and throughout the hunger strikes, that all of it was written in the H-Blocks.[14]

Brendan Hughes himself had played a crucial role in discouraging a precipitate hunger strike in the preceding years. Now he devoted just as much energy to dampening hopes that the O'Fiach and Daly talks with Atkins would produce anything decisive. In this he was correct. The main practical role of O'Fiach's intervention was to lend the H-Block protest an international credibility and respectability which it had previously lacked, stiffening the prisoners' resolve and suggesting that movement was possible if enough pressure could be exerted.

Another morale building minor victory came at the end of August when Atkins announced that he was prepared to give protesting prisoners the same rights to compassionate parole, for instance to attend funerals of family members, as other prisoners. He also allowed them to choose 'closed' visits, where they would be physically separated from visitors by a screen, as an alternative to being body searched. The concessions were dismissed out of hand by the prisoners. Now they were more than ever convinced that a hunger strike, and only a hunger strike, would get them what they wanted.

The mounting disorder and violence associated with the H-Block movement forced the IRA to condemn the 'hooliganism' which surrounded the 9 August anti-internment demonstrations; the dragon's teeth which would produce the street 'hood' gangs that sprang up amongst ghetto youth after the hunger strikes were now being sown. However in the prisons even this development, which was in reality alienating support, could raise unrealistic hopes that the H-Block issue held a revolutionary potential.

These hopes were fed when six US state legislatures voted to support the blanketmen and, in an amazing gaffe, which the IRA never forgot, NIO prisons' minister Michael Alison stated that special category status had been conceded in response to the street disorders of 1972.

All this conspired to feed the myths of blood sacrifice which Bobby Sands had tapped in his writings and which were reworked in *Trinity*. As the year wore on Joe Austin[15] noticed that some of 'the prisoners believed that the hunger strike had the makings of actually being another 1916 scenario'. In this atmosphere not only a solution but perhaps an end to the long war and a chance to be on the side of historic destiny seemed at last in sight and the numbers of prisoners on the blanket rose dramatically. After sticking around 360 through the spring it had risen to 468 at the end of October. Prisoners were for the first time transferring in large numbers from other blocks to the protesting areas and by the autumn H3, H4, H5 and most of H6 were filled with blanketmen. O'Fiach, Sinn Féin, the relatives and other local observers were well aware of the dangers of this situation. Seeking to build on the European Commission's call for flexibility and generosity the Protestant Irish Council of Churches warned that the prison rules could not deal with the situation but that an 'official study' of prison conditions might find a way round it. For his part O'Fiach secured from relatives an assurance that if there was movement on just two of the demands, clothes and work, then the prisoners would abandon their protest.

When the bottom line was transmitted to Atkins he made it clear that he saw it as a demand for political status which he was not prepared to negotiate on.

The leadership on the outside were still largely opposed to the hunger strike, wary of risking everything on so chancy a venture, fearful of the reaction and reluctant to see men whom many of the younger northern leaders knew personally dying or facing defeat in such dismal circumstances. In a frequently quoted communication Gerry Adams told Bobby Sands that the leadership was 'tactically, strategically, physically and morally opposed to a hunger strike'.

Yet the massive investment of resources in the H-Block campaign did mean that the Provisionals at large were, as they put it, 'captured' and a process of continuous resessment was under way. The organisation on the outside, especially the urban northerners, were now almost as badly hamstrung by the protest as the men on the blanket. Its propaganda and mobilisation value had peaked and would decline unless it was transformed by a qualitative change in the protest itself. Besides this the exhaustion of alternatives had created a situation which had been theoretically contemplated for at least a year in which the pressure for a hunger strike would be unstoppable and in which, whatever the niceties of the prisoners' position as IRA volunteers, an open breach with at least a section of them would be on the cards. All this sprang into focus when the British rejected what Fr Alec Reid described as the cardinal's efforts to substitute the moral clout of the Roman Catholic church for the IRA's more traditional methods. The very pressure to find a solution, once it was resisted by the British, turned in on the IRA and the prisoners themselves. Early in October decisions long planned as theoretical fallbacks rapidly entered reality. Liam McCloskey recalls:

> When the talks between Cardinal O'Fiach and Bishop Daly and the NIO failed Brendan Hughes learned that they had failed on a visit and within one hour, when the first lock-up came at half past four, he announced that there would be a hunger strike. We had a few weeks to think about it and we were told anyone going on it was to put their names down and be prepared to die, that it wouldn't be a glory run for 40 or 50 days and we were asked to think about it and if we thought we could do it to put our names down.

Bobby Sands, who had long contemplated this step but was left off the strike on the grounds that he would be needed to take over as OC once the fast got under way, took personal charge of the practical arrangements. Again McCloskey recalls his experience as a blanketman:

> I couldn't make up my mind whether I could die or not. Every time I came to the point of actually dying I drew back, I left it, I just decided to put it out of my mind and then the day that Bobby Sands sent a note down the wing, down through all the cells — there were small holes in the walls we were able to pass notes through — we were told to put our names down if we wanted to go on it.
>
> The two men in the cells below me put their names down. I decided there and then, we had been through so much together, we may as well go through the hunger strike and I thought I'll only know if I can die when it comes to it. I decided just to take the risk of death at that stage.

There then began a process of winnowing down the list of seventy or so who were prepared to die. The initial selection was on a geographic basis to maximise support. Organisational considerations meant that a place was reserved for the smaller INLA. According to Sinn Féin there were several stages of vetting in which the layers of OCs and the outside leadership would tell prisoners they were unsuitable but would relent if the individual prisoners insisted. This process is similar to that adopted by the IRA in recruitment for some operations or units.

Mary McDermott, then a Sinn Féin member, was a regular visitor to Andersonstown man Kieran Doherty. They first met when she volunteered to take some of the brief daily visits allowed during his appeal against conviction for possession of explosives and hijacking a car in the course of an abortive bombing mission in Balmoral Avenue. After the appeal was rejected he kept sending her visiting passes until his death. Unknown to her there was, for Doherty, a special bond between them. Her son Sean, then a twenty-year-old IRA volunteer, had been shot dead at Doherty's side as they attempted to hijack a police reservist's car after placing a bomb in West Belfast's Conway Hotel on 5 April 1976, just four months before

Doherty's eventual capture.[16] A third member of the bombing party, Armagh jail OC Mairead Farrell, was the only person to be arrested on the mission. Afterwards Doherty ignored IRA security precautions to attend Sean McDermott's funeral.

She recalls a visit as the selection process was in train:

> At that time you wouldn't have known anybody; covered in long hair, wispy beards, filthy and unwashed. When they were coming out from the blanket they were given just any uniform, it didn't matter whether it fitted or not. They seemed to be put in some sort of electric dryer at too high a speed, all full of creases, and great heavy boots with no laces, they must have thought they would strangle themselves with the laces on the way out.
>
> But Kieran was still protesting, as strong as anything and he was talking about the hunger strike, telling me that this hunger strike was necessary and so on, but he didn't tell me for a good while that he was going on it. When he told me he said, 'You know my name is down for hunger strike?' and I said, 'Are you sure?' He said 'I'm only number 7 so it is a toss up. The Irps[17] don't know if they are putting somebody on it or not but if the Irps decide to put somebody on then I will have to step down but if they don't I'm going on the hunger strike' and he said, 'Would you tell my father and mother?' So I did. I told his father. I went up to the PD[18] and I told him Kieran was going to go on hunger strike if the Irps didn't put anyone on. Then about a week or some length of time like that went on and everybody heard that that fellow John Nixon from Armagh, he was an Irp, was going on the hunger strike. So I thought to myself, 'Kieran won't be on it.'

On 10 October the blanketmen announced that a hunger strike, not for the five demands, but demanding 'as of right, political recognition and that we be accorded the status of political prisoners' would commence on the 27th. They went on: 'We claim this right as captured combatants in the continuing struggle for national liberation and self-determination . . . Our widely recognised resistance has carried us through four years of immense suffering and it shall carry us through to the bitter climax of death, if necessary.'

The announcement brought an immediate reaction from the cardinal who flew back from the Synod of Bishops in Rome to meet Atkins amidst speculation that a cabinet sub-committee had agreed to abolish prison uniform in all jails in Northern Ireland. Instead Atkins offered to 'substitute civilian type clothing for prison uniform'. The concession, essentially a change to a smarter and more varied uniform, was dismissed as meaningless by the prisoners and the hunger strike went ahead as planned.

Darkie Hughes, John Nixon, Sean McKenna, Raymond McCartney, Tommy McKearney, Tom McFeely and Leo Green were put on strike straight away. Seven, as they saw it, 'like the seven of 1916' whose execution by the British after the Easter Rising had provided the spark that was to be fanned into the Irish War of Independence. Most of them were extremely fit men despite their years on the blanket. John Nixon in particular had a powerful physique and constantly exercised in his cell. The exception was Newry man Sean McKenna who had been kidnapped by the SAS south of the border in 1976 and badly beaten by the police at Bessbrook before signing statements implicating himself in a number of attacks on the British army and RUC. As the prisoners were to learn, any weakness, even one that was not obviously troublesome in normal conditions, would be accentuated by the effects of starvation and would have a marked effect on the individual's performance in the later stages of a hunger strike.

There was no shortage of potential mediators in the dispute and the heightened tension was already making itself felt outside the prison. Fr Reid, who had played an important part in arranging the earlier contacts with the church, had become ill and was replaced by another Redemptorist from the order's headquarters on Dublin's Orwell Road who worked to involve senior political figures like John Hume and Charles Haughey in pressure for a settlement.

Opinion quickly polarised around the issue. West Belfast MP Gerry Fitt and the English Cardinal Basil Hume appealed for Britain to resist the pressure from the prison. SDLP leader John Hume was coming under pressure in his own city of Derry from the Provisionals who characteristically supplemented appeals for humanitarian concern with straightforward intimidation when they organised a one-day work stoppage there and, two days later, placed pickets on Hume's own home to protest against SDLP 'inaction'. Despite or perhaps because of the pressure on people living in nationalist areas to display H-Block posters or support demonstrations, the SDLP did make contact with the IRA through clergymen and eventually arranged a meeting in Dublin, ostensibly to dissuade them from blowing up the cross-border electricity link whose absence was costing electricity consumers in both states in excess of £10 million a year.

The hunger strike ended its first month with the news that a demonstration in Dublin had attracted up to 12,000 people and that southern public opinion was split down the middle on the issue of political status.[19] In this atmosphere three Belfast women (Mairead Farrell, Mary Doyle and Mairead Nugent) in Armagh jail joined the strike on 1 December and a few days later the seven male strikers were segregated to new cells in a reserved wing for medical monitoring. There Hughes received word from Hume who now had all-party backing in the Dail for a meeting with Atkins in which he pressed the British to use the European Commission's judgment as a hook for reforms in the areas of uniform and association which would meet the prisoners' minimum bargaining position. Hume's approach was followed, on 4 December, by a statement from Atkins spelling out the state's core opposition to the five demands as measures which would give 'the protesting prisoners control over their lives in prison' and 'legitimise and encourage terrorist activity' but adding that he was willing to 'discuss the humanitarian aspects of the prison administration in Northern Ireland with anyone who shares our concern about it' as the Commission had suggested.

The hunger strike was, as its advocates had predicted, dividing society around the H-Block issue and putting the IRA in a position where it could shape the overall political agenda from behind the bars of the Maze. In an attempt to seize the initiative thus presented riots were staged near Hume's home in Derry to protest at the lack of progress in the talks with the result that Atkins refused to negotiate directly with the protesters.

Another major mobilisation was in Dublin where at least

2,000 people demonstrated in support of the prisoners on the eve of the Anglo-Irish summit which was held there on 8 December. Haughey, who had publicly rebuked Sile de Valera for accusing Britain of callousness, raised the issue in the meeting, but the centre of discussion was elsewhere and, with Carrington present, Irish minds were still on the Rhodesia/Zimbabwe precedent. Earlier Irish suggestions that the country's traditional neutrality might be abandoned in return for unity were fleshed out by suggestions that an Anglo-Irish defence pact could replace it in the meantime and the obstacles to Ireland joining the British Commonwealth of Nations were capable of removal. A communiqué was issued to the effect that there would be joint studies of 'possible new institutional structures', security, the economy and citizenship rights. Armed with these the next meeting of the two premiers would, the communiqué said, give 'special consideration to the totality of relations within these islands'.

Pundits had a field day with this pregnant phrase and, in the North, Ian Paisley led a 'Carson Trail' series of marches to mobilise Protestants against the long predicted sellout of their interests. But in the event these seemingly momentous matters came to nothing; instead the grievances of the blanketmen reached out to capture Thatcher, Haughey and their Ulster strategy as surely as it had captured the IRA. Until it was resolved and its effects absorbed movement was to prove impossible in Anglo-Irish relations and the unionist position was to remain as secure as even Paisley could have wished.

Despite Atkins' statement in the Commons the summit was followed by a process that seemed to the prisoners very close to negotiations with the British. The conduits for this process were the clergy and the civil servant in charge of prisons, John Blelloch, who made a visit to the jail on 10 December to explain to the seven hunger strikers the reforms that were already available to them should they choose to abandon their protest. These included measures on visits, letters, association, civilian type clothes and compassionate leave already announced. Although Blelloch was unable to bargain with the men or even to meet the non-hunger striking OC, Bobby Sands, it appeared to the hunger strikers that they were being given an authoritative statement together with an opportunity to make an input through messages to the clergy and to Hume.

As so often before, significant political initiatives were accompanied by attempts by the Provisionals to apply additional pressure. On the eve of Blelloch's visit to the prison the IRA attacked police in Strabane, injuring three officers and a civilian. On the day that the civil servant spoke to the prisoners there were violent clashes in Toomebridge and twenty people were arrested after H-Block demonstrators blocked the main Belfast to Derry road.

By this time Sean McKenna's condition was deteriorating rapidly and tension was rising within the prison. On the 12th, six UDA members (Robert Adams, Norman Earle, William Mullan, Thomas Andrews, Samuel Courtney and Samuel McClean) embarked on a hunger strike for segregation of loyalist and republican prisoners and the next day McKenna was visited by an eye specialist as fears mounted that he was losing his sight.

The advanced condition of McKenna put the remaining hunger strikers in a position where they would soon have to decide on whether to allow him to die although they were themselves in danger and negotiations were still going on. In an effort to panic the British away from using this dilemma as a pressure point, plans to increase the numbers on hunger strike were brought forward. On the 15th, as McKenna sank further, twenty-three more prisoners embarked on the fast and it was announced that seven more would follow on the 16th.

As the announcement was made O'Fiach, who had been briefed by the clergy on the prisoners' reaction to Blelloch's paper, pointed up the disadvantages to the state of McKenna's death by warning of major violence if any hunger strikers died and again met Atkins. He told Atkins that the UDA hunger strike gave the British additional room for manoeuvre since concessions would now be seen to be even handed. In what the strikers hoped was a further recognition of their position and a sign of weakening on the British side, Atkins now postponed a statement which he was due to make in the Commons so that they could see it first. The fact that the British had done exactly the same thing with the statement which abolished special category status seemed to have struck nobody as the paper was brought into the jail by the Dublin based Redemptorist on 18 December, the 53rd day of the hunger strike.

The position of McKenna was uppermost in the minds of the weakened men who would decide whether the British offer was enough to save his life. By now he was lapsing in and out of consciousness. On the morning of the 18th he lay with his eyes rolling in his head and in his occasional moments of lucidity asked how long he had to live. When he was told that he had been given twenty-four hours he expressed determination to continue before again lapsing into coma.

The Atkins speech delivered to the prison envisaged the ending of the hunger strike and opened with the words: 'The seven republican prisoners, who were in the 53rd day of their hunger strike today took food.' It was the first time that any British minister had referred to them as anything but criminals. There were accompanying documents, one of two pages and one of thirty-four. They contained the key phrases that prisoners coming off protest would be put in clean cells and 'within a few days clothing provided by their families will be given to any prisoner giving up his protest so that they can wear it during association and visits. As soon as possible all prisoners will be issued with civilian type clothing to be worn during the working day... They will also immediately become entitled to eight letters and food parcels and four visits. Prisoners will be able to associate within each wing of the prison blocks in the evening and at the weekends.'

The hunger strikers were being presented with a picture of a situation in which the British would refer to them as republicans, McKenna would live, they would have their own clothes in a few days and they would be allowed freedom of association. Hume, who had stressed these very points, had sent them a message that if they were given an offer that would meet their bottom line demands he would visit them himself. He was not there, but then the Provos were not sorry to see the 'domestic cockroaches' carved out of the kudos for regaining status and they were told that a senior civil servant would shortly be over from London to answer any questions, effectively to negotiate.

At the last minute it was revealed that there had been an upset in the mandarin's travelling arrangements and he would be delayed until the next day, by which time McKenna would probably be dead. There was now tremendous moral pressure on the prisoners to settle. If, as it now appeared, they were being offered what they had asked it would be wrong and damaging to the movement to let the weakened McKenna die for the sake of a delayed flight.

The next morning Sean McKenna woke to find tubes attached to his body and, thinking he was being force fed, began ripping them out. He stopped when his mother Brigid told him that he was being treated in the military wing of Musgrave Park Hospital and the strike was over. The other six leading hunger strikers were in good shape and there were victory celebrations in nationalist areas across the North. As McKenna, his condition still touch and go due to potassium deficiency, was moved to intensive care in the Royal Victoria Hospital the news came through that the women and the loyalists had also come off the hunger strike and Bobby Sands, in his capacity as OC, was meeting the prison governor, Stanley Hilditch.

NOTES

1. *Magill,* September 1980.
2. Matt Merrigan (southern area officer of the ATGWU), Sean McBride, Siobhan McKenna, the writer Anthony Cronin, Albert Fry (President of Conradh na Gaelige) and Eddie McAteer (the leader of the Nationalist party) were amongst those who agreed to act as sponsors at this stage.
3. *National Smash H-Block Minutes,* 3 February 1980.
4. They were Eilis O'Connor (22, North Belfast), Eileen Morgan (22, Newry), Rosemary Callaghan (20, East Belfast) and Anne Bateson (23, South Derry County).
5. 'It is my belief that Armagh is a Feminist issue' *Irish Times,* 17 June 1980, reproduced in *The Best of Nell,* Attic Press 1984.
6. The same group of relatives met Fianna Fail Euro MP Sile de Valera who promised 'to do all she could privately' and who continued to brief Haughey on the H-Block situation from this point on.
7. Handwritten notes on the National Smash H-Block Armagh Committee meeting of 23 March 1980 in the Linenhall collection.
8. A joint communiqué following a meeting between Thatcher, Carrington, Atkins, Haughey and his foreign minister Brian Lenihan read in part: 'While agreeing with the Prime Minister that any change in the constitutional status of Northern Ireland would only come about with the consent of a majority of the people of Northern Ireland, the Taoiseach reaffirmed that it is the wish of the Irish government to secure the unity of Ireland by agreement and in peace.'
9. The words of Senior Assistant Chief Constable Michael McAtamney, explaining the training of the SSU and E4A in court in June 1984. Cross-examined, he confirmed that 'out of action' meant 'permanently'.

10. Headquarters Mobile Support Unit.

11. An illegal assassination commando of the legal loyalist paramilitary UDA.

12. He was the son of Major Ronald Bunting, a former right-hand man of Ian Paisley.

13. cf. *Sunday Times*, 22 March 1981. The IRA finally admitted the murder in a statement in January 1982 describing Valente as a 'central RUC informer for a number of years'.

14. The demand for communications was such that there was some evidence of outside mass production of accounts of life in the H-Blocks, perhaps with the prisoners connivance. For instance the author has a number of copies of a document entitled 'A Day in the H-Blocks' which purports to give a blow-by-blow account of a day in the life of a prisoner, his thoughts on his family and the political situation. However each copy is 'personalised' to different areas of the province with the name of the prisoner, the names of a relative, his work place and other details changed to suit the target area in much the same manner as an advertising mail shot.

15. Interview with the author, December 1985. Joe Austin was the chairman of the Belfast H-Block Committee during the hunger strike and was, at the time of the interview, Northern Organiser of Sinn Féin.

16. Interview with the author.

17. A contraction of IRSP used as a generic term for the Irish Republican Socialist Party and the Irish National Liberation Army.

18. PD Club, Prisoners' Dependents' Club, a social club in Andersonstown near the Dohertys' home.

19. In an RTE/*Fortnight* opinion poll on 27 November it was found that 45 per cent of the sample supported political status, 39 per cent on principle and the remainder as a matter of expediency; 45 per cent were firmly opposed to the granting of status and 10 per cent expressed no firm view.

7

To the Death

'Today's troubles will look like a Buckingham Palace garden party, compared to what will happen if Bobby Sands dies on hunger strike.'

Phil Flynn.[1]

As the victory bonfires blazed on the Falls, doubt and recrimination were not far off. On the night the hunger strike ended SDLP Councillor Paddy Devlin returned home from an evening out with his wife Theresa to find West Belfast in uproar. His home had been surrounded by a mob and his son, alone and worried, had spent the evening on the 'phone to relatives in England.

Devlin had been the defiant butt of Provo anger and frustration for years. An IRA man from 1936 to 1950, he regarded the Provisionals as a violent and bigoted organisation. Although well to the left of his party he had held a cabinet post in the Sunningdale executive and had registered the highest vote of any candidate in Northern Ireland in the most recent council elections. His was just the sort of independent voice within the nationalist community which brought out the Provos' most fascist tendencies. Already his children had been tied to lamp posts in an effort to get him to mend his ways, his daughters had had to register under assumed names at colleges outside the area and his son had been beaten on the way home from school.

Such treatment was no novelty for non-IRA supporters in ghetto areas. When houses or cars were taken for IRA operations they belonged to those who did not buy *Republican News* or otherwise support the Provos. Individuals who did not toe the line also found that, in areas of at least 30 per cent unemployment, they were ostracised from the growing financial infrastructure of black taxi services, drinking clubs and fringe businesses.[2] In a society where the state offered little, many allowed themselves to be convinced. However self-respect, stubbornness and his habitual bluntness prevented Devlin from caving in or even from appealing to those who, like Gerry Adams, he had helped and who were well thought of by the IRA. He believed 'once you rang them you were showing that what they were doing was hurting and you were in their hands. You were showing weakness and you were encouraging them to do more.'

There had been mobs at his door before. During his term in the power-sharing executive Maire Drumm had led regular Saturday morning demonstrations against his 'treachery', but this time the crowd had been bigger and angrier. They had, as near as his son could make out, wanted him to go to the City Hall and support them, perhaps by resigning his seat. It did not augur well for the future and it did not sound like a movement which was fully convinced of the triumph it was so furiously celebrating.

In the prison there were problems in making the settlement stick because the decision to end the hunger strike had been taken by the hunger strikers and not by the prison command structure headed by Sands. This encouraged the authorities to negotiate piecemeal with individual prisoners and created room for dissension which was most strongly manifested by the INLA. They were only about thirty men but their OC, Patsy O'Hara, indicated that they had four volunteers who would, if necessary, start an independent hunger strike for political status and they steadfastly refused to take part in any ordered withdrawal from the blanket protest. Besides this, the most able and charismatic prison leader, Hughes, had been marginalised and, as his replacement, the bright but less experienced Sands was thrown in the deep end with a vague, rushed agreement that was not of his making. 'The Dark' as Hughes was known, had been a senior officer in the Belfast brigade and came from a strong republican family in the Lower Falls. When he was arrested in 1974 he had been passing himself off as a businessman, complete with conservative suit and briefcase, running an office on Belfast's elite Malone Road. The office had turned out to be the IRA headquarters for the city and to contain plans for the evacuation of entire Catholic areas if the ongoing Ulster Workers Council strike should escalate.

Bobby Sands, on the other hand, was part of the wave of Catholic youth hardened into IRA men by adversity and discrimination. In 1962 his family, who were not republicans, were forced out of the mixed area of Newtownabbey where they lived. They moved to Rathcoole where the young Bobby Sands mixed again with Protestants, playing for a time on the religiously mixed Star of the Sea football team and joining a mixed workforce in his job as an apprentice coach builder. However Rathcoole was fast on the way to becoming the hard-line loyalist ghetto that it is today. In 1968, two years into his apprenticeship, he was intimidated out of his job. Two years later bigotry and constant harassment forced the family to move to the dreary overspill ghetto of Twinbrook where, before the year was out, he was active in the IRA and had been jailed for possession of weapons. In 1976 he was released and got married but was soon back in the hurly-burly of the commercial bombing campaign, leading an IRA unit and being taught the skills by Joe McDonnell, another future hunger striker. Before the year was out the two men had been captured on the same operation.

In his writings, *The Birth of a Republican*, he sets out an idealised past where he imbibed republicanism at his mother's knee, had the seeds of political understanding planted by a republican teacher and joined a local IRA unit composed of the classmates he grew up with. In reality the bulk of his career as a republican, and his only prolonged experiences of influence within the movement, had been in jail. Latterly the single mindedness required to sustain the blanket protest was a far cry from the flexible negotiating and leadership skills needed to steer a way clear of the four-year-old log jam. The fact that his authority had been undermined in the settlement and the undercurrent of romantic fatalism revealed in his writings made his position still less tenable.

This difficult and deteriorating situation affected Hughes deeply and he suffered from severe tension headaches, appearing to blame himself for the deaths that were to follow. The burden of doubt and imagined guilt was not always eased by the movement: as Jimmy Drumm recalls, 'there were suggestions by people who wouldn't bloody well go on hunger strike that they backed down. The lads honestly thought that the way the thing was worded they had got their demands. There was a good basis for it; if the British government and the NIO had moved on it they could have been resolved. But they didn't, they dug their heels in.'

Like Morley in the negotiations to end status, Sands was initially afforded practical recognition by the authorities. As soon as the hunger strike was over he was allowed to consult with Hughes and the others. The hopeful passage was the one, already quoted, in which Atkins said that prisoners coming off the protest would be given their own clothes within a few days and prison issue civilian type clothing as soon as possible; the presumption was that they would get their own clothing first and that they could then ignore the outfits which the authorities were buying for them. The question of what precisely would be involved in 'prisoners giving up their protest' remained open, although a passage mentioning a few days delay for cleaning up suggested flexibility. A meeting to thrash out the practical details with the OCs of the other four blocks was arranged early the next morning, but within two days relations between the authorities and the prisoners had again broken down. Disregarding Sands' attempts to control events the authorities proceeded to move prisoners to clean cells as part of the steam cleaning process and to explain to them individually what was on offer. In most cases the blandishments were ignored and the cells wrecked to underline the point that no progress was possible unless the authorities worked through Sands as OC: the issue of control was central.

The prisoners were now as confused as anyone else by the settlement. As the hunger strike went on the numbers of protesting prisoners had briefly risen to 505 but fifty-three of them had conformed before it ended and thirty-four more had followed suit when they were moved to clean cells.[3] As the moves continued the likelihood was that more would conform at each opportunity. But yet a body of prisoners, including the INLA, were unwilling to make any concession of principle, or to wear the prison issue clothes as a preliminary to being given their own. The pressure for a resolution, which had already brought a trickle of prisoners into the new regime and which the authorities counted on to force the blanketmen to concede, was once more pushing the prisoners towards a hunger strike.

The next move came on 10 January when, after hearing details

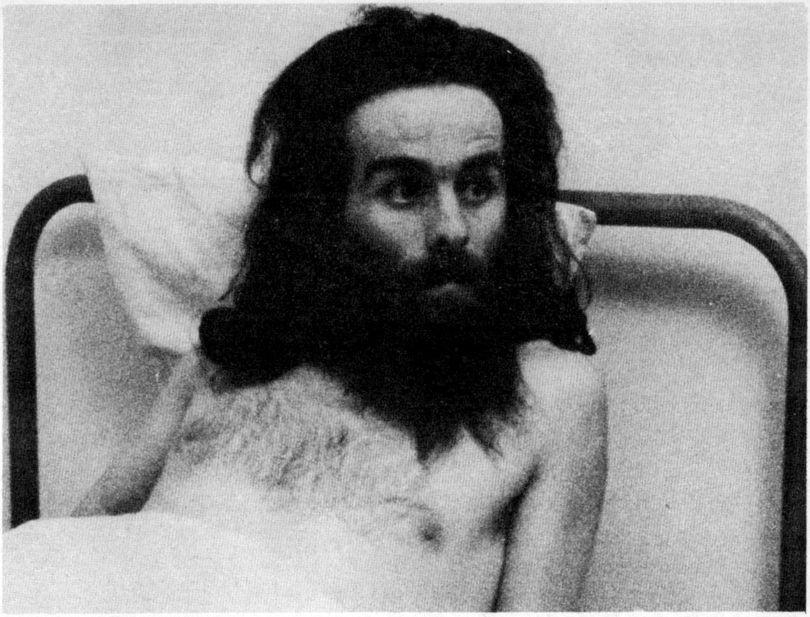

Granada TV

In the H-Blocks of Long Kesh. One of the early blanketmen (*above*). Rosary beads hung on a bell in the H-Blocks during the dirty protest (*below left*): many prisoners did this to guard against any temptation to ring the bell to call prison officers and abandon the protest. A blanketman (*below right*) writing on the wall of his waste-encrusted cell, August 1979; this was the first photograph smuggled out of the blanket blocks.

Pacemaker Press Int.

Pacemaker Press Int.

Crispin Rodwell

H-Blocks demonstration in Belfast (*above*). Unlike unionist demonstrations, H-Block protests were banned from Belfast city centre. People's Democracy leader Fergus O'Hare is arrested at one such demo in March 1981 (*below left*). Pat McGeown (*below right*).

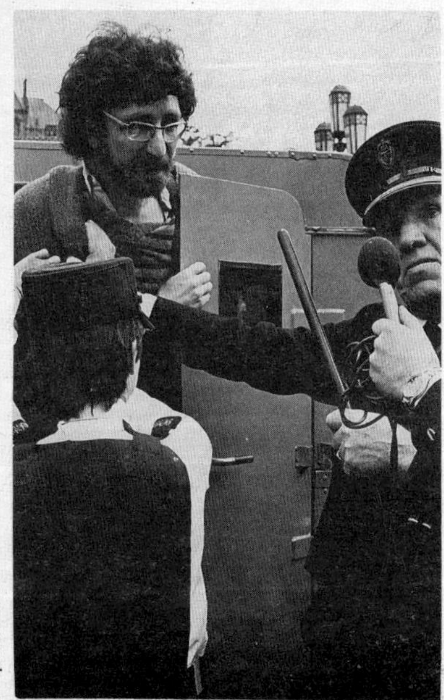

Crispin Rodwell

TV South

Andersonstown News

Tom Conachy

Outside Long Kesh. Blanketman Joe Maguire and his wife Eileen and two children after his release (*above left*). His fellow blanketman Liam Berkery is met (*below*) on his release by (left to right) Marie Moore (H-Block information centre), Martin Lawlor (third from left), Liam's sister and his mother Moyra, the anti-supergrass campaigner. Paddy Agnew (*above right*), former blanketman and TD for Louth (photographed in Dundalk).

Andersonstown News

Crispin Rodwell

Broadening the battlefield: Politics, propaganda and the armed struggle all go hand in hand in the modern republican movement. (Left to right *above*) Tom Hartley, Kathy Bundred, Steve Bundred, GLC leader Ken Livingstone and Gerry Adams during a visit by the Bundreds and Livingstone to Belfast. The platform party at the 1986 Sinn Féin ard fheis is shown (*below*) during the crucial vote to drop abstentionism: (left to right) Joe Cahill, John Joe McGirl, Martin McGuinness, Gerry Adams, Brendan Curran, Danny Morrison. 'Heavy gear' (*above right*): a South Armagh IRA man aims an M60 machine gun at a British army helicopter in May 1980. The future INLA hunger striker Mickey Devine pictured (*below right*) masked in the foreground at an Official IRA roadblock in Derry, 1970. A display of arms by the IRA during the annual march to mark the anniversary of internment, 10 August 1980 (*below far right*).

Crispin Rodwell

Pacemaker Press Int.

Willie Carson

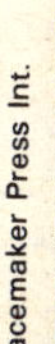

Pacemaker Press Int.

Crispin Rodwell

A blanketman's relative shows communications wrapped in cling film (*above*) which she had smuggled out of the prison after being passed them during a visit. One of the communications (*below*) written on a sheet of toilet roll.

Crispin Rodwell

Crispin Rodwell

Francis Hughes' father and brother shoulder his coffin, flanked by mourners and an IRA guard of honour.

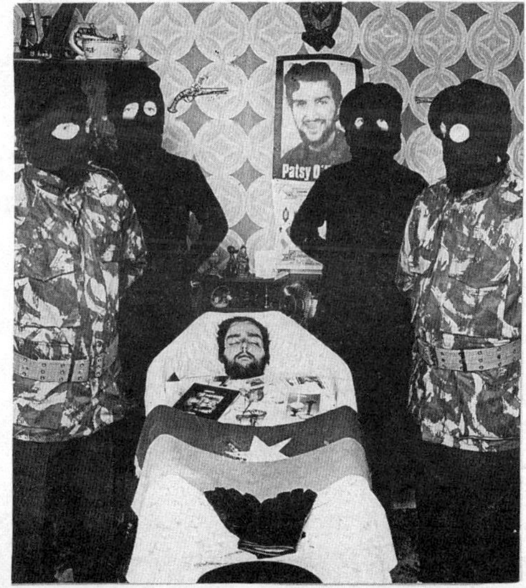

Willie Carson

Father Denis Faul

The dead hunger striker Patsy O'Hara flanked by an INLA guard of honour (*left*).

Bobby Sands

Tom McIlwee

Martin Hurson

Joe McDonnell

of a new statement by Atkins in the Commons the previous day. Sands requested a meeting with the governor, Stanley Hilditch. Atkins had said that the agreement which ended the hunger strike had meant that the prisoners would accept prison issue clothing to demonstrate conformity but that instead of keeping to this they fouled the clean cells into which they were moved. Sands' meeting resulted in an uneasy agreement on two moves from dirty to clean cells involving ninety-six men in H5 and H3, where he himself was Block OC. His intention was for the prisoners to slop out for a week to show conformity, being immediately granted 50 per cent of lost remission and a parcel a month; the next weekend they would wash, shave and ask for their own clothes. Since conforming prisoners were allowed to wear their own clothes from Friday evening to Sunday morning the question of prison issue clothing need not arise until the move from the blanket was completed and could be settled later. However Sands was less than hopeful that this would happen and a statement was issued condemning the 'treacherous manner in which the British government has handled the protest since the ending of the hunger strike' but underlining the wish of the prisoners 'to end the protest in a principled fashion'.

The authorities asked for a week's further delay in implementing this exercise in evasion. When the week was up, on Friday 23 January, twenty of the ninety-six prisoners washed and shaved and asked for their own clothes whilst making it clear that they would do no prison work except cleaning their cells and full-time education. They were then told that they could not have them unless they first collected the personalised prison issue clothing and moved to furnished cells. By the 27th all ninety-six rioted, causing £13,000 worth of damage, and began fouling their cells. They were then beaten and moved to new accommodation, many of them being kept overnight in cells which were filthy and awaiting steam cleaning. The issues in dispute between the IRA and the government were at this point insurmountable. If things continued as they were prisoners would periodically be presented with opportunities to abandon the protest and it might eventually be whittled down to a hard core who could be indefinitely ignored. Indeed by 5 February the total of protesting prisoners was down 109 on the peak and of these fifty-three had abandoned the protest since the end of the hunger strike. The IRA, Whitehall reasoned, had no option but to knuckle down, in view of the failure of the previous hunger strike and the slow attrition of their remaining protest.

Mary McDermott's visits to Kieran Doherty show the initial confusion and the eventual disgust of the hard core as the terms of the settlement became clear:

> That hunger strike ended shortly before Christmas. I got a visit from Kieran very early in the new year and it was snowy, it was cold, it was freezing. In the meantime he had washed and they had been given this suit of civilian clothes from Marks and Spencers bought by the authorities. I remember sitting in this little box and seeing Kieran Doherty coming out and I thought, 'Oh my God, am I seeing things — this fine looking, good looking fellow'. He stood well over six feet high and I said to him, 'The only thing wrong with you Kieran is that your hair is too short' for his hair was cut very, very short and he was shaved clean. I thought they were lovely clothes, they looked nice, fawn pullover and brown trousers, brown suede shoes. He looked really marvellous.
>
> I said, 'Well good heavens, you won't want me to visit you any more', I says 'a good looking fellow like you dressed up like this won't want to be seeing me.' His face contorted and he said, 'this is prison uniform, I don't want it. This is prison uniform.' I said, 'well it looks lovely on you' but he didn't like that, he didn't like that at all. He was in *gear* as he called it, this was prison gear. This doesn't mean anything.
>
> He was very disturbed that day because he wanted to know, they hadn't heard anything, I think, about any result from the first hunger strike. It had ended and that was it and they were in a kind of a limbo for about a fortnight or three weeks.
>
> They didn't know anything, they hadn't been told anything and their relatives didn't know anything and they weren't happy. They weren't contented and they had these clothes and they didn't want them because they weren't their own, they were the authorities' and they were the prison uniform and they might take a different shape but as far as he was concerned that was it.

> So by the time I got the next visit I suppose it would be about a month. Well then the rumblings were on again. He was back to square one, he was back in the same way that he was before the first one. He was giving his name down. I thought, 'I hope he doesn't die' that's the first thing it was. It sounds a very selfish thing to think but I thought, 'I hope he doesn't die, all that hardship. I hope to God he doesn't go on it.' I said, 'ah Kieran for God's sake surely you don't want to go.' He said, 'It will have to be brought to a successful conclusion. Someone will have to die.' I said, 'Oh Kieran, for goodness sake. There is too many republican dead. You will end up like all the others', I said, 'the graveyards are full of republican dead and people don't even remember the names.' I said, 'They are news for five minutes and that is the end of it.'[4]

The prison OCs and the outside leadership believed that a second strike was likely to result in deaths and to end in less than total victory, but by the time the 27 January riot took place the decision had already been taken to proceed. However, hopeful precedents were drawn by some from a recent apparent back down by Thatcher in face of industrial action by the National Union of Mineworkers and an uneasy compromise had been reached with the outside leadership, who were largely opposed to another hunger strike. Their collective feelings was that the initiative was lost and it would be hard to mobilise mass support again. Initially they agreed to support the strike only on condition that it was limited to four men. Sands announced the decision in a note passed around the block telling the prisoners:

> I accept now that men will sacrifice their lives on this hunger strike. But you must all cast aside everything for total unity within these blocks — unity and steadfastness. You should, when a comrade dies, remain steadfast. Because, comrades, at the end of the day men will die, for the responsibility of ending this protest for once and for all will not lie with dead comrades, but with you.[5]

Sands, who left a two week gap between himself and the next hunger striker, felt that he, at least, would die, and discussed the moral implications with a number of priests. He answered Father Dennis Faul's criticisms in the words of Christ, 'Greater love hath no man than this, that he lay down his life for his friends.' Faul replied 'there is no answer to that Bobby', but later realised that there was an answer; the hunger strike would involve more deaths than those of the participants. Pragmatically, Sands told another priest that it was impossible to delay any longer because a communication for the Dublin leadership outlining the strategy for the hunger strike had been intercepted by police outside the prison.

When the prisoners read Sands' 27 January communication many of them had already been involved in discussions of possible alternatives but had concluded that none, short of surrender, remained. This time the process of selection drew on the experience of the previous hunger strike. Pat McGeown, who initially opposed a second hunger strike and estimated that it could produce up to seven deaths, says that prisoners had been vetted for the type of offences they had committed in an attempt to present a sympathetic profile and to avoid the appearance of grieving relatives of IRA victims on TV screens. However a number of volunteers with records that might not appear attractive to non-republicans, were included because of their own determination to participate. For example, police claimed that Francis Hughes had killed twenty-six members of the security forces and dubbed him 'The Belaghy butcher'. Another such man, Brendan 'Bic' McFarlane who was jailed for his part in the Bayardo Bar attack, was left off the strike and given the role of the new OC. McFarlane is a strong minded and disciplined man. This time there would be no doubt who called the shots and, as the prisoners were to stress, the buck would most unequivocally stop with him.

This time too there appeared to be little room for outside mediation. In the statement announcing the hunger strike O'Fiach and the bishops were condemned as part of the 'moral blackmail' exerted on the prisoners to end the previous strike. What was required was pressure pure and simple on the British. A number of objectives were set including industrial action in the Republic involving, at a minimum, the blacking of British goods and ships. Later, it was hoped, constitutional nationalists in the north could be driven to withdraw from the councils and other institutions of government and the Republic could be forced into severing diplomatic relations with Britain, bringing the country to the brink of civil and international war.

When the official announcement for the hunger strike was made Sands, who had agreed with the OCs that all the demands might not be met, explained his vision to his fellow blanketmen. Liam McCloskey, who was on the same wing, recalls:

> On the night that it was announced he said that he wouldn't be prepared to die for five demands only but that through the hunger strike he would hope to gain more support for the IRA: if he died it would incense the Irish people, make them angry and draw support for the IRA: if he lived it would show that Margaret Thatcher could be beaten and again draw support for the IRA. Either way the IRA won; our backs were against the wall; we had to go on hunger strike but Bobby wanted the hunger strike to be for a wider thing and all the men agreed that it should be used to its full potential.

Taken with the earlier communication the message was clear, those who went on hunger strike were engaged in an operation of major importance to their IRA comrades in the jail and outside it; they must be prepared to die and those who did not must be prepared to accept the death of others rather than give in. On the second day of the hunger strike the end of the dirty protest was announced, halting its slow attrition and concentrating all the prisoners' hopes on the four hunger strikers. The attitude of the Northern Ireland Office, fresh from one hunger strike victory and convinced, as Margaret Thatcher was later to say, that the IRA was playing its last card, was emphatic. 'If they insist and carry it on', Humphrey Atkins said, 'they will die.'

When the hunger strike began on 1 March it was estimated that Bobby Sands' condition would become critical around the anniversary of the 1916 Easter rising and a day of industrial action was planned to coincide with it. In the event Sands' decline was more protracted and the National H-Block Armagh Committee proved unable to mobilise trades unionists in any number. At one point the Northern headquarters of both the Irish Congress of Trades Unions and the Irish Transport and General Workers Union were attacked in frustration. The industrial organisation had, as one republican report ruefully commented, 'been left to hare brained activists'. Instead the major focus of the early hunger strike was to be provided by the unexpected death of the independent Fermanagh/South Tyrone MP Frank Maguire. The constituency was one of the bitterest in the north, where the electorate voted in solid orange and green blocks and the nationalists had a 5,000 vote advantage provided they did not split the vote by putting up more than one candidate.

Maguire, a wing OC of IRA internees in the 1950s, had been very active on prisoners' issues; he did not actually abstain from attending Westminster but he rarely bothered his head going there and never got round to making a maiden speech in his seven years as an MP. Not a conventional politician, he once told a TV interviewer who asked him what he offered the unemployed that there was plenty of work around. However he had a reputation as a good constituency man who could always be contacted in his Lisnaskea pub, and his majority increased in the two elections he contested. It was the ideal opportunity for a H-Block candidate to highlight the issue Maguire had held so dear.

Bernadette McAliskey, herself a Tyrone woman, declared an interest. On 24 January she had become the latest, and last, H-Block activist to be shot by loyalists. Three UDA men were charged with her attempted murder but their ability to find her remote farmhouse home, where they smashed down the door with sledgehammers before shooting Bernadette and her husband Michael, and the presence on the scene within minutes of a British army unit, who had been watching her house, invited theories that the authorities had at least been aware of the attack. All this made her a strong and sympathetic contender.

Others declaring an early interest were Maguire's brother Noel and the Irish Independence Party's Frank McManus, who had held the seat from 1970 to 1974. The SDLP had stood down in Frank Maguire's favour but their local leader, Austin Currie, had run against him as an independent in 1979. The calculations of all these various groups were thrown into disarray when Sinn Féin announced, on the suggestion of the prisoners but without consulting the H-Block Committee, that they were 'firmly considering' fielding a candidate.

From this point on, the pressure was on amongst nationalists to find a single Catholic candidate to avoid splitting the vote and amongst the unionists to agree a single Protestant to capitalise on the hoped for confusion in the Catholic camp. In reality the result amongst unionists was a foregone conclusion. The OUP, by far the largest party locally, provided Harry West who held the seat on a split nationalist vote from February to October 1974 when Maguire took it off him. However Paisley, who was bidding for hegemony in the unionist camp through a series of rallies predicting imminent Irish unity and/or civil war as a result of the Thatcher-Haughey talks, put forward a 'unity' candidate, Roy Kells. A part time UDR lieutenant himself, Kells highlighted the sixty Protestant members of the security forces whom the IRA had murdered in Fermanagh since 1971. Although he eventually withdrew, the bitterness created between the two unionist parties as well as amongst his UDR colleagues and the families of the dead weakened West's position.

The nationalist decision was more difficult. An SDLP meeting in Irvinestown on 21 March attended by party chairman Sean Farren was strongly in favour of fighting the seat. However, under the urging of Fermanagh members, opinion eventually swung round to backing Noel Maguire, who had announced that he was standing regardless of anyone else, rather than split the vote. The IIP took a similar decision, removing McManus from the race.

Bernadette was cleared out of the way by a visit from Sinn Féin's Jim Gibney on 18 March. He told her that Bobby Sands was willing to run and that Maguire would shortly announce that he was standing down in his favour. That evening a local radio station rang McAliskey to ask her her position and she said that not only would she stand down for a prisoner but she would sign his nomination and 'work the shirt off my back' for his success.[6] Maguire, who was asked to stand by the Bishop of Clogher and told the SDLP that he would do so two days before nominations closed, was also visited by the Provisionals. As the 20 March deadline for nominations approached, everyone was hedging their bets. Sinn Féin had decided that Sands, who had by now lost over 17lbs and was in the prison hospital for observation, would not run unless he had the field to himself and Gerry Adams had lodged no papers for him. He had them in his pocket along with a precautionary handwritten note explaining why the hunger striker was withdrawing from the election. Maguire's nomination was in and another Sinn Féin member had, unknown to the party at large, lodged an extra set of nomination papers for Sands. Currie, who was prepared to lodge his papers as an independent if Sands got a clear field, had a man posted in Maguire's bar to tip him off if there was any last minute change of heart. Then, just 13 minutes before nominations closed at four o'clock, an apparently angry Maguire walked into the electoral office and withdrew his papers. His companion pushed a camera man aside and his niece Serena, Frank's daughter, stood sobbing outside. As he emerged he declined to call on voters to support Sands but in the pub the phone was tied up so that it was impossible to get the message to Currie.

Allegations of physical intimidation were made, although Maguire forbade the Bishop of Clogher to make a public statement to this effect and later backed Sands. But whatever methods of persuasion they had used, the Provos had what they wanted, a clear run and all that that implied. 'At the time', says Jimmy Drumm, 'things were getting pretty critical in Long Kesh. There had been mass parades, mass everything, but Maggie Thatcher wasn't moving. The whole story going round was that these people had no support so if they didn't support him it was going to be an awful slap in the teeth.'

The SDLP were furious at the outcome and advised their supporters to boycott the poll. Divisions within the party were increased by Currie's go-it-alone tactics and the discovery that Councillor Tommy Murray, who unknown to the party had retained his IRA membership since the '50s, had signed Sands' nomination papers.

From the very outset, Sinn Féin were determined to broaden support beyond what was available to the IRA. On 15 March South Derry man Frank Hughes had joined the protest to be followed the next day by Raymond McCreesh from South Armagh and Patsy O'Hara from Derry City, who was now replaced as INLA OC by Mickey Devine, making up the full complement of four hunger strikers agreed with the leadership. The main emphasis on the campaign, hammered home again and again in election literature, was that a vote for Sands could save the four men's lives.

Sinn Féin and the IRA were played down in the literature and Sands stood under the banner 'Anti H-Block Armagh Political Prisoner'. The handout most widely used during the election carried endorsements from Noel Maguire ('a vote for SANDS is a vote for the dignity of human life'), Bernadette McAliskey, Frank McManus (IIP), Tommy Murray (SDLP), Neil Blaney (the Independent Fianna Fáil TD for Donegal who left Fianna Fáil proper after the 1970 arms trial) and Owen Carron, a Sinn Féin member and a nephew of John Carron who had represented Fermanagh at Stormont as a Nationalist from 1965 to 1972.

The leaflet made no mention of local issues, though UDR harassment was raised in the course of the canvassing. Instead it said that Sands' life could be saved by a vote of 32,000, that failing to support him was a vote for 'West and Paisley', that the reader should not stand by and let prisoners die and, more subtly, that Bobby Sands was only 'borrowing' the votes for one election. The leaflet, which was larded with references to the cardinal's interest in the H-Blocks issue, concluded:

> The blanketmen and the women prisoners are BORROWING this election in an attempt to illustrate your support for the prisoners and your opposition to the British government.
>
> BOBBY SANDS' intervention in this election permits the basis of the broadest possible platform for unity among those people who oppose unionism and British rule.
>
> His life and his comrades' lives can be saved if you elect him. Under no circumstances, following this election will the seat, by default or British court order, be allowed to fall to Harry West.

Every effort had been made to get electors over the hurdle of supporting an IRA candidate; they would only be lending their vote for one election to save a life.

At a series of rallies around the constituency Sands' mother, who never spoke, and his sister Marcella, who spoke eloquently of the need to save her brother's life, appeared with a range of Irish sporting and language enthusiasts. The possibility of actually winning the seat was only taken seriously after an 6 April supporters' rally in Enniskillen which included individuals from the SDLP, the IIP, the GAA, Conradh na Gaeilge, as well as Noel Maguire and the republican minded Fermanagh-born priest Joe McVeigh who had recently returned from his parish in New York.

The immediate run-up to the election was punctuated by two major outside events, one negative and one positive. The IRA, which had been largely inactive in the early months of the year, backed up Sinn Féin's campaign against the ongoing census by robbing a number of census collectors at gunpoint. On 7 April in Derry, where census forms had been ceremonially burned a few days earlier, a 26-year-old collector, Carol Mathers, was shot dead in what was said to be an accident, creating a good deal of anti-republican feeling. The next day the election effort was buoyed up by the announcement of support from Sile de Valera, Neil Blaney and a group of non-alligned Euro MPs who were backing Sands' candidature.

In organisational terms the campaign now boiled down to bringing the nationalist vote out. The Unionist candidate, Harry West, fumbled any chance he had of eating into the 10,786 anti-IRA Catholic votes which Austin Currie had garnered in 1979 by placing cynically contrasting advertisements in the Catholic and Protestant papers with the pope's condemnation of violence prominent in the Catholic version. Sands' chances lay in stopping as much as possible of this middle ground vote from taking the SDLP's advice and staying at home or spoiling their ballots. It was a classic exercise in campaign management which gave Sinn Féin members a chance to learn the ropes from old hands like Bernadette McAliskey, the IIP's Pat McCaffrey, Tommy Murray and others with a more conventional political background than their own. Gerry Adams, whose only previous experience of elections had been as a young campaign worker for Billy McMillan in 1964, updated his skills by running the Dungannon office and most of his entourage were also active in the campaign.

In the event their efforts were successful and Sands was

elected with a 1,446 majority. It was down 3,541 on Maguire's but represented a remarkable achievement in the circumstances and was arguably the main watershed in Northern Ireland's history since Bloody Sunday. The decision of the SDLP not to stand had undoubtedly prevented the Unionist from getting in and saved them from a severe and possibly violent backlash in the constituency. However, it had given a major leg-up to a party that could prove their grave-diggers, Provisional Sinn Féin.

On the unionist side, extreme forces also benefited. Paisley was in the ideal position of having graciously withdrawn in the interests of Protestant unity and still seeing his Official Unionist rivals losing to the IRA. For ordinary Protestants across the province it was taken as evidence that, as the extremists had always preached, most Catholics supported the IRA. Harry West summed up the feelings of many when he told reporters that it was 'very uncomfortable to find you are living among 30,000 people who support the gunmen' but was trumped by the Sands camp when Kevin Agnew, a well-known republican solicitor, addressed the cheering crowds as 'fellow terrorists' and Bernard O'Connor, of Amnesty International fame, promised the same crowd 'victory on the H-Blocks, victory on the streets, victory throughout the country, when we see the heels of the last Englishman out.'[7]

The Paisleyite Carson trail rallies against the Haughey/Thatcher talks were given a temporary boost and Haughey himself received the message that H-Block was indeed an important issue. He announced at the next day's Fianna Fáil ard fheis that the north would most definitely be an issue in the next election, but plans for the election itself were quietly shelved while ways were sought to take the heat out of things.

The election was far from fulfilling its promise of saving Sands' life, although the movement on the outside did tell the prison leadership that this was a moment when the strike could honourably be ended. Sands himself, now about two stones lighter, received the news with equanimity. On the outside a wave of rioting in Belfast, Lurgan and Cookstown set the scene for a build-up of street and IRA violence that dramatically reversed the steadily falling graph of violence of the past four years.

Like the entire hunger strike the election brought far more direct pressure on Irish nationalist leaders than the British, who suffered international embarrassment and scrutiny but no actual threat to their political survival. The British response was to repeat their opposition to political status, to reject moves to eject Sands from the Commons but to introduce legislation preventing prisoners standing in the future. The protesters' hopes were pinned on creating a crisis in nationalism which would leave the republicans in the pivotal position and force the Catholic and nationalist establishment to act as a lever to move the British. The response was a damage limitation exercise centering, in the first instance, around the European Commission of Human Rights.

Hume, who had always seen the Commission's criticisms of British inflexibility as a possible way out of the impasse, suggested on 14 April that Sands should refer his case to it. After this the authorities moved to furnish the former blanketmen's cells and rumours circulated that members of the Commission might mediate on an individual basis only to be quashed by one blunt statement from Atkins that 'there is nothing to mediate about' and another from Sands, who was by now on day 47 and weakening fast, that he regarded Hume's intervention as 'a stunt'. Despite this the SDLP issued a statement condemning British inflexibility after meeting a delegation from the National H-Block committee. In the interim there had been increasing violence at H-Block demonstrations, some of which were barred from Belfast City Centre, and one boy, Paul Withers aged 15, had been fatally wounded by a 'plastic bullet' whilst stoning police during rioting in Derry.

Both the cardinal and Haughey were now seriously worried by the drift of events, prompting O'Fiach to suggest once more that the Maze be brought into line with Armagh and that the wearing of prison uniform be made optional. In the Republic, Sile de Valera, who had been cheered at the Fianna Fáil ard fheis for her stance, took advantage of an invitation from Sands to visit him along with her fellow Euro MPs Neil Blaney and Dr John O'Connell. De Valera had, she said, 'the express permission and approval' of Haughey for her mission.

Of the three only O'Connell, who had negotiated in previous hunger strikes, attempted to persuade Sands to abandon his fast and was told that the only man who could negotiate on such matters was Brendan McFarlane. Undeterred, the three held a press conference at which they asked for an urgent meeting with Mrs Thatcher, or failing that, her deputy William Whitelaw. The request brought a stinging rebuff from Thatcher who was on a trade mission to Saudi Arabia. 'It is not my habit or custom', she said, 'to meet MPs from a foreign country about a citizen of the United Kingdom, resident in the United Kingdom. If they wish to make any representations they should do so through their own government in the customary way.'

The snub was accompanied by a marked deterioration in Sands' condition. By the 22nd he had been on hunger strike two days longer than Sean McKenna and could only keep down iced water. Hume continued to urge an informal intervention by the ECHR and the papal envoy to Dublin, Dr Gaetano Alibrandi, followed a condemnation of violence from the pope by indicating that he would be personally willing to visit the Maze if asked.

A process of diplomatic fence-mending now seems to have taken place with Dolores Price being released from prison on health grounds on the same day, the 22nd, that Haughey summoned the British Ambassador to Dublin, Sir Leonard Figg, to meet him in his office. No public statement was issued following the meeting, which was presumed to centre on Thatcher's outburst, but it was followed by a statement from Atkins to the effect that he would welcome and facilitate a 'formal or informal' intervention.

On the heels of this statement Haughey, who had a few days earlier refused to meet relatives of the four hunger strikers, rang the Sandses saying that he wanted to see them as a matter of urgency. The worried family, who now feared that Bobby might soon enter a coma and be beyond consultation, went straight to Dublin and met Haughey that evening in his spacious Kinsealy residence. In Marcella Sands' uncontested account,[8] they were seeking public support for the five demands but instead found that Haughey had the papers for a formal application to the European Commission of Human Rights on the table before him. The Taoiseach gave her the impression that an application would be a mere formality, allowing Britain off the hook and most probably resulting in the acceptance of the essence of the five demands in time to save her brother's life. The paperwork (specifying the rights to life, to freedom from inhuman treatment and freedom of expression) was ready for her to sign. As soon as she did so it was sent via Haughey's private telex to the ECHR in Strasbourg.

The announcement was treated with something less than jubilation in the prison. It became known as the prisoners learnt that former US Attorney-General Ramsay Clark and Fr Daniel Berrigan, two American supporters of the protest, were refused admission to the Maze. It also raised fears of a breach with the families. The ECHR's previous judgment had rejected all of the five demands and had stepped outside its own terms of reference to rule against any special status for IRA convicts. Dallying with it at this point would imply acceptance of that ruling and could be another 'exercise in brinkmanship' designed to bring an end to the hunger strike and to save Sands' life without the demands being clearly met. At the same time an outright refusal to meet the commissioners would be seen as a slap in the face for grieving relatives and evidence of Provo unwillingness to seek a solution. The tactic adopted was to demand conditions for a meeting which could only be met if the British were indeed ready to cave in; if Sands was to meet the ECHR he must have with him not only the jail OC Bic McFarlane but also Gerry Adams and Danny Morrison as advisers from the movement on the outside.

The Commission delegation comprised Professors Carl Aaage Noergaard of Denmark, acting President of the ECHR, and Torkel Opsahl of Norway as well as Hans Kruger and Michael O'Boyle of the ECHR's secretariat. En route to the Maze they had been briefed by the British side in London and by Marcella Sands and Pat Finucane, Sands' legal representative and the brother of blanketman Seamus Finucane. On hearing Sands' conditions they had a brief meeting with McFarlane, who repeated the demands for external 'advisers' and learnt that the Commission's proceedings were likely to be lengthy. After consulting with Sands for about ten minutes McFarlane told the Commissioners that the position was unchanged and the talks ended.

During the various meetings it had emerged that rather than

investigating on the spot the commissioners wanted Sands to take over Marcella's application, and then to start proceedings with a special meeting in five days time. The bottom line was that if Sands was to survive to pursue his application he would have to abandon his hunger strike. Within a few days the Commission made it clear that, despite pleas from Haughey for an 'eleventh hour humanitarian solution', they could not now act on Marcella's application. The prisoners' worst suspicions of a re-run of December 1980 appeared to be confirmed and in a statement from Owen Carron the Provisionals made it clear that, as they saw it, the blame lay with Haughey alone who, they said, had 'misled' the family. It had long been clear that no internationally recognised standard entitled the prisoners to their five demands or to anything but normal criminal status. Now it was also clear that the issue could not be fudged but would instead be decided by the motivation and the political clout of the two sides. With this clarification the already slim chances of outside mediation shrank to vanishing point.

However Sands was to receive two more outside visitors before his death, neither of whom made any real attempt to interfere with his patently willing sacrifice of his life or to criticise the British government's position on the five demands.

The first was the pope's personal secretary, Newry born priest Mgr John Magee who held talks with Peter Blaker of the Foreign and Commonwealth office and prisons minister Michael Alison before meeting the hunger strikers themselves. When he visited Sands on the 28th, the 58th day of the hunger strike, the former blanketman was in a very advanced state of starvation. Fluoride and other impurities in the water supply were enough to sicken him, but he could keep down spring water. He had come close to dying a few days earlier but was, according to Sinn Féin, alert again, and periodically consenting to be rubbed with oils to prevent his skin breaking at the joints. A radio was available for him to keep abreast of events and he lay upon a water bed, a difficult and complaining patient but one who left no doubt of the depth of his determination to pursue his protest to its grim and increasingly inevitable conclusion. The envoy's visit was the subject of intense church politics with the British Cardinal Basil Hume denouncing the hunger strike as violence and being largely backed in this view by Archbishop

Bruno Heim, the papal envoy to Britain. After seeing the determination of both sides to maintain their position Magee had little to offer but prayers and a large gold cross, a present from the pope which seems to have been a source of comfort to Sands in his last days of life.

The final outsider to see Sands alive was Don Concannon, the Labour spokesman on Northern Ireland and one of the architects of criminalisation when an NIO minister. He was also subject to intense pressure from within his own party where a group of MPs, led by Ernie Roberts, believed that the differences between the government and the prisoners were now small. After making it clear that his party was opposed to special status he too left on 1 May, defeated by the implacable forces that were ranged in opposition in the prison hospital.

Desperation outside the prison was now increasing. Rumours were circulating in Catholic areas that in the event of Sands' death there would be a loyalist invasion and these were mirrored by parallel fears in Protestant areas of a Provo pogrom.

On the nationalist side these fears were skilfully exploited by republican propagandists, half convinced that they were true but in any case eager to feed a siege mentality which would increase their own control at street level. From mid April the pro-republican *Andersonstown News* was reporting secret UDA and UVF conclaves and warning its readers that 'the loyalists are prepared to make a move. In the past the nationalist people have been told to be prepared. The crunch may be coming soon.'[9] The panic grew when, at the end of April, the UDA, fearing attacks on Protestants, brought an estimated 2,500 men on to the Shankill Road, where most of West Belfast's Protestants live, in what they described as a 'purely defensive mobilisation exercise'.

By the beginning of May plans were well advanced for the defence and, if necessary, the evacuation of isolated Catholic areas like Short Strand, the 3,000 strong green enclave in orange East Belfast. An IRA spokesman in Short Strand told Associated Press that he had 'worked day and night to muster our people. They are now ready for anything that is coming'.[10] Even in the relative security of Andersonstown a Sinn Féin organised Civil

Defence Association was flooding the area with scare leaflets advising householders to hoard food, fuel and other necessities, warning them that the RUC were stopping 'provision lorries' from entering the area and ironically advising local people not to panic. In South Armagh some Newry schools were reported to have suspended their lessons to provide crash courses in first aid.

These fears of Protestant invasion fed on the bitter memories of the attacks on Clonard and other interface areas in the early days of the troubles but were known by anyone with any contact with loyalists to be groundless. Devlin, an active leader of the Irish Transport and General Workers Union who had worked hard to build up the largely Catholic union's Protestant membership, was one such person and took the opportunity of a TV interview to condemn the network of street committees and to discount the rumours they were circulating as an attempt to stir up sectarian fear and hatred. In the most vindictive passage of his hunger strike diary Sands had personally condemned Devlin, seeing his refusal to support political status as evidence that 'he is not, nor ever has been a trades unionist, more like a unionist'. The statement was also linked in Provo minds to one by the Secretary of State Humphrey Atkins in which he warned that the IRA planned to burn some areas, probably Short Strand, and blame it on the loyalists, to use children in confrontations with the security forces and to create an atmosphere of panic from which they would emerge with a stronger hold on the areas they considered their own. The result for Devlin was, that in his words:

> One Saturday morning a big man came round dressed in a black suit and a cap. I had never seen him before but he said he was the chairman of the local defence committee. He said, 'You are putting out statements and they are not acceptable to us and we want you to let us know any time you are doing this in the future so that we can . . . ' I don't know whether he said censor them or what and I said, 'Will you fuck off and give my head peace. Who are you coming round to me, the cheek of you' or words to that effect.

This stormy session was followed by a more friendly meeting with future Sinn Féin councillors Alex Maskey and Tish

Holland, both of whom he knew well, who advised him to make statements urging prison reforms on whatever terms he thought appropriate. Devlin was by now in deep trouble, but unlike many others facing similar pressure he could not find it in him to back down.

Towards the end of April around twenty republicans, including Tom Cahill the chairman of the Belfast H-Block Committee, were lifted in apparent anticipation of Sands' impending death. As it grew closer other voices were raised against the slide into violence which all saw coming. On the 3rd, at a 15,000 strong rally in Toome, Oliver Hughes told how, on a visit to his brother Frank, he had been frightened by the sight of Bobby Sands, lying on his back like a dead man, his face black and Father Magee's crucifix in his hands. Even in the face of this harrowing news, Mrs Rosaleen Sands appealed for calm and Bernadette McAliskey asked for not a single stone or bomb to be thrown.

It was not to be. Plans had already been laid and the bombs stockpiled. When Sands died at 1.17 am on 5 May orchestrated rioting convulsed nationalist areas of Belfast and Derry. The biggest security operation since internment swung into operation, putting 7,000 police, 5,000 reservists, 7,000 UDR men and 11,000 soldiers on standby. Six hundred extra soldiers were flown in from the spearhead battalion. There were no invasions by the loyalists but there were three casualties. At the top of the New Lodge Road, an isolated Catholic area of North Belfast, a retarded man, carried away by the carnival atmosphere of violence, joined in the stoning of a milk float and killed the driver, Eric Guiney and fatally injured his fifteen-year-old son Desmond, both Protestants who lived a few streets away in neighbouring Tiger's Bay. Elsewhere in the city a policeman, Philip Ellis, was shot dead by an IRA sniper. The ratchet of violence which had been wound down in 1980 to allow for negotiations was now being cranked up for the confrontation and polarisation which prisoners and IRA were alike convinced provided them with their only chance of a favourable result.

NOTES

1. Speaking at the April 1981 Easter Commemoration in West Belfast's Milltown cemetery. The chapter title formed the front page headline of *Republican News* on 7 February 1981.

2. Black taxis: London style 'black hacks' which operate a bus service along the Falls Road under the auspices of the Falls Taxi Association. The service was introduced in 1972 after Citybus vehicles became a target for petrol bombers and later the UVF was associated with the setting up of parallel services in loyalist areas. Over the years an estimated 300 buses, valued at £10 million, have had to be withdrawn from service as a result of attacks and the black taxis have been the main beneficiaries. Each driver pays a set amount to republican charities each week. During the hunger strike one driver recalls that at a meeting in the Lake Glen Hotel 'A 'RA [IRA] man just got up and made a speech. He said, "I think that there should be another £3 on the road money to bring it up to £8" and everybody started cheering.' More important to IRA finance was an network of drinking clubs which were initially run illegally but later got licences under the Registration of Clubs Act. The IRA cut came in the form of undeclared sales averaging about 10 per cent of total turnover. IRA-linked businesses included slot machines (which were placed in pubs, taxi offices and shops as an alternative to asking cash donations) and building firms. Here the basic fiddles were protection charges to main contractors, putting 'dead men' (non-existent workers) on the books and the operation of forged or dubious 'exemption certificates' which enable a sub-contractor to defer payment of PAYE contributions until the end of the tax year. A proportion of workers claiming supplementary benefit could then be employed at suitably reduced rates and, at year's end, the sub-contracting firm could disappear. Taken together, these enterprises allowed the Provos to exercise a good deal of patronage and provided a network for the employment of ex-prisoners.

3. Figures on prison numbers are those supplied by NIO ministers in *Hansard.* The clothes provided by the prison authorities consisted of trousers, pullovers, shirts and shoes in a range of colours.

4. Interviews with the author.

5. The communication is quoted at length in Tom Collins *The Irish Hunger Strike* (White Island, 1986).

6. Downtown Radio News, Thursday, 18 March 1981.

7. *Irish Times* 11 April 1981. This account of the election campaign is also indebted to the reports in *Magill*, the *Irish News*, the *News Letter, Republican News* and the *Fermanagh Herald.*

8. Given in *Republican News, Iris* and John Feehan's *Bobby Sands and the Tragedy of Northern Ireland.*

9. *Andersonstown News*, 18 April 1981.

10. The AP interview was published in US papers on 2 May.

8

Nothing but the Five Demands

I am becoming increasingly worried and wary of the fact that there could quite well be an attempt at a later date to pull the carpet from under our feet and undermine us — with the concession bid of 'our own clothes as a right'.

This, of course, would solve nothing. But if allowed it could, with the voice of the Catholic hierarchy, seriously damage our position . . . the issue at stake is not 'humanitarian', nor about better or improved living conditions. It is purely political and only a political solution will solve it.

Bobby Sands (Day 10 of his diary).

The question of not winning the five demands no longer exists. Having paid Mrs Thatcher's blood price, we will not take no for an answer.

National H-Block Committee (5 May 1981)

The replacement of Bobby Sands with Joe McDonnell, a man who had been arrested with him following the Balmoral Furnishing Company bombing in 1976 and who had refused to join the 1980 hunger strike with the words, 'I have too much too live for'[1], crossed a psychological barrier, bringing the hunger strike past its first four volunteers.

According to Pat McGeown, still OC of H6 and involved in the major strategy discussions, from now until early June was a period when the prisoners seriously discussed ending the hunger strike in line with the outside leadership's initial decision that it should only involve four men. During this period, detailed strategies were drawn up for a range of possible ends to the strike and the tactics that would follow any degree of success or failure with which it met. Models were created under which, Joe Austin says, 'the hunger strike could more or less run automatically'.

Up to seventy volunteers for hunger strike were now claimed and, with this base to work from, the continuing reassessment was able to draw on first-hand knowledge of the effects of the hunger strike process.

Sands had maintained a diary for the first seventeen days, in which he records the loss of approximately one-twelfth of his body weight. In that time acute hunger pangs gradually gave way to lassitude and a freezing coldness as surface body fat was used up and organic ketones and adrenaline dulled the appetite. Around twenty to twenty-five days talking became more difficult, but, given a sound constitution and the prisoners' target intake of five pints of water and salt a day, severe physical ill-effects would only become apparent when about 25 per cent of body weight was lost after forty to seventy days. By this point normal reserves of fat and protein would be gone and the body would be drawing on more basic tissue to sustain life, using up about 200 grams of muscle a day. Now any weakness in the kidneys or internal organs could prove crucial. If this hurdle was passed the vitamin deficiencies could begin to affect sight, perhaps irreversibly. As the stomach lining began to suffer the dangers of dehydration as well, the attack on the senses would, after day 40, be accentuated by the onset of Nystagmus, a distressing loss of muscle control in the eyes caused by the body's attempts to extract vitamins from non-vital muscle tissues. This lasted four or five days, accompanied by vertigo, retching and nausea. Fluids would also be difficult to keep down and, after a while, only spring water could be stomached. Some prisoners fought against the lack of co-ordination in the eyes by fixing their gaze on a single spot or using their hands as blinkers. Francis Hughes, 'The Boy from Tamlaghtduff', who remained cheerful to the end and even regaled visitors with rebel songs, constructed blinkers of gauze for this purpose. Liam McCloskey exhibited classic symptoms at this stage:

> I hadn't any ill-effects from the hunger strike until day 42. When I was watching television my eyes began to flicker causing everything in my line of vision to be unsteady. A couple of minutes later I began to vomit green digestive fluid from my stomach. Over the following week my eyes deteriorated and the vomiting became more and more frequent. It was at its worst on Friday night with continuous heaving — but I had nothing to throw up. From then on with my eyes growing duller, the vomiting eased up and after a couple of days stopped, by which time I was

> almost blind. By Wednesday I was totally blind and had great difficulty walking due to damage in a nerve centre at the top of my spine which affected the balance and co-ordination. Between the two things I was pretty much bed ridden.

As Nystagmus receded the final assault began on the vital muscles, including the heart and diaphragm, which would eventually result in the loss of the ability to breathe or a seizure. Skin would dry and the body waste to the extent that there was a danger of bones literally poking through and prisoners might have to be placed on water beds or sheepskin rugs and rubbed down with oils or other embrocations. Stomach cramps, troublesome in the early weeks, would disappear to be replaced by headaches and painful ulcerations of the mouth and throat, giving rise to heart rending debates about the use of medication. In the last day of his life Patsy O'Hara pushed away the cotton wool with which his sister Elizabeth sought to moisten his parched lips, fearing that it was medication. In the case of Kevin Lynch his mother recalls:

> Before Kevin died a man said, 'Is it all right, Mrs Lynch, to give Kevin a mouthwash?' and I said, 'I wouldn't know'. I didn't know if it was all right or not, and he asked my son Patsy and he said he didn't know either. Then Father Murphy [a prison chaplain] said 'That's all right'. It was a wee blue bottle and a very tiny brush for the ulcers were in his mouth, awful ulcers, and his throat. Father Murphy said, 'That's all right, there's nothing goes down'. He went over to Kevin to the bed and, it's as if I am looking at him now, Kevin held the mouth tight closed and Father Murphy said, 'Kevin, are you not going to take the mouthwash' and Kevin shook his head. Father Murphy said 'that's enough, he doesn't want it'. The lips were bleeding but he wouldn't even let vaseline on his lips. I wouldn't like to see my worst enemy, and I thank God I have no enemies, in his place tonight for I think I'd have too . . .

During the course of starvation naturally occurring substances which mimic the effects of morphine, endomorphins, are periodically released into the system and it is thought by some that bodily adrenaline can be converted to adreneultin, a hallucinogen whose action, particularly in conditions of vitamin B6 deficiency, can resemble mescalin for brief periods. Such bodily actions, combined with prolonged reflection and the loss of the faculties of sight and hearing, may be the biochemical backdrop to the periods of abnormal clarity and insight, the feelings of transcendence and the later disorientation experienced in varying degrees by those on hunger strike. McCloskey, who went through a religious experience around the time of the hunger strike, remembers considering his position in the absolute perspective of infinity, a microcosm closed in itself by blindness and uncommon experience. In these circumstances loyalty and commitment were the decisive factors, solidarity combining with fear of letting comrades down and the inertia of terminal exhaustion.

Meals were brought in as normal to the starving men, who thought them larger and more appetising than usual, but were invariably left untouched at the end of the bed. Prison staff say that no special effort was made over the rations but that where food would often be cold and greasy by the time it reached the H-Block wings it could be heated up in the hospital ovens. In other ways too the prison hospital, a separate single storey building, was more congenial than the H-Blocks. When the hunger strikers were moved there after the first three or four weeks they immediately gained the substance of the five demands. Radios were provided in the rooms and association was permitted in a TV room between 6 and 8 each evening. This meant the hunger strikers heard and saw the main local news bulletins and listened to occasional messages thinly disguised as record requests on the radio. They knew as much about events as the general population, and would applaud IRA actions as they watched TV. There was also regular contact with Sinn Féin personnel, at first Jim Gibney and later Joe Austin, and, in addition, messages and even copies of *Republican News* could be smuggled in. When death appeared imminent, and in a few cases this was more than a week before it actually occurred, families were given constant use of a smaller room adjoining.

The attitude of prison staff was generally better than it had been in the blocks, though both families and staff have confirmed that at least one officer went out of his way to cause discomfort to hunger strikers when he moved them and some officers were frightened by the determination and courage of their dying IRA charges. 'It showed that they made formidable enemies', one officer commented. By and large searches for tobacco and other contraband tended to be more cursory, as one officer put it, 'I would find baccy but it is no use worrying about their health.'

In these terminal stages visits were sad affairs. Again Mary McDermott's recollections of Kieran Doherty in the nine days before death are particularly vivid:

> He didn't see me, he said 'the head lamps are gone.'
>
> After 30 days he had been sitting up in bed and apart from the fact that his jaws were sunken, you would think that he was all right . . . now he was gaunt to the extent of being really frightening and there was a prison orderly there who was a nice lad. One time Kieran wanted his pillows adjusted and he wasn't able to, the orderly had to sort of fix him up and give him a drink from his cup. . . . And you could hear the water just rattling down inside. It was pure skin and bones. You could hear the noise. It was horrible. Hear the noise of the water going down inside him but he was still talking. I wouldn't say he was quite so hopeful now but he still had a bit of hope.
>
> I was more or less doing the talking because he wasn't really able. There was no point in saying 'don't go on hunger strike' at this stage so I was saying 'everybody is doing what they can, you know, we are contacting this one and that one and the other one and so on and so forth' and I said 'I'm sure that they will give in to your demands.' He would say, 'oh demands, there is a lot more to it than that.' I remember that. He said 'there is a lot more, there is more to it than that.' He didn't talk very much for he wasn't able, he really hadn't the energy and I didn't want him to talk too much because I felt every word that he says is taking away his strength.
>
> His eyes were closing and I said, 'Kieran, just you close your eyes, keep them closed if you want to. I'll talk.' I'd talk on about something to try and keep the thing going. It was very difficult because I felt it was pointless saying, 'This has been tried' and 'that has been tried' and 'the other has

been tried', yet there he was dying and still he would like to hear something.

So the time passed and I went away. He said to me, 'don't worry about me, don't worry about me' and I went away after half an hour or so.

And then he happened to be alive the next Friday... well, I went and it really was the most horrific thing that I have ever seen or ever hope to see again. We have all heard of Terence McSwiney the Lord Mayor of Cork and learnt at school that he was so many days on hunger strike and we knew all this verbatim but you never really knew what it actually meant until you saw...

He was lying in bed and he was just alive, you know he was breathing, but he was far worse, thinner than he had been the week before and he was getting blood blotches on his face, you know those blotches as if you got a knock. He didn't of course but that was the way it looked. He was terrible, his face was red, he was making a noise. He was breathing and it was making a noise. I suppose it was a weakening of his muscles, what people call a death rattle. There was no flesh at all. He was just like an absolute skeleton and he couldn't see. He said 'who is it?' and I told him and then he knew but he was staring, just staring into space. He wasn't able to turn his head to look at me but he just held on to my two hands and he didn't say anything about it, he wasn't able. He didn't ask 'is there any hope' or 'what's happening'.

I don't know whether he was fully conscious or whether he was in a sort of trance between this world and the next, if there is one, but he was lying there and he said to me, 'Oh yes,' he said. It's the first thing he said, 'Sean was a great soldier, he was shot dead beside me.' Now that was the first and only time that he ever mentioned to me that he even knew Sean, because Kieran wouldn't tell you the time of day if it didn't concern you. Yet he told me that and I wondered why. I thought to myself, 'Well he knows he is dying. Does he want to tell me or is it that he is not himself, that he is not as much on his guard as he would be normally?'

It was terrible as the orderly lifted him up like that and he said, 'water, water' or something like that. They

> gradually moved him round a little bit and he stared on and as if to say, 'well, I'm determined to do it and that's it.' I think he knew at that time they weren't getting anything. He died from sheer loyalty.

Hunger strikers were weighed daily and, through the sophisticated system of communications and visitors, kept the movement on the outside fully informed of their condition and thoughts. The traffic of information was two-way with visitors reporting to Sinn Féin offices to be given communications to be taken to the hunger strikers, some of which contained information on the likely course of the hunger strike, pointers on how to handle possible interventions by relatives and comments on the attitudes of individual relatives or friends at meetings outside the prison. Before the hunger strike commenced all those who went on it had volunteered and been made aware of what was involved; some were individually discouraged and all were given time to reconsider in light of the painful symptoms and likely death that awaited them. However, once the decision was taken it was expected that they would abide by collective and individual commitments and not abandon the fast unless its causes were removed to the satisfaction of the OCs.

Great care was taken to maintain lines of communication between the hunger strikers, the outside and the prisons to prevent feelings of isolation and to ensure that each part of the organisation was fully aware of the whole picture. Jimmy Drumm was often stationed in the prison car park to brief and debrief visitors whilst other Sinn Féin personnel gave meticulous reports of the successes and shortcomings of external activity in support of the hunger strike. Joe Austin, who fulfilled this role from mid May, says:

> The motivation for me visiting the prison was communication. Basically it was to monitor the condition of the prisoners, to provide a link with the outside world and to keep them accurately informed of what was happening outside . . . there was an emotional and personal thing involved and there was also the political considerations that I had responsibility for . . . The relatives, because they were relatives, would have come in and said, 'There were 10,000 in Cookstown last night' because, I suppose, those

people felt there was a need to keep the spirits of the prisoners up. That combination of inaccurate information was a very dangerous thing, because somebody could say that victory was around the corner and it actually wasn't around the corner. My job was to go inside and say, 'There were 10,000 people in Cookstown last night and the Brits are not about to move.'

The position of relatives as a possible alternative to the IRA command structure for ending the hunger strike was grasped by not only the British authorities, nationalist politicians and the Roman Catholic Church but also by the Provisionals. Families who showed interest were encouraged into a range of protests and meetings which both helped the build-up of pressure and kept them occupied without endangering the integrity of the protest.

On the propaganda front the death of Bobby Sands brought international interest back with a vengeance. There was a twenty-four-hour black on British shipping in New York docks. Over twenty-three nations sent camera crews, sixteen from the US alone. Seven hundred reporters and photographers descended on Belfast and his funeral[2] brought up to 100,000 people onto the streets. It also won the Provisionals a long cherished and never to be repeated goal, recognition by a government, that of Iran, whose principal diplomatic representative in London, Abdolrahim Gavani, travelled to Northern Ireland for the funeral, missing it by two hours. A message from the Tehran municipality that a street near the British embassy had been named after 'the heroic death of the IRA freedom fighter Bobby Sands' was also received.[3]

The issue was once more denting Britain's image abroad, all but evaporating the wave of anti-IRA feeling engendered by the killing of Lord Mountbatten. In a survey of sixty-four newspapers in twenty-five countries[4] the majority (thirty-six) thought that Britain should at least start talks with Dublin with a view to withdrawal. Only a single newspaper, the right-wing Turkish *Tercuman*, supported Thatcher's handling of the crisis. However international embarrassment did not amount to overwhelming political pressure. Friendly governments said little and, despite a few dissident MPs, the British opposition parties supported the government position. The press was, in general, supportive with one influential columnist (John Junor of the *Sunday Express*) expressing the hope that 'every other IRA hunger striker will go on the same sort of protest and stay on it till they are all in wooden suits.' What mooted criticisms there were confined themselves to the handling of the crisis and were offset by demands that the BBC restrict or slant its coverage of the hunger strike, demands which provided the background to a later decision by Granada TV to withdraw a 'World in Action' documentary on the hunger strike after the IBA decided to censor a sequence showing Patsy O'Hara lying in his coffin flanked by armed INLA men. Most decisively an opinion poll[5] showed that 92 per cent of English and Welsh voters were opposed to the granting of political status. A disturbing reminder of the vulnerability of British institutions was provided by the explosion of a 7 lb 'sleeper bomb', similar to the one later used in Brighton, at Sullom Voe oil terminal in the Shetland islands minutes before Queen Elizabeth opened it, but still, from the distance of Downing Street there was little attraction, and no votes, in concessions to the IRA.

The people who could feel real and immediate pressure were, as ever, Irish nationalist politicians and the Catholic Church, though even here there was no enthusiasm for an outright Provo hunger strike victory. Faced with the declared Provo 'strategy for success of destabilising the six and twenty-six county states, and thus forcing the British government to grant the prisoners' demands',[6] they sought to find some mediating body, with an ECHR intervention being briefly revived after the death, on 12 May, of the second hunger striker, Francis Hughes.

Hughes was an exceptionally audacious and resilient man whose early death, after only fifty-nine days, was probably linked to the rigours which surrounded his capture in 1978. Originally a member of the Official IRA he had left the organisation after its 1972 ceasefire and set up an independent commando unit in his native South Derry which was, a year later, accepted en masse into the Provisionals. For the next five years he was almost constantly on the run, mainly in the company of Dominic McGlinchey and Ian Milne. He operated in full combat gear and frequently rang the British army to tell them where he was, acquiring such notoriety that most IRA attacks in the area were, with some justice, blamed on him. His eventual capture came after a shoot out with the SAS in which his left hip was shattered. Despite this he made his way to the nearest cover, 300 yards away, and lay bleeding copiously through one of the coldest nights of the year. At this point he was the most wanted man in Ireland but when he was discovered by a British army patrol the next afternoon he managed to decieve them as to his true identity, refusing all medication until he reached Musgrave Park military hospital. Three operations to save his leg resulted in its being shortened by an inch and a half, leaving him dependent on a crutch to walk.

Sentenced to a total of 83 years this adamant personality left room for little doubt that he would carry on to the bitter end, telling medical staff, 'I'm dying, I'm dead, that's it' and never complaining about conditions. Emerging from the prison after Hughes' death his brother Oliver told newsmen, 'Maggie Thatcher has murdered another Irishman and created another martyr.' The violent contrary emotions aroused by Hughes was illustrated by marks found on his face after death which, an eye-witness has confirmed, may have resulted from a number of kicks directed at the corpse before it left the prison.

The death and funeral were surrounded by heavy rioting, still mainly confined to Belfast and Derry, and the decision of the RUC to divert the remains away from the West Belfast crowds who were waiting to greet it caused ill-feeling with the family. That day an apparently innocent girl, fourteen-year-old Julie Livingstone, was killed by a plastic bullet as she made her way home and a British soldier was seriously injured. A worried John Hume was in London meeting Margaret Thatcher who, after what was described by Hume as 'not an easy meeting', agreed to assist the ECHR if it could be re-involved.

After the last fiasco, families and prisoners were unwilling to make a fresh application and interest briefly centered on the Irish government whose foreign minister Brian Lenihan discussed the matter in Strasbourg with the British. However he made no application and in the end the intervention came to nothing more than an abortive agreement by the ECHR to consider two points outstanding from the last application. A few days later an attempt to involve Amnesty International collapsed when its Secretary General, Thomas Hammarbert, made it clear that the hunger strikers were not 'prisoners of conscience' in any accepted sense.

This new evidence that the IRA did not have an objectively sustainable case for political status coincided with equally convincing evidence that the hunger strike was delivering hearts and minds in the nationalist ghettos and the signs of the first possibilities of a crack in the hunger strike itself.

British hopes of a break were at first centered on two men, Brendan McLaughlin and Raymond McCreesh. McCreesh, a South Armagh man who had been arrested with future hunger striker Paddy Quinn after a gun battle with British soldiers, began his hunger strike on 21 March. Rumours were leaked by the authorities that he might not see it through. The details of what occurred remain controversial, the family seeing themselves as the victims of a set-up and the prison authorities maintaining that the hunger striker had expressed a wish to drink milk to medical staff.

What is uncontested is that on 16 May prison chaplain Father Tom Toner gave Raymond McCreesh the last rites and shortly afterwards the medical staff asked the family to come to the hospital. They said that Raymond had not been taking water and was in a confused state. In answer to questions he had indicated that he would take milk or some other nourishment but after speaking to his family he continued his hunger strike until his death on 21 May. The BBC and *Time* magazine both alleged that his brother Brian, a priest, had talked him out of eating. Fr McCreesh threatened legal action against the BBC, maintaining that his brother's wishes were clear and demanding the removal of two members of the medical staff. In a cable to Mrs Thatcher he asked her to respect his brother's dignity and save his life. A short time later a small camera and tape recorder were found in Raymond McCreesh's room and speculation continued as to whether they were bugs placed by the authorities or, as the NIO hinted, a ploy by the IRA to get propaganda material. In fact, the INLA had introduced the camera into the prison for Patsy O'Hara's use. Jimmy Drumm, who spoke to the family immediately after the visit, believes that Father McCreesh simply ascertained his brother's wishes.

Patsy O'Hara also died on the 21st. This time his mother had actually resolved to intervene and two days before his death had told him, 'I don't care about Ireland or the whole world, you are the only thing that matters to me — everything else has failed and now I am the only one who can save you and I am going to do it' and had even conveyed her decision to the outside leadership who said they would back her in it. The next day she was forced to change her mind by his clear instruction to 'let the fight go on'.

Such tragic scenes underlined the vicious predicament of families in a situation in which a relative's reasoning powers and contact with reality were impaired by vitamin and mineral deficiencies. The argument could, and would, be made that the family must stand by the prisoner's wishes, if necessary disregarding what were no more than the ravings of a tortured man; alternatively it was argued that the family must act at a time when a prisoner might not be able to express the will to live as strongly as he wished. The dilemma of the families and prisoners increased as the hunger strike progressed and it was seen that further deaths would have only a cumulative effect. The case of Sean McKenna, plucked by Darkie Hughes from the edge of death and now recovering, showed that permanent damage would not necessarily result from advanced starvation. Shortly Brendan McLaughlin was to put the first dent in the theory that all hunger strikers would, like O'Hara, preserve their determination to continue to the end.

McLaughlin began his hunger strike on 14 May to replace Patsy O'Hara and it soon became clear that he could not survive long on it due to a perforated ulcer. On the 24th Sinn Féin indicated that they would back him in either continuing or abandoning his fast. On the 26th he accepted medical treatment but Sinn Féin stated that he would continue to refuse food. The next day he was accepting nourishment and Sinn Féin announced that they supported his decision because 'to have continued in his present condition would have meant almost certain death before the full effects of a long hunger strike could be felt by the British government'. Two days later he was replaced by Tyrone man Martin Hurson.

Whatever about the British government the people of Northern Ireland were now certainly feeling the effects of the protest. On the 19th another young girl, twelve-year-old Carol

Ann Kelly, was fatally wounded, shot by a British army plastic bullet hours after an IRA landmine had killed five soldiers near Newry and on the 21st another round of rioting was sparked off by the deaths, in a single day, of Raymond McCreesh and Patsy O'Hara. The next day, with the controversy raging about the diversion of O'Hara's body, and as one man was killed and twenty injured by plastic bullets, Northern Ireland's local government election results were counted.

Sinn Féin had taken a decision not to stand, advising their supporters to vote 'H not X', and the IRA had made some efforts to cause disruption, shooting a soldier in the arm at a West Belfast polling booth and organising rioting. As a result of all this, polling was down but a number of smaller parties standing on pro-prison tickets did well. In particular the Irish Independence Party picked up twenty-one seats whilst PD and the IRSP gained two seats each in nationalist areas of North and West Belfast. Moderate parties like the SDLP and Alliance, or those campaigning on social issues like the Workers Party Republican Clubs, suffered and, on the loyalist side, Ian Paisley's DUP overtook the Official Unionists. Devlin, whose record breaking majority was transformed into a wafer thin margin, retained his seat but, like others who opposed the Provisionals, came under pressure in the aftermath of the election, finally leaving his Andersonstown home for good on 25 May.

The sectarian polarisation of society around the prisoners and the constitutional issues gave weight to those within the Provos arguing for 'electoral intervention' and the success of smaller parties on the backs of the hunger strike campaign left a sour taste in the mouth. It also concentrated the minds of the Catholic Church and constitutional nationalism on the need to devise some formula for ending the hunger strike to prevent a slide into anarchy. However Margaret Thatcher, on a visit to Belfast, felt no such pressure. It was, she said, 'the IRA's final card'. In reality, as Joe Austin put it, 'she was dealing the IRA a whole new deck'.

In the prison Kevin Lynch had joined the hunger strike to replace his INLA comrade Patsy O'Hara and, judging by the leading hunger striker Joe McDonnell, morale was high. When British Liberal leader David Steel visited him in the prison hospital, he told him his only complaint was about the food.

If the northern nationalist establishment had been the first to feel the chill wind of Provo electoral intervention their southern counterparts did not have long to wait for their turn. A series of false alarms were ended by the announcement, as Raymond McCreesh and Patsy O'Hara died on 21 May, that the Republic would hold its general election on 11 June.

By the end of May it was clear that there would be no repeat of the gains of fringe groups campaigning on prisoners' issues in the northern local elections. A brief flurry of interest around the possible candidature of Bernadette McAliskey was killed off by the announcement that nine prisoners would be standing.[7] From the start the particular target was Charles Haughey both because of the kudos that would flow from displacing a premier or governing party and because of the bitterness created by his failed interventions and refusal to give his unequivocal backing to the five damands. During the campaign the Taoiseach's electioneering efforts were disrupted repeatedly by H-Block squads whose actions Bernadette McAliskey described as 'undemocratic and politically and physically dangerous'. At one stage he was hit by an egg and in a more serious incident an INLA bomb was found at the Fianna Fail election headquarters in Castleblayney shortly before Haughey was due to arrive.

In the south, H-Block seemed of fringe interest though rising numbers had attended demonstrations as the deaths mounted and there were isolated outbreaks of rioting, most seriously on 12 May when marchers had clashed with gardai riot squads after the death of Francis Hughes. Haughey played down the dangers of the intervention, pledging that the hunger strike would not interrupt his steady progress on the Anglo-Irish front, but was said privately to fear the loss of five seats.. In the background there were moves by the Catholic clergy to achieve a settlement through the intervention of the Irish Commission for Justice and Peace, a body set up by the Irish bishops in 1967 which had previously been active mainly on third world issues. On 3 June the ICJP counterposed 'three suggestions' to the prisoners' five demands as a possible means of ending the hunger strike. They were:

1. That prisoners in the Maze, who are at present permitted to wear their own clothes for a greater part of the

time should, like the prisoners in Armagh, be allowed to do so at all times.

2. That some moves might be made to increase opportunities for association while making it clear that military training, or any other activity that would be illegal in society at large, would not be tolerated in the prison.

3. That the question of prison work should be reviewed both in order to ensure that the work is of the greatest possible cultural and educational value and that no work of a demeaning nature is demanded.

As these proposals began to gather support from the Catholic hierarchy, starting with Bishop Edward Daly of Derry, the prisoners finally rejected the idea of ending the hunger strike and instead announced a further escalation because, they said, 'the existing four man relay strategy allows the British a recuperation period during which they enjoy the lessening of pressure'. The extent of this escalation, which aimed at putting one prisoner a week on protest to plug the so called '40-day gap', was not known until after the Republic's election by which time Tom McIlwee had replaced his cousin Francis Hughes on hunger strike and the Provos had scored a major propaganda coup with the escape from Crumlin Road jail of eight remand prisoners.

The accepted wisdom in the Republic was that the prisoner candidates would not greatly affect the poll but, in the event, their 2.3 per cent of the national vote proved to be sufficiently strategically concentrated to ensure the election of two TDs. Paddy Agnew, a man written off by the pundits, topped the poll in his native Louth whilst Kieran Doherty scored 9,121 votes in Monaghan, securing another seat. In Waterford Kevin Lynch missed taking a third seat by around 300 votes. Both the seats were lost by Fianna Fail reducing Haughey's total to 78 against the combined Fine Gael/Labour total of 80, the other six seats being made up of the two prisoners, Joe Sherlock of the Workers Party, Jim Kemmy of the Democratic Socialist Party and two independents. With the tacit support of Kemmy and Sherlock Fine Gael and Labour were able to form a government.

During the count the British government had published an amendment to the Representation of the People Act seeking to stave off a repeat of Fermanagh-South Tyrone by preventing prisoners standing in elections. As the results came out, South Armagh man Paddy Quinn, who had been arrested with Raymond McCreesh after an ambush on the British army went wrong in June 1976, brought the total number on hunger strike to six and it was announced that from now on one man would join the fast each week. The seventh was to be INLA man Mickey Devine, who joined on the 22nd.

The election results and this new escalation created a situation in which established order, especially in the nationalist community, was under threat and it was becoming likely that a very large number of hunger strike deaths might occur. At the annual Wolfe Tone commemoration in Bodenstown the least reticent of the urban northerners, Danny Morrison, expressed the confident and uncompromising mood induced by the rising political temperature:

> Day and daily, politicians and newspaper editors and bishops bemoan the destabilisation north and south which the hunger strike has created via the new layers of fresh support it has mobilised. And it has undoubtedly increased support for the IRA . . .
>
> The election of prisoner candidates, whose profile as IRA men their opponents and the media emphasised, and the recent local government elections in the north, show that the mood of the people is changing. They are far from war weary and not so far from victory.

The Irish Catholic Church did indeed face real practical and theological problems now that actual death had replaced the slow build-up of prolonged hunger strike envisaged by Sands as the primary means of pressure on themselves and on Britain. The Catholic bishops acted quickly to spell out their moral position, imploring 'the hunger strikers and all those who direct them to reflect deeply on the evil of their actions and their consequences'. In clear condemnation of the IRA they went on: 'The contempt for human life, the incitement to revenge, the exploitation of the hunger strikes to further a campaign of murder, the intimidation of the innocent, the initiation of children into violence . . . all this constitutes an appalling mass of evil.' They recommended the ICJP proposals, associating them with the authority of the pope by recalling the responsibility which, in the Drogheda speech, he laid on governments not to allow conditions to continue which would give an excuse or pretext to the men of violence.

The members of the Commission were Bishop Dermot O'Mahony, Jerome Connolly, Brian Gallagher, Father Oliver Crilly from Maghera (relative of both Tom McIlwee and Francis Hughes) and Hugh Logue, a leading SDLP figure and friend of Kevin Lynch's family. Collectively they represented the best chance of an agreed settlement and had they but realised it, the nearest the Provisionals would get to mobilising the power and influence of the entire nationalist community around the prison issue.

The Commission prepared the ground carefully, meeting with representatives of Fianna Fail, Fine Gael and the Irish Labour party on 19 June and opening contact with some hunger strikers' families before making any approach to the British. The so called 'gap' until Joe McDonnell entered a critical phase would be filled with the Commission's efforts to find a solution which would stick with both sides.

At their first meeting with Northern Ireland prisons' minister Michael Alison on 23 June it emerged that there might now be some movement on the prisoners' demand to be exempt from wearing prison clothes, provided that their dress could be vetted by the authorities to prevent the use of uniform and other unreasonable attire (women's clothes were actually mentioned). Aware of a statement issued by Gerry Adams over the prisoners' names in which he called the ICJP's three suggestions an 'unacceptable dilution' of the five demands, Father Crilly arranged to meet his second cousin Tom McIlwee in the jail. As a result of this meeting it emerged that the prisoners had not drawn up the Adams statement and a more hopeful one, saying that they would welcome the intervention of the ICJP or 'any other body' which could arrange for them to 'talk to the British government to bring about a just settlement to the hunger strike', was issued. On the strength of this the ICJP again met Alison on the 26th. Both sides agreed that the clothing issue was resolved in principle. Discussions now centred on the details of how association could be achieved without endangering prison security by allowing large numbers of prisoners to wander about at will. The solution proposed was association amongst the twenty-five or so prisoners on each secure wing for around three hours a day. The outstanding item on the shopping list was the question of prison work where a redefinition seemed possible.

The apparently swift progress of these meetings was illusory. Deep reserves of intransigence and mistrust as well as powerful political considerations existed on both the British and the republican sides. Shortly after Crilly's meeting with McIlwee an eighth hunger striker, Laurence McKeown, joined the protest on cue and Sinn Féin issued a statement saying that the British were 'deliberately creating an illusion of movement' in an effort to break the protest. This seemed to be borne out by a 30 June statement from Atkins, which though conciliatory in tone and making a commitment to 'yet further development' in prison reform, made no concrete pronouncement on what exactly such development might entail.

The ICJP later felt that Alison, the man on the ground, had acted in good faith[8] but that he had been overruled by Mrs Thatcher, recalling his statement at one meeting that 'there is a lady behind the veil'. According to former British government sources the Prime Minister did take a personal but not a sufficiently detailed interest in the negotiations, tending to view any willingness to negotiate on the part of the prisoners as a sign that the hunger strike was breaking down. Unlike the miners the hunger strikers could put no effective pressure on her administration and it would have taken crippling pressure to induce her to recognise, much less give public commitments to the IRA. However it seems that the concessions which followed the hunger strike's eventual end were available at this stage, and that the government's reservations concerned being seen to be forced into them. A number of ways round this difficulty were considered by the local administration, including getting a senior prison official from outside the province to make a televised statement of what was likely to occur once the hunger strike was ended.

The position on the Provisional side was if anything more complicated. The pre-strike predictions of several deaths had been fulfilled, but it is in the nature of a military organisation to accept casualties in furtherance of its ojbectives and the political pessimism that the hunger strike would drag the IRA down with it had been confounded. The strike had not only moved the IRA centre stage, allowing an escalation of the military campaign hand in hand with electoral victory, but had made it possible for the plans of the urban radicals for a restructuring of the movement to proceed apace. Structures were being changed, organisational lessons learnt and dead wood cleared away in the constant activity. Moreover, the sense of unity which this produced vindicated the urban northerners, allowing the Prisoners of War Committee, which they dominated, to take the lead. The last clear opportunities to end the hunger strike short of victory, the election of Bobby Sands and the cut-off point of the first four hunger strikers, had been rejected by the prisoners themselves and, with these past, the political price to be paid for an unsatisfactory conclusion was arguably higher than that required to continue the fight.

The precedent being looked to on all sides was the ending of the 1980 hunger strike. A further meeting with Alison on 3 July produced a prediction from him that if the prisoners removed the duress of the hunger strike they would be allowed to wear their own clothes as of right. This changeover would be facilitated by allowing the prisoners to remain on the blanket until their own clothes arrived, thus avoiding the difficulties of the December changeover. The ICJP proceeded to put this to the strikers who said that McFarlane must be involved in future talks and told the ICJP that their proposals were too vague. However that evening, Saturday 4 July they issued a prepared and seemingly conciliatory statement, in which Brendan Hughes was said to have had a hand.[9]

Answering Atkins' 30 June statement, it assured the British that the prisoners were not seeking control of the prison or even differential treatment from other prisoners; they would be happy for the five demands to apply to all inmates. The once central hurdle of clothing seemed to have been crossed; freedom of association was defined to mean association on the wings for indefinite periods with occasional provision for visits between wings; the demands on exemption from prison work and educational facilities were telescoped to mean a re-definition of work to allow a choice of unpaid cleaning duties and education classes instead of the normal paid tasks; the fifth demand, for restoration of remission, was opened up for discussion. Segregation from loyalists was, rightly, assumed to flow from the other changes in the interests of the avoidance of conflict during association. However the prisoners demanded that a competent official come into the prison to talk directly to them as had been promised at the end of 1980 and this, once again, was to prove too much for the government to swallow.

Instead Atkins concentrated his efforts on using the ICJP to 'clarify' the position to the prisoners on the basis of a gentleman's understanding. In the light of the disappointments of 1980 the trust needed for such a course did not exist.

The meetings of 3 July between the ICJP and Alison had taken a marathon eight hours. During this time Joe McDonnell's wife Goretti and other relatives were with the new Taoiseach, Garret FitzGerald, and his deputy Michael O'Leary. The Taoiseach liaised closely with the ICJP and had unsuccessfully asked Thatcher to have the meeting brought forward in view of the poor condition of McDonnell. FitzGerald, who seemed to expect a breakthrough and had ministerial Mercedes on stand by to take the families north, briefed the relatives fully on details of negotiations which had been withheld in the earlier stages by the ICJP in the interests of confidentiality. The relatives, some of them impressed by what they had heard, went home under their own steam in the early hours of the 5th. Later that day they met the ICJP in a West Belfast hotel where the details of what had occurred were once more withheld. By now the prisoners' 4 July statement had been issued and the next day the ICJP again met the relatives, this time put them fully in the picture, saying that they would return to the prison.

McFarlane, mindful of the exclusion of Bobby Sands in 1980, took part in this meeting at his own insistence and Danny Morrison was also admitted to the prison to consult with the hunger strikers. However Joe McDonnell, on day 58, was too weak to attend. In view of his grim state, and apparently without any firm agreement from McFarlane, the ICJP set about the task of getting a senior official — they were trying for John Blelloch — into the prison to nail down the concessions and to end the hunger strike in time to save McDonnell's life. A planned statement from the ICJP outlining the negotiations so far was now shown to Alison who accepted its drift, asking only for one minor change in the wording and describing the concessions on matters other than clothing as 'illustrative only'. An official would, he said enter the prison by mid-morning on 7 July. At his request the ICJP withheld the statement to await this development. A prison chaplain told the prisoners to expect an official by 10.30 am on Tuesday the 7th and a visit from the ICJP later in the day. That evening no new hunger striker was named although it was now exactly a week since McKeown had joined.

When by 11.40 am, no official had appeared the ICJP called a press conference for 1.00 pm to try to force the pace. A few minutes before it was due to start they were assured by 'phone that an official would come. As a result they sent journalists home, saying nothing. At 4.00 pm they were informed that detailed drafting was being carried out on a document to be given to prisoners and, within an hour, it began to look as if a document would be sent but no official.

Still later Alison's staff said an NIO official would shortly go into the prison with the governor who would read out a document. However in another call at 10.00 pm Alison himself said that the visit had been delayed to the morning for reasons that were to the prisoners' advantage and agreed to an immediate meeting. When the ICJP arrived at Stormont the minister claimed that he had been overruled — 'Frankly I was not a sufficient plenipotentiary' — on the matter of sending in the official that morning. He then guaranteed that one would arrive by 8.00 am next morning, July 8th, and assured the Commission that Joe McDonnell, now entering day 61, was in no immediate danger.

At 5.12 am McDonnell died. Five hours later the long awaited official, a Mr Jackson, arrived with the prison governor Stanley Hilditch, and, visiting each hunger striker individually in his cell, presented a statement from Atkins. It contained no firm commitment, on clothes it said only that 'we would not rule out the possibility of further developments', and appeared watered down. There were no questions from the prisoners, the gesture had been far too little and just a few hours too late. As

Pat McGeown, the man destined to replace Joe McDonnell, recalls:

> When Joe McDonnell died it meant that you had gone from the first group of hunger strikers to the second group where they would follow on at weekly or two weekly periods with deaths. This meant that you didn't have a clear line where you could ever actually say 'right, we'll break it there' and the whole thing took on a momentum of its own to a degree from that point.

Late in the morning an angry ICJP called their long delayed press conference, revealing the details of what had been discussed, including a document which Alison had agreed to be a correct account of their negotiations and which appeared to meet the prisoners' main demands.

At this point it was clear that, whatever its intentions on the prisons, the Thatcher administration would not make commitments to the IRA or its prisoners. Yet even though the hunger strikers had been attracted by the ICJP proposals and had considered ending the fast, the IRA, inside or outside the prison, would not accept second-hand assurances given to intermediaries. In their eyes the position was analogous to the rushed settlement to save Sean McKenna's life. Their eventual minimum position was that they would end the protest in return for guaranteed negotiations over a period of two to three weeks. A less obvious analogy, in terms of IRA attitudes, was the situation which followed the Feakle talks when, in the absence of written guarantees, the leadership were unwilling to move, or perhaps unable to carry the movement, from a known situation to an unknown one.

The Provos could hope to nail the British government down in this way only if they became what they purported to be, the representatives of the Irish nation. Any serious attempt to assume that role brought them into immediate conflict with the nationalist and Catholic establishment which was now beginning to realise that if the intolerable strains being placed on their leadership and on the community as a whole were to be removed it would have to be by means other than open negotiation.

NOTES

1. According to *Belfast Graves,* National Graves Association 1985.

2. Media figures from Liz Curtis, *Ireland and the Propaganda War,* Pluto 1984.

3. There were a number of messages of support from some of the smaller Middle Eastern factions, though not the PLO proper, and European left or terrorist groups. In terms of international links the period of the funeral also coincided with a visit to the Middle East by William 'Blue' Kelly and Denis Donaldson, a future head of Sinn Féin's foreign affairs department. In August the duo were arrested at Paris' Orly airport where they were charged with using false papers. They told police that they had spent some months in a camp in the Lebanon.

4. *Sunday Times,* 31 May 1981, 'Is Britain Losing the Propaganda War?' by Philip Knightly.

5. The issue of the BBC's role was debated in the Lords on May 15th and taken up by a number of influential right-wing commentators including Paul Johnson. The poll, by MORI, was published on the day of the Lords debate. It also showed that whilst only 18 per cent of the sample supported Irish unity only 35 per cent supported the continued presence of British troops in Northern Ireland.

6. *Republican News,* 16 May 1981, reporting on the proceedings of an emergency open conference on the hunger strike on 12 May. The article stated that 'there urgently needs to be popular street riots, the erection of barricades against the British forces, and other violent acts of disobedience building towards the establishment of no-go areas in the nationalist ghettos; plus of course the armed action of IRA volunteers against military occupation forces' but warned that the national H-Block Committee would not be suitable body to organize the necessary 'rioting and shooting'. Gerry Adams told the conference that 'sporadic uncontrolled rioting on a small scale forms no part of this strategy and is counter productive'.

7. They included: hunger strikers Kieran Doherty, Martin Hurson, Kevin Lynch and Joe McDonnell; former hunger striker Sean McKenna; Armagh OC Mairead Farrell; as well as former blanketmen Paddy Agnew, Tony O'Hara and Tom McAlister.

8. ICJP press statement, 8 July 1981.

9. The text of this statement is given in Appendix 6.

9

A Devious and Conniving Priest?

> Sinn Féin could balls ahead because that is the way they go on but the intelligent man has to sit down and reassess the situation: especially when there are loads of people dying. There were people dying in the prison and there were people dying on the streets. Children were being blasted with plastic bullets because the security forces had complete *carte blanche* to go into Catholic areas, break up women saying the rosary, shoot kids — wee Carol Ann Kelly, Julie Livingstone, those wee ones had their heads blown off.
>
> Another thing that was coming through to me as a priest that had to work with youth was that the youth were being filled by Sinn Féin and by the whole situation with a black, black hatred of Protestants and English people. As a Christian minister interested in education I couldn't allow that to happen.
>
> Father Denis Faul.[1]

Fr Denis Faul was in France when he heard the news of Joe McDonnell's death. It was unexpected and over the next few days the bulletins chronicled an ugly litany of death and violence on the streets of Belfast, sowing doubts in the priest's mind about his present priorities.

The headmaster of a Catholic boys' school in Tyrone, Faul would, in most societies, be regarded as a theologically conservative churchman, a pastor of unusual diligence and a man of acute social conscience. In the circumstances of Northern Ireland he had been a thorn in the side of the authorities since the early troubles and the string of closely researched polemics[2] on security force abuses which he had penned with Armagh prison chaplain Fr Raymond Murray had landed him the title 'The Provo Priest' in the British media. In fact he was regarded with suspicion by the Provisionals since the mid 70s and was increasingly frozen off platforms which they controlled.

His credibility was strongest among the victims of arrest, interrogation, and security force brutality and their families whose cases he championed at every opportunity. His primary motivation for this was his belief that the church must sharpen its social teaching and stake its claim as champion of the oppressed against the political extremists who were ultimately in conflict with it for leadership of the Catholic community.

His feelings on the hunger strike were mixed. A frequent visitor to the prison, where he said mass, and to the prisoners' families he felt strongly about the conditions in the H-Blocks and had discussed the strike with Sands before it started. He held that if the fast was aimed primarily at redressing grievances and not at death then it was not sinful or suicidal. After six deaths and the announcement that there would be a funeral a week to keep up the pressure, this view was shaken. In his mind the protest was assuming the grotesque dimensions of a 'death strike' in which a stream of coffins was the dominant feature.

The death of McDonnell heralded vicious organised rioting. In the two days following it the security forces were fired on on thirty occasions and in a hundred more instances they were attacked by blast, petrol or acid bombs.[3] In the first evening a thirty-year-old woman, Nora McCabe, was killed by an RUC plastic bullet and sixteen-year-old John Dempsey was shot dead amongst a group of youths who were attempting to drive a stolen Ford Transit full of petrol bombs into the Falls Road bus depot. Dempsey was a member of the Fianna, the junior IRA; the death underlined both the IRA input to the escalation of rioting and their use of young people at the sharp end of the fighting.

The next day brought another two fatalities, one a policeman and the other Danny Barrett, a completely innocent youth who was shot by a British army marksman when he left his tea to sit on the low garden wall of his Ardoyne home. Future supergrass Christopher Black, who was organising rioting for the IRA that evening, later testified that Barrett had not been involved and that there were no disturbances on the street where the boy lived until after his killing. Tests showed that he had not handled a weapon.

More trouble flared at McDonnell's funeral on the 10th when the army pursued the IRA colour party after a volley of shots were fired over the coffin, cornering a number of men in a house in Agnes Drive and wounding two of them, including Gerry Adams' younger brother Paddy.

After giving a major interview on French television Faul

experienced what he described as 'an awful desire to go home. A feeling that the Irish people were suffering and I shouldn't be away, I should be there.' He returned on 12 July, the date of the annual loyalist Orange Order demonstrations. This year the festivities were accompanied by two disturbing pointers, a statement from the prisoners that there was no further role for intermediaries and the discovery of an INLA bomb factory near the start of the Belfast march.

At 4.10 the next morning a seventh hunger striker, Martin Hurson, died as a result of kidney failure after only forty-five days without food. His swift decline was linked to beatings he received during interrogation by the regional crime squad when he was arrested in 1976 and from prison staff during the first of the forced washings in 1978.[4] Hurson's life ended as toxins reached his brain and, despite his emaciated state the agony was such that it took four staff to hold him down, one of them weighing seventeen stone. At the inquest his family complained that they were not told of the danger in time to intervene and save Martin's life without risking permanent brain damage. In fact his complications had been apparent since late June and he suffered seizures, which usually responded to treatment by placing a paper bag in front of his face to cut down his carbon dioxide intake, at the rate of two or three every twenty-four hours for some days before he died.

Faul had discussed the problem of prisoners who were not physically fit for hunger strike with Brendan McFarlane after the McLaughlin crisis and again shortly before he went to France in late June. Now he raised it once more. This time the discussion ended in a twenty minute shouting match in the prison canteen before mass and the normally unflappable McFarlane accused the priest of blaming Hurson's death on him personally.

Before this argument, Faul had further reason to question his own qualified support for the hunger strike tactic. He had visited Mrs Bridie Lynch in Dungiven, an extremely devout Catholic and the mother of INLA hunger striker Kevin Lynch. Mrs Lynch now believes that the IRA acted properly towards the prisoners on hunger strike but at the time she was, like some other relatives, inclined to blame them for keeping it going. This feeling was aggravated by the barrier which the blanket protest had placed between herself and the youngest son on whom she doted and the shoddy treatment she had received at the hands of the INLA in the early stages of his hunger strike.

A very dedicated and determined young man, Kevin Lynch had refused to put on a prison uniform for visits for most of his sentence and during these years her only firm news of his condition had been from Father Faul who saw him at mass. After a trip to Lourdes Mrs Lynch returned to find that Kevin had sent her out a visit at last, and she regarded this change of heart as little short of miraculous. After that, visits continued on an intermittent basis and before one of them she received a call from the IRSP to meet one of their members in the prison car park. Although she did not know him the man who met her was Seamus Ruddy, later to disappear in Paris after an INLA interfactional feud over relations with the French *Action Direct* group.[5] Ruddy asked her if he could get into her car and in answer to her husband's observation that times were bad he replied 'indeed they are, Raymond McCreesh could be dead tomorrow and Patsy O'Hara on Friday and Kevin is taking his place.'[6] The parents were left speechless and when they went into the prison Mr Lynch told Kevin that they would not accept or support his decision to go on hunger strike. At this Kevin grasped his mother's hands and said 'Mammy you never let me down in your life and I never needed you more than I need you now. I want to do what I am doing because you have no idea how we are getting treated in here and I think you never will. We are locked up from Christmas to Christmas, you never see fresh air, you haven't a bed to lie on, not even a pair of shoes. I want to do what I am doing for what I believe in and for the rest of my comrades.' At this she told him, 'Kevin, whatever you want I will always pamper you' and returned home in a daze realising that she was now committed to supporting him through the nightmare of death by starvation. In Kevin's terms his parting injunction to stand by him meant refusing to intervene when he lapsed into coma.

The far from unique anguish of this devoted and prayerful mother affected Faul deeply, especially as he was convinced that the hunger strike could not achieve its objectives and that further deaths were both pointless and inevitable. This had come home to him in a conversation with the auxiliary Bishop of

Armagh, Seamus Lennon, in which he had heard the details of a meeting between himself, the cardinal and Mrs Thatcher which took place on 1 July. The cardinal had already declined to meet Thatcher when she visited Belfast towards the end of June and the eventual meeting did nothing to dent the impression of an ignorant and insensitive woman with no particular knowledge of Irish affairs. They had argued and from the report Faul had no doubt that the Prime Minister meant what she said and would not move further on the five deamnds. On 14 July he attended Martin Hurson's wake and left believing that Sinn Féin had taken over and exploited proceedings. The fact that the family did not share his criticisms only convinced him that they were used all the more deeply.

Over the next fortnight Faul saw the last efforts of mainstream nationalism to resolve the crisis fizzle out, first the ICJP's initiative and later an intervention by the International Red Cross. Garret FitzGerald's first reaction to McDonnell's death and the pointless visit of Jackson and Hilditch to the dying men had been to announce that the British had 'made a complete mess of things'. After meetings between the Taoiseach and the ICJP and relatives, Bishop O'Mahony announced that acceptance by the British of the ICJP document discussed with Alison provided 'a way forward to a solution without further loss of life'. His high hopes were countered by immediate demands by Gerry Adams for unequivocal backing for the hunger strike to he manifested in the expulsion of the British ambassador from Dublin, the withdrawal of the SDLP from the councils and a direction from the cardinal to Catholics that the British government was at fault. Further attempts were made to retrieve the situation in a meeting arranged at FitzGerald's insistence by the British ambassador in Dublin between high ranking British and Irish politicians.[7] James Dooge continued the push with a meeting with Lord Carrington in Brussels. It bore fruit when the civil servant in charge of prisons, John Blelloch, entered the Maze on 16 July to tell the prisoners to expect a visit from the International Red Cross. Another visit by an NIO official, a Mr Blackwell, to explain the situation if the fast ended occurred at 2.00 am on 21 July on the initiative of Father Michael McEldowney but ended with the hunger strikers refusing to see him because he would not agree to the presence of McFarlane.

The Red Cross delegation met the prisoners with McFarlane two days after Matt Devlin replaced fellow Tyrone man Martin Hurson. They explained that they had a wide remit to study prison conditions in the province and hoped to be instrumental in bringing the British into negotiations. The whole exercise was promptly dismissed by the prisoners as brinkmanship, though they acceded to the Red Cross team's request for an elaboration of the 4 July statement by issuing a new and marginally more hardline version on 6 August. Atkins followed with a curt four-point statement in which he ruled out negotiations but expressed willingness to 'clarify with the hunger strikers any remaining doubts that they still have about what will happen when the protest ends'. The Red Cross intervention petered out over the next few days in the absence of any movement on either side, as did an attempt to involve US President Reagan in bringing pressure on Britain through the offices of the Irish ambassador to Washington, Sean Donlon.

At the same time, the Sinn Féin side was making its own attempts to move the hunger strike up the British and Irish political agenda. In Dublin there was heavy rioting when crowds tried to reach the British embassy in Ballsbridge and 120 gardai and 80 demonstrators were injured. In London Ken Livingstone, the new left-wing leader of the Greater London Council, received Alice McIlwee, mother of hunger striker Tom McIlwee, at London's County Hall. Despite statements from Livingstone that the 'H-Block protests are about the struggle to bring about a free, united Ireland. They have my support' and that the IRA were not criminals or lunatics, this initiative misjudged the British mood badly, unleashing a torrent of press abuse on Livingstone's head. In a month unionists had arranged for him to meet three children orphaned in the McIlwee brothers' blast incendiary attack on Ballymena and by the autumn he had retreated to the extent of saying that 'anyone who lets off a bomb is clearly criminal'.[8] In Dublin, where only 400 had turned out to demonstrate after Joe McDonnell's death, the unwelcome spill over of northern violence helped turn public opinion against the hunger strikers' cause.

On 27 July FitzGerald held a last meeting with relatives at which he refused to expel the British ambassador. The next day Faul began to turn his misgivings into proposals for action by mobilising the relatives as a separate force, encouraging them to intervene by persuading their loved ones to come off and, if all else failed, to take them off when they lost consciousness. In reaching this decision he had prayed long and hard to his mother Nan who had died a year earlier and who was, he said, a devout woman 'who did not regard public opinion as being a barometer of what you should do'. Attempting to break the hunger strike meant that Faul would have to be similarly immune in the opinions of those he had worked with down the years. As he explained it:

> I had a fairly high profile among the prisoners and their families. Now I was going to have to intervene and lose all the influence that I had built up during the previous ten years. I knew that I would have to lose all that to bring the hunger strike to an end and I knew then that I would be blamed by the prisoners themselves and their leaders outside the prison and probably by some of the relatives. It was a big decision to come to. It was a kind of kamikaze effort, a suicidal effort in terms of popular esteem amongst the Catholic community.

After early mass he rang first Mrs Lynch and then Fr Michael McEldowney, the zealous Dungiven curate, who agreed to organise the Derry relatives for a meeting in the O'Neill Arms hotel in Toomebridge at 6.00 pm. Faul spent the rest of the day travelling the country to contact relatives and past colleagues from his various civil rights initiatives. In Dungannon he met up with his friend, the Armagh chaplain Fr Raymond Murray as well as roping in independent councillor Jim Canning who had brought relatives to meet the NIO on 21 July. In Maghera he enlisted Willy and Betty Noone, two RAC campaigners and in Belleek he visited the family of Paddy Quinn, now on day 45 and sinking fast. From them he learnt that one of the regular Sinn Féin organised meetings for relatives was scheduled for 2.00 pm at the Lake Glen hotel in West Belfast so he suggested that they inform both the other relatives and Sinn Féin. If it was to be a kamikaze mission the red scarf was now firmly around Faul's temples and the flying bomb was taxiing for takeoff.

At Toomebridge all those whom he approached turned up. Of the families only Kieran Doherty, who had now survived a day longer than any hunger striker to date, had no relatives present. However Doherty's circle was represented by his girlfriend Geraldine Scheiss, a woman who had caused problems for Sinn Féin at a previous relatives' meeting where she hinted that the Provisional leadership, and not the prisoners, were taking the ultimate decisions on the hunger strike and highlighted the decision, in the midst of the ICJP talks, of all the prisoners to change their previous solicitors to Pat Finucane.[9]

Others at the meeting included Fr Crilly who in the course of the day visited his cousin Tom McIlwee to suggest that the hunger strike be suspended to allow British intentions to be monitored by an independent committee, and Bernadette McAliskey, who told a less than welcoming Faul that she was a distant cousin of hunger striker Matt Devlin.

Faul lost no time in pinning the blame where he now thought it belonged, with Sinn Féin and the IRA. As he now explains it, his view was that joining a hunger strike was a little like joining the IRA, you volunteered in the first place but once you were in you followed orders. He backed this up to the relatives with an account of a conversation he had with McFarlane in which he was told that the buck stopped with Gerry Adams. He argued that the hunger strike was now hopeless, that it had achieved all it could hope for in the ICJP talks and that the only moral position was to end it, something which the IRA had the power to do. Against this it was argued that the prisoners had themselves volunteered and that it was for the families to stand by them in their decision. As Faul's argument gained ground McAliskey suggested that Sinn Féin be contacted for a meeting and one of the relatives, Laurence Quinn, called their Belfast office, which called back saying that Adams couldn't travel to Toomebridge for reasons of security but would meet them in Belfast.

At Sinn Féin's Falls Road premises they found Margaret and Alfie Doherty, the parents of Kieran, waiting for them. The Dohertys are a well known couple in republican circles in Andersonstown where Alfie once worked as a floor tiler at Sinn Féin's Eire Nua co-op and were amongst the firmest supporters of the Provo standpoint in the current crop of families. Faul knew Mrs Doherty as an articulate woman who had worked effectively with him on a H-Block delegation to France.

When the meeting got going after 11.30 Faul repeated his conversation with McFarlane, upon which Adams produced a communication from McFarlane which made the point that the OC's comments were in the context of Bobby Sands' demand that Adams be present if he met the European Commission of Human Rights. Though agreeing, Faul found the precise timing of the conversation far from crucial. He pressed on with his central assertion that since the hunger strikers were mostly members of the IRA they were, as McFarlane had indicated, subject to outside direction. Concessions were now available from Britain but would plainly not be guaranteed before the hunger strike ended. Therefore the IRA army council should tell the protesters that their case was hopeless and order them off the hunger strike. Adams maintained that the hunger strike had been started by the prisoners against outside directions and the IRA had no power to do as Faul suggested. He added that, sitting as they were in Sinn Féin offices on the Falls Road, it would be difficult to contact the IRA and the army council could take five days to convene.

Frustrated at the academic turn the discussion was taking, Faul tried to get round Adams, saying he made his case so ably and was so highly thought of that he would be the best possible person to go in and ask the hunger strikers to come off as a group. In Adams' eyes this was tantamount to withdrawing support from the strikers, some of whom were old friends. Besides, he countered, Faul shouldn't look past himself in a job of this nature. The meeting was punctuated with appeals from the Quinn and Lynch families that their relatives might not understand the desperation of the situation, and from Mrs Doherty to the effect that Faul was undermining support for the hunger strike and threatening her son's life. Fr McEldowney urged the relatives to tell the press of Adams' reticence upon which Bernadette McAliskey, who had been broadly supportive of the relatives' position in Toomebridge, offered to give an account which would be damaging to the priests and which would attack the church for failing to support the hunger strike. When the meeting broke up around 2.00, Faul and some of the others had the impression that Adams would, after all, go in and either order the prisoners off or ask them to suspend the hunger strike to test British intentions. Later in the morning Adams rang to ask if Faul could, as promised, arrange the visit and if it would be possible for two other men to go in as well. Faul agreed, making the arrangements through the cardinal. Strangely Sinn Féin sources were warning journalists not to expect too much from the visit.

The two men were Seamus Ruddy of the IRSP and Owen Carron, Bobby Sands' election agent who was due to fight the Fermanagh-South Tyrone by-election on 20 August. Faul's heart sank when he heard Carron's name because he feared that the prisoners would feel obliged to hang on until after the election. Pat McGeown, one of the hunger strikers who met Adams, makes another point. 'The only thing on the horizon' he said 'was Owen Carron's election and after that there was really nowhere that the hunger strike was going.'

The trio met McGeown, Tom McIlwee, Laurence McKeown, Matt Devlin, Paddy Quinn, Mickey Devine and Brendan McFarlane at the prison canteen at 5.15 pm. Kieran Doherty and Kevin Lynch were too ill to attend but Adams met Doherty between 7.45 and 8.20, missing Lynch, who was not fit to be disturbed, but speaking briefly to his father and Alfie Doherty before returning to the main group in the canteen between 8.20 and 9.15.[10]

The visits, in Adams' account, were remarkably light hearted and amiable affairs. The starving men joked about Owen Carron's election suit and Adams' liking for the spring water provided at such great expense by the British government but left him in no doubt of their determination to continue the fast. He explained to them that he 'felt duty bound to satisfy the clergymen and all those who were pressurising their families'. With this preamble he told them bluntly, 'You could all be dead. Everyone in this room could be dead' and asked them if they were motivated by loyalty either to those who had died or to each other, making the point that 'we could go out and announce it had ended or that any one of them had finished it'. The prisoners, who had discussed Fr McEldowney's proposals to Tom McIlwee the previous evening, assured him that they were individually and collectively determined to continue not out of any sense of loyalty but for the five demands. Doherty, on his own, turned down a similar offer from Adams to go out and announce it was over saying that he thought he had a week's life in him and that he would not eat unless the five demands were met. He too joked with Carron about the election.

What Adams did not do was to order or direct the prisoners to come off the hunger strike or suggest, as many of the prisoners knew or would soon find out, that although the family's feelings might have been brought to the fore by Faul they were not invented by him. Four of the eight men to whom Adams talked were to be taken off the hunger strike by their families over the next three weeks. One of them, Pat McGeown, regards Faul's role as one of back stabbing but explains:

> With the early families there was always strong hope. Six months later that strong hope was very hard for us to keep in their minds in that they had seen people die one after the other. Even Joe McDonnell, whose wife I talked to, had that problem. Joe was about to die, well they didn't know he was about to die but they knew he was in a fairly bad position. It was a critical time for the hunger strike. The decision 'do I pull him off and actually weaken the whole basis for the solution or do I accept that he takes the chance and maybe you do end up with a solution tomorrow morning'. Those were the sort of life and death issues that people were involved in.
>
> Then it got into one after the other dying with no apparent critical situation and no crisis situation and no major attempts at negotiation. The families became more downhearted and less fully in support. That was the weakness of the hunger strike. Did Father Faul voice that or encourage the families to voice it more than they had already voiced it? I don't think so because I think they had already started before Faul really got saying anything. It was always there.

If this vital point was grasped, that like everything else the hunger strike carried the seeds of its own destruction and had now run its course, then Faul's invitation to order an end to it was no bear trap. It was instead a real chance to take charge of the situation, giving Adams the opportunity to lift the whole question out of the realm of personal determination and moral fibre, to display statesmanship and save life. In any case it was soon to become clear that the protest had not the dynamic to win further concessions on the prison issue or even to create a crisis which would force mainstream nationalism to fall fully behind Sinn Féin and become a lever against the British. Instead the 'whole new hand' dealt by the unwitting Thatcher was dangerously close to being overplayed. In the grim dialectic of the hunger strike all the forces which had been built up so rapidly were now turning on the Provos and the prisoners themselves, making it increasingly difficult for them to extricate themselves from the situation with the gains which they had bought at such awful personal sacrifice intact. As so often before, the Provos would now face the problem of exploiting these contradictions to turn their chips into money.

After hearing what had happened in the prison, Faul and many of the relatives were far from happy and a heated meeting ensued with Joe Austin of Sinn Féin and Seamus Ruddy of the IRSP. The upshot of this was a statement expressing disappointment with Adams' performance and the formation of a new committee to monitor British performance and exert pressure. Before this committee could meet Paddy Quinn, who had a weakened liver, took a sudden turn for the worse.

At lunch time as Bridie Lynch, Margaret Doherty and Geraldine Scheiss and other members of the families of the two most advanced hunger strikers sat in a waiting room they could hear Quinn's screams of agony as his own family were sent for. After arriving Mrs Catherine Quinn said simply, 'I was at my son's bedside on the 47th day of his hunger strike. He was screaming and struggling. The lack of oxygen to his brain was causing terrible epileptic fits. I couldn't bear his suffering.'[11] Mrs Quinn had already discussed her next move with Faul. She called the doctor who administered vitamin shots and the screaming stopped instantly. Quinn was taken to hospital and placed on an intravenous drip. When he came round he accepted nourishment and he is now a free man, fully recovered and living in Belleek.

When Mrs Quinn came out two hours later the pathetic line

of Lynch and Doherty relatives were elated that her son had been saved. One delighted woman turned to the mothers and said, 'Which one of you ladies will be the next to take your sons off?'

The call was to be echoed by the Bishop of Derry, Edward Daly, who described Mrs Quinn's decision as 'a motherly and Christian action' commending it to others. However Mrs Quinn herself gave no such advice for the situation was not to be that simple. Both Mrs Lynch and the Dohertys had been strictly enjoined by their sons to do no such thing and, on the day of Daly's statement, Kevin Lynch died quietly in his sleep as he had asked.

Kieran Doherty's hunger strike had been a particularly protracted and difficult one because he had rallied for what the inquest described as an unknown reason as he approached the danger time around the time of the Justice and Peace initiative. The result was that on day 70, the day before Paddy Quinn was saved, he still enjoyed considerable periods of lucidity and his father Alfie Doherty had, asked him at 4.00 pm if he would like to end his hunger strike.[12] Mr Doherty remembers his son telling him that his hearing and mind were slipping and adding 'when my mind goes stand by me unless we get the five demands. Don't do anything, don't sign anything unless we get the five demands.' However the day after Quinn was given treatment Kieran Doherty's girlfriend Geraldine Scheiss emerged from the dying man's room at around 2.00 pm to tell his mother and the prison chaplain, Father Tom Toner, that Kieran had twice asked her to get him tablets 'for my body'. Ms Scheiss became quite distressed and tried to get tablets herself when Mrs Doherty would take no action until her husband came, which was some hours later. By the time that Alfie Doherty arrived his son was unconscious but he says that he spoke to another of the chaplains and after this consultation during which the chaplain went to see Kieran he decided to abide by his son's last clear wishes not to intervene.

Although none of this had appeared in print Alfie Doherty that day slammed the prison chaplains for 'pressurising the prisoners' rather than the government, adding 'my son is no dupe; he understands clearly what he is doing and the consequences of his actions. My family welcomes any meaningful initiative which is based on support for the prisoners' position and which is aimed at achieving a principled settlement to the hunger strike.' On 2 August, Kieran Doherty died in his sleep after 73 days on hunger strike, the longest of any prisoner in 1981.

As these sad events unfolded in the Maze the IRA's hunger strike battlefield was once more narrowing. After hearing details of the Faul inspired meetings in Toomebridge and Belfast FitzGerald tapped the unease at rioting in the Republic to issue, on 31 July, a strongly worded statement in which he said: 'the responsibility for failure does not lie only with hesitation or delay on the part of the British. On the contrary, there is no doubt that intransigence was shown by the other side just when it seemed likely that the British, however belatedly, were proposing to take an initiative.' He revealed that the Irish government had been in almost daily contact with Britain since 30 July, accusing the IRA leadership of sabotaging his efforts as they became public and 'facing all those concerned with a stark choice between total concession to their demands and the deaths of further hunger strikers'. He pledged 'implacable opposition' to the Provos and called upon them to use their military command structures to order an end to the hunger strike which, he said, they were exploiting.

The next evening Faul's new committee, now named the 'Help the Prisoners Committee', met in Fr Murray's home in Armagh under the leadership of the cardinal himself. Its membership included some of those who had been at Toombridge, including Bernadette McAliskey and Jim Canning, as well as the solicitor Oliver Kelly. Its collective approach probably approximated to that of the families at this time, commending the prisoners' 4 July statement as a basis for settlement, urging the British to make concessions and the following morning calling through the cardinal for the prisoners to end the hunger strike. For his part Faul called a meeting of the relatives of all protesting prisoners in the Redemptorist Hall at Clonard, West Belfast, for 7 August.

The period surrounding these meetings was filled with death and the secret preparations for the coming autumn bombing offensive against Britain. As Quinn was saved a former policeman, Thomas Harpur, was murdered by the INLA in Strabane. On the day that the committee met, thirty-six-year-old Peter Doherty was killed by a plastic bullet standing in his West Belfast kitchen and on the day of the cardinal's statement a British soldier lost both legs in an IRA rocket attack on the Falls and two policemen were killed by a landmine in Tyrone.

On the 4th, Liam McCloskey joined the hunger strike to replace his friend and cell mate Kevin Lynch despite criticisms from Faul and his mother that his health was poor. The same day a youth was struck on the head by a plastic bullet. The SDLP decided, despite opposition from Currie, that it wouldn't field a candidate against Carron in Fermanagh-South Tyrone. The 5th saw the province convulsed by a co-ordinated bombing campaign and by the 7th a group of relatives had returned from a meeting with FitzGerald that was so unpromising that they staged a sit-in at his office and had to be cleared by police. Meanwhile Atkins had just rejected a prisoners' statement offering to clean the blocks as part of prison work and asking to be met half way. The relatives were now more than ever torn between fear of undermining whatever chances the protest still had and the feeling that those chances had evaporated. Jimmy Drumm, who had the task of liaising with the relatives and who now had little faith that the hunger strike would achieve any more, recalls how one woman, after being told her son would be on hunger strike in forty-eight hours, said to him 'that is another one condemned to death'.

Before the meeting started Faul met Gerry Adams and Tom Hartley of the Sinn Féin Prisoners of War Committee privately in the Clonard monastery itself. They appealed to him to avoid disunity and Hartley told him that the political consciousness of the people had changed since the death of Bobby Sands. Faul said this was nonsense and warned them that if there were many more deaths the Irish people would turn against them, adding that far from manipulating events he wanted to let the relatives have a say. In the main meeting, which was attended by some 300 people, he saw that Hartley had a point.

During it Faul had little to say — he was barracked more or less solidly from start to finish by what he describes as 'fanatical women' but noticed that the mothers of the remaining hunger strikers were for the most part quiet. 'At that stage', he says, 'I determined, having given Sinn Féin an opportunity in full confidentiality of ending the thing honourably and saving lives, just to get the relatives one by one to end it.'

Next day a ninth hunger striker, Tom McIlwee, died after 62 days and the remaining relatives said that their determination was stronger than ever. A day of co-ordinated rioting followed in Belfast, Derry and Strabane. There were silent vigils in Belfast and Derry of 400 and 300 people respectively and, for the umpteenth time, H-Block demonstrators were barred from Belfast City centre and seven people, including two councillors, were arrested at the city hall.

In the prison the hunger strike ground on against the background of these diminished demonstrations. On the 10th, Pat Sheehan, a bright twenty-three-year old who had dropped out of a promising academic career less than a year before being arrested on explosives charges in 1978, joined it to be followed later by twenty-five-year-old Jackie McMullan, another academically gifted youth who had replaced an early vocation for the priesthood with membership of first the Fianna and then the IRA and was convicted of attempting to murder a policeman in 1976. But by now doubts about the wisdom of the continued protest were again growing amongst the surviving hunger strikers, only one more of whom was to die. According to Pat McGeown, 'a certain number of the hunger strikers had arrived at the same conclusion and were saying "look, possibly the whole thing needs to be reviewed". We had a discussion of whether or not the hunger strike should end. I think what Faul had done put everyone's back up against a wall and actually for us to have ended it would have looked as if we were giving in to Denis Faul's pressure.'

The moment passed and at 7.52 am on 20 August twenty-seven-year-old 'Red Mickey' Devine from Derry was the last hunger striker to die after telling his relatives to sign nothing. The death came less than an hour after polling opened for Owen Carron's by-election in Fermanagh-South Tyrone and later in the day Pat McGeown's hunger strike ended after serious and unforeseen complications robbed him of consciousness after forty-two days without food. His wife Pauline said[13] that she had been called to the hospital with his parents and had been praying at his bedside with the prison chaplains when 'Pat took bad and started convulsing in pain. I could not bear the sight of him suffering so much and decided to call on medical supervision to relieve his agony.'

Faul was relieved by her decision. Leaving everything else aside, the McGeowns were close to Gerry Adams whom Faul saw as an opponent but who McGeown says put similar points to the hunger strikers privately as Faul was putting publicly. Mrs McGeown had herself been a strong critic of Faul's own role in trying to break the hunger strike. Now Faul says: 'I worked on the Foxes and the Sheehans. Some of them directly, some of them through the media. When I would hear a fellow was bad I would go on the media and say, "I think his parents want him to come off. He is not well" because I knew this was what they really wanted. There was no point in any more of them dying, it was senseless. That went on for a while. They were coming off.'

The call for the IRA to order an end to the hunger strike took its toll on public opinion, prompting it to state that it was free 'of the oppressive discipline of a regular army' and the main Sinn Féin hope lay in Carron who, even taking into account the other candidates' claims of personation, impressively increased Bobby Sands' tally by 786 votes in a field that included the Alliance and Workers Parties as well as the OUP and fringe 'Peace Lover' and 'General Amnesty' candidates.

The victory shaped the Provos' overall development. Carron had beaten back an early bid by the ever willing McAliskey and the IRSP to contest the seat on a prisoners' platform and once more forced the SDLP to stand down. For world and unionist opinion the victory established the Provos as the most visible force in northern nationalism and, a decisive gain for the urban northerners, started Sinn Féin on the path of electoral involvement.

In terms of the prisoners it achieved little. If anything it prolonged matters as Carron, who was said to be convinced that he couldn't win the five demands on his own, trudged the well worn rounds of delegations and rejections with the relatives in tow. He succeeded in seeing Alison for what he frankly described as an 'amicable but worthless meeting' and later Haughey who, *Republican News* commented, showed 'that he values a connection with the H-Block hunger strikers'. Carron was, by all accounts, plausible but could not hope to persuade Thatcher to give concessions to Sinn Féin that were denied to O'Fiach and FitzGerald.

Alison made the point by hitting the roof over Carron's stress on segregation from loyalists, announcing that a sixth demand had appeared out of thin air and citing it as evidence that granting the original five would not satisfy the prisoners. In fact, as Alison knew and Carron insisted, segregation followed from the implementation of free association and was mentioned in statements from the early stages.

FitzGerald said roundly that he would meet any politician except Carron. 'If Free State premier Garret FitzGerald cannot be embarrassed into meeting the prisoners' advocate Owen Carron' *Republican News* was to ask, 'what hope is there of forcing the British government and its Northern Ireland Office into negotiating directly with the protesting prisoners?'[14]

Meanwhile the hunger strike continued to decline with families intervening as prisoners slipped beneath consciousness and the protesters briefly considering legal means to prevent this. Matt Devlin, McAliskey's distant cousin from Ardboe, was next to reach a crisis. Faul had visited his mother and found her upset that he was still on hunger strike. He told her, 'Mrs Devlin, you son is coming to the danger point. You need to be ready. The minute you get word from Long Kesh go straight down and authorise the doctor to intervene. There is no sense in this any more.' The next day Mrs Devlin was called to the prison and found Matt in agony. Several men were holding him down as he screamed his life away on his 52nd day without food. She took Faul's advice.

Laurence McKeown, a strong man who endured seventy days without food, was taken off by his family on 4 September. The same day the IRSP, who had caused Sands such problems, announced that they could not maintain their one to four ratio with IRA hunger strikers. The British had proved 'far more intransigent than expected' and to continue at the present rate would mean the death of their twenty-eight blanketmen within six months. The announcement came at a H-Block conference at Dundalk which decided optimistically to broaden the campaign into women's groups and trades unions but rejected, in a debate marked by 'floor stampers whose undemocratic antics had nothing in common with the democratic traditions and principles of republicanism', several proposals that successful H-Block candidates should attend the Dail and Westminster.

The next morning Kieran Doherty's friend John Pickering brought the number on hunger strike up to six. The hopes of trades union involvement suffered a blow when on the 10th, the British TUC registered only one vote in favour of a motion supporting the prisoners but, on a more hopeful note, Sinn Féin announced that £0.25 million had been received in donations in North America.

Gerard Hodgkins joined the hunger strike, which was now clearly on its last legs, on the 13th as Tory wet Jim Prior replaced Atkins as Secretary of State. Prior's move was part of a purge of moderates from the cabinet and in his case was intended to clear his former post in Employment for Norman Tebbit, a man who rejoiced in the nickname 'the Chingford boot boy'. A top line Tory grandee from the shires, Prior retained significant political clout, even in his Ulster exile. This enabled him to command a freedom of manoeuvre denied to the lacklustre Atkins in return for withdrawing his threat to resign and fight Thatcher from the backbenches. He brought three of his fellow wets, including the Irish-born Lord Grey Gowrie who took charge of prisons, with him.

In his first public pronouncement in Ireland Prior staked his reputation on bringing political life back to the province. The situation appalled him. It was immediately clear to him that the hunger strike was blocking any sort of political progress and that 'Mrs Thatcher was dictating the pace from London without really understanding what was happening'.[15] His advisers in the NIO believed that the whole thing could have either been avoided or, once started, ended with 'a little more finessing'.

His first port of call in the province was the Maze which he toured for three hours on 17 September with his wife Jane who had a keen interest in penal reform and was deeply affected by what she saw. During the visit he looked in on the most advanced hunger striker Liam McCloskey, without McCloskey being aware of it, and later attempted to speak to a number of blanketmen. Surprisingly in view of the current demands for face to face meetings with the British this opportunity for some level of negotiation was ignored. Prior found that 'all the prisoners who had been on the blanket were told, I think by McFarlane who was clearly a great power in the prison, not to speak to me. So I spoke to them. One or two of the younger ones were desparate to try and talk but they were told not to so they said a few words and then they shut up.' He confined himself to telling them briefly of his desire to bring the hunger strike to an end without going into any specific proposals.

On the 19th he found himself surrounded by H-Block protesters at the back of Derry's Guildhall. Despite his RUC escort he adopted a direct approach, borrowing the protesters loud hailer and making a brief speech to them in which he said that, although he was making no promises, he would try to resolve the crisis without further loss of life. The gambit worked and the crowd dispersed without incident.

At the time the strike was undergoing a brief revival. Carron had, on the 18th, led a delegation of ninety-two blanketmen's relatives to London on the invitation of Lord Gifford. After an abortive attempt by Scottish MP Ron Brown to includc him on a delegation to meet Thatchcr, Carron predicted that the hunger strike would be resumed in three months if it broke down without a settlement and that the remaining seven prisoners would resume it if taken off by their families. Michael McCloskey, brother of Liam, added that both the families and the prisoners were determined to continue.

On the 21st the number of hunger strikers was brought up to its target number of eight by the addition of Belfast man Jim Devine. Two days later Hugh Sheehan, father of Pat, led a delegation to Bishop Philbin's residence where he handed in a petition and denied that the families were losing heart in the hunger strike. However the Carron-led rally was short lived. The next day Bernard Fox, who had been retching violently for a week after only thirty-two days on hunger strike, developed a blocked tube to his kidnies which threatened to kill him within hours. He made the decision to come off the hunger strike himself, removing the dilemma from his family. Later the same day Liam McCloskey's mother said that she would intervene if her son became unconscious and was no longer able to take decisions on his own behalf.

The image of the starving McCloskey is fixed in Prior's mind as one of resolute fanaticism, but inwardly the prisoner was going through the strike without any hope of success. Although fully resigned to death his commitment to the INLA had been seriously weakened and in the early days of his hunger strike he had made it clear that he wanted no paramilitary funeral. McCloskey was also undergoing a religious conversion but he says:

> I was totally at peace with the thought of going to death. I think as time went on, deep down in my guts I knew I was wrong to die for the reasons of the hunger strike but I hadn't the courage to face that. Once you were on hunger strike I think it would have taken more courage to actually stop of your own accord than to keep going because it seemed so much like losing face and backing down when other men had died. I just kept on praying and hoping that I wouldn't have to die yet I was prepared to die. I was caught between two poles . . . The writing was on the wall at that stage anyway. A lot of men had come off in the few weeks before that and the whole hunger strike was beginning to crack. I knew deep down that it was beaten. I think that most of us knew that. We were caught in our own trap where there were ten men dead and we felt we had to keep going and look for a way out of it.

Despite these doubts the inertia of the situation was such that he had no intention of coming off. As he approached coma on the morning of Saturday 26 September, he reasoned that if he pulled out now somebody else would only have to start the whole process again. That day a local priest came into the room and asked him to come off the hunger strike for his mother's sake, saying that Kevin Lynch had told him that he didn't want him to die as he had. The priest then showed his mother into the room. She told him that she would take him off when he became unconscious. She added that she had consulted an eye specialist in Belfast who had told her that if he lapsed into coma he would probably be blind for life. McCloskey says:

> My first reaction was, no, keep on going and my thought was partly the eyesight and partly that I had no right to

leave it to my mother to take the decision herself, that I had to do it and stand over it. It was too easy a way out to just leave it to her . . .

He ended his hunger strike at this point, consenting to vitamin shots which acted so quickly that his eyesight was returning as he travelled by ambulance to Musgrave Park hospital. Until the other prisoners ended their hunger strikes he felt deep guilt but he has never since regretted his decision.

Faul, who had spoken to McCloskey's mother before her visit, was about now asked by Jim Gibney of Sinn Féin to address a meeting of relatives in the Lake Glen on Sunday. The surprising invitation was issued, according to Jimmy Drumm, in response to the growing accusations that Sinn Féin was manipulating the families. On Sunday morning the *Sunday Press* carried a swingeing attack on Faul's involvement in the hunger strike.

When he arrived Faul asked Gibney, Drumm and other Sinn Féin personel to leave the room, saying that they had had their say in the papers and that he would have his now. They agreed and the meeting got off to a stormy start. A member of the Fox family, who blamed a media interview by Faul for undermining his brother's hunger strike attacked Faul and was joined by relatives of Jackie McMullan who also resented his role. However, as the meeting progressed things got onto a more even keel and the relatives ended by asking Faul to arrange a meeting with Lord Gowrie, which he did there and then.

The next day Gowrie met the relatives with a brief from Prior to indicate that the same concessions as had been offered to the ICJP were available but that no change would be made until the hunger strike ended and that even then the five demands would not be met. Gowrie, a man of easy aristocratic charm, got on well with the relatives but stuck strictly to his brief. As the meeting went on rumours started to circulate in republican circles that the hunger strike was to end within the week.

The remaining strikers now issued a statement condemning Faul as 'conniving and dangerous'. On Wednesday he went with the cardinal to meet Prior who levelled fully with them on the extend of concessions, which were still what had been offered in July. The one point of movement was on restoration of lost remission where the Secretary of State increased the existing 20 per cent on offer to 50 per cent, despite impassioned pleas from Faul that he should make it 100 per cent. Faul felt Prior was 'a stupid bugger' for missing this opportunity to show some generosity but Prior says he was advised that he could not exceed the terms of an earlier agreement under which loyalist protesters had lost 50 per cent of their remission.

The next day, Thursday, Faul arranged for one of the remaining hunger striker's relatives to visit his son who told him that the fast was not ending. A statement was now issued by five of the six remaining families saying that they would intervene if their relatives became unconscious.

This was the last blow. On Saturday morning the prisoners issued a statement saying that they had been 'robbed of the hunger strike as an effective protest weapon principally because of the successful campaign waged against our distressed relatives by the Irish establishment (the SDLP and the Free State political parties) which took no effective action against the British government and did everything to encourage feelings of hopelessness among our kith and kin.'

The hunger strike had ended.

NOTES

1. Interview with the author. The chapter title is the description applied in an essay of his role in the Sinn Féin journal *Iris*.
2. See bibliography for a partial list.
3. Statement from the Chief Constable, 11 July 1981.
4. See Chapter 4.
5. According to INLA sources, who add that Ruddy's crassness on this occasion was one of the factors precipitating a split in the organisation. In the case of IRA prisoners Jimmy Drumm, who had overall responsibility for dealing with the families, normally called to the home some time before the hunger strike was due to start and maintained close contact thereafter.
6. I am indebted to Mrs Bridie Lynch for her detailed recollections.
7. It involved acting Foreign Minister John Kelly and Minister-elect James Dooge on the Irish side as well as Humphrey Atkins and the Lord Privy Seal, Sir Ian Gilmour, representing Britain. It took place in London on Friday 10 July.
8. *The Sun,* 16 October 1981. He made similar statements on BBC's 'Nationwide' and in a letter to *The Times*. The children were the sons of Mrs Yvonne Dunlop who was burnt to death.
9. At least one of the previous solicitors, the leading civil rights lawyer and former internee Oliver Kelly who had represented Kieran Doherty and another blanketman, John 'Pickles' Pickering, felt that his clients did not arrive at this decision independently.

10. The details given of these visits, which are not disputed, rest almost entirely on Adams' own account in *Republican News* (1 and 8 August 1981). The details of the Toomebridge and Falls Road meetings are based on the recollections of some of those present as well as an account given by Bernadette McAliskey, in defiance of an undertaking not to speak to the press, to *Magill* (August 1981).

11. *France Soir,* 5 September 1981.

12. I am indebted to Alfie Doherty for his account of some incidents during the last three days of his son Kieran's life. The account has also relied on details from other witnesses to events, including Fr Toner.

13. In statement at the time.

14. *Republican News,* 12 September 1981.

15. Interview with the author, 18 January 1986.

10

The Ballot and the Armalite

> There was, when we fought the Stormont and Westminster elections, even when we fought the Bobby Sands election, a reaction against it for quite understandable reasons. If you wanted to count the number of people who were wholeheartedly for those political initiatives you could do it on both hands.
>
> Gerry Adams.[1]

Father Denis Faul firmly believes that he was used by the IRA and Sinn Féin to cut the Gordian knot of the hunger strike. He believes the Provos, or a section of them, were convinced that further deaths would begin to turn the tide of public opinion against them and that was why they invited him to a meeting of relatives, knowing that he would try to persuade them to break the strike.

This analysis is denied by Sinn Féin who regard it as tantamount to saying that they sold the hunger strikers down the river. What is clear is that Faul had tapped feelings that already existed amongst both prisoners and relatives, that he was not alone in his reading of British intentions and that the hunger strike would have, sooner or later, collapsed on terms that may well have been less favourable to the entire Provisional project. It is also clear that, whatever the intentions of those involved, the circumstances in which it did end cast Faul in the role of a scapegoat who took much of the blame with him into the desert, deflecting the recriminations which might have followed a more protracted hunger strike.

Even in these circumstances the final tally of gains and losses was not immediately clear. The extent of the prison reforms was spelt out in a statement from Prior on 6 October which was supplied to the prisoners and was supplemented by a personal visit from Gowrie to the prison on 14 October. All prisoners could wear their own clothes, with the proviso that platform heels, useful for disguise, and the 'uniform' colours of black, dark or olive green and navy were banned. Association was permitted between the fifty or so prisoners on adjoining wings and 50 per cent of lost remission was restored to each former protester who conformed to the new rules for three months. To ease the changeover there was a month's grace in which no remission was lost for failing to conform. The remaining grey areas were work and segregation.

On work, the prisoners objected to contributing by their labour to the conditions of their confinement. The ICJP had floated a number of suggestions for getting round this, including putting them to work building a chapel, and the protesters themselves wanted to have education re-defined as work. On 2 November the governor imposed lost remission at the rate of ten days a month, loss of some association and the loss of a visit a month on sixty-eight men who refused to take part in work. In fact, however, there was not enough work for them to do and the majority opted to go along with the stystem, attending the workplace but doing little when they got there. This arrangement allowed the authorities to save face and to issue statistics claiming full conformity.

Segregation was handled by the expedient of fighting with the loyalists during association until the two sides were separated. Inevitably the authorities accused the various paramilitary groups of colluding to achieve a shared aim of segregation. The saga took a new turn in December when loyalists in Crumlin Road went onto the roof rather than take further abuse from the republicans. The protest ended when some of what were considered to be the most militant republicans were transferred to the Maze and 200 republican inmates from the Maze were moved to Magilligan to make room for them. The result is described by Twister McQuistan, a former UDA inmate in Magilligan:

> If you argued with one of them you were were arguing with fifty, these guys were dedicated. They had done blanket protests, dirty protests and they had done hunger strikes. They seemed to have the attitude that they were some kind of elite regiment and when they came down they started getting into the loyalists. The loyalists went on their protest to get away from them. There were hospital cases and they went hell for leather. When the NIO came up with this col-

> lusion thing I was laid up in hospital with scars down my back from being scalded and my ear was hanging off. I was a UDA commander in the prison and I might be a bit staunch but I wouldn't collude with anyone to kick my ear off.

The loyalists blamed McFarlane and lifers were told 'that if they got their hands on him they were to do their best to kill him.'[2] Over the next few years these battles resulted in bombs being planted by republicans in the Maze laundry (27 April 1982) and C Wing of Magilligan (February 1984) as well as a number of injuries on both sides and a series of loyalist protests of which the most serious was a hunger strike involving seven UDA prisoners and three UVF prisoners in September and October 1984.

For most of the period republicans achieved *de facto* segregation in the Maze H-Blocks. In Magilligan there was virtual segregation with loyalists and republicans working at different times. As the British had feared, this set-up facilitated paramilitary organisation, culminating in the mass breakout of September 1983 when thirty-eight IRA men escaped from H-Block 7 which was exclusively populated by republican prisoners. However the official report on the breakout,[3] the biggest in British or Irish penal history, found that it could have been avoided had not the prison authorities become complacent due to the good relations within the block. Sir James Hennessy found that some members of the IRA command (including Bic McFarlane, the escape organiser Bobby Story and Gerry Kelly) had been appointed orderlies. The visiting area was not secure, some visits were so private that sexual intercourse took place during them, and McFarlane himself had kept the same cell for three years. The internal discipline of the prisoners was such that a small group of perhaps eight men had been able to reduce tension in the jail over a period of months, thus putting staff at their ease, to plan the breakout in secrecy from the other prisoners and to rehearse parts of it before putting it into operation. A total of five guns, one of which was used to kill a prison officer, had been smuggled in from the outside. Twenty-four officers were overpowered as part of the break. One was killed. The prisoners piled into the food lorry, one of the service vehicles whose routine trips was used for the movement of communications, and took it through perimeter security. It was only outside the wire that sixteen of the prisoners were recaptured. Routines had been allowed to build up over the years and the prisoners were so seldom moved that cohesive groups were able to exploit the chinks in the system.

In the balance sheet of the hunger strike the protesters had scored a victory and the substance of their demands had been conceded in fact if not in theory. As the authorities argued, these demands, especially segregation, had left them with less control of the prison that before. However the loss of control could have been overcome by better security within the jail.

The effects on the movement outside the prison were more complex. The hunger strike came in the course of a long-term run down of IRA activity which continued after it ended.

Initially there was an escalation of violence generally. Leaving aside the ten dead hunger strikers the year's violent death list reached 101 and the figures of those injured touched 1,442. Shooting and bombing incidents amounted to 815 and 298 respectively.[4] These figures are down on most previous years and were to continue to fall as the IRA's strategy changed from all out war to what Gerry Adams was to describe as 'armed propaganda'.[5] However the hunger strike was followed by the revenge killing of hardline Official Unionist MP Rev. Robert Bradford, who had made the mistake of saying he prayed for an epidemic in the H-Blocks, and a resumption of the bombing campaign in Britain which was originally intended as a means of pressure had the hunger strike continued through the autumn.

The first *Republican News*[6] after Adams' visit to the prisoners did in fact carry a statement from the IRA saying that it would like to see the hunger strike concluded in a principled way and saying it was up to the hunger strikers whether they continued or not but adding that the prisoners 'do not have the basis for a permanent settlement and obviously we sympathise'. The IRA went on to say that it had come under pressure from members and supporters 'who believe that the IRA should pay the British government in kind for the deaths of comrades and for the deaths on the streets. That the IRA will do that goes without saying.' The promised action came quickly and appears to have been largely the work of a new active service unit including Paul Kavanagh, Tommy Quigley, and British police believed, Eibhlin Glenholmes. At least some of its members had been in place since 1979 and there were supply lines stretching through the Low Countries, where future Brighton Bomber Pat Magee had been living, to the US as well as to Ireland and a large explosives and arms dump in Oxfordshire. In October a bomb outside Chelsea Barracks killed two civilians, a week later retired Royal Marines Commander Lt Gen. Stuart Pringle was killed by a bomb attached to his car and on the 26th a sophisticated device in the Oxford Street Wimpey bar killed bomb disposal expert Kenneth Howarth as he attempted to disarm it. A further bomb followed in Oxford Street and by the beginning of November the IRA claimed in an interview[7] that they would disrupt central London every day from then till Christmas. However this seems to have been a deliberate blind for the IRA's intention to concentrate on more prestigious targets. In November three major operations failed to find their intended targets, one the home of the Attorney-General, Sir Michael Havers, the second inside Woolwich Arsenal where it was set off by a dog and the third at Greenwich Gasometer.

Attacks on Britain continued sporadically with an explosion that killed eleven soldiers and some horses in Hyde Park in July 1982, a spate of London city centre bombings in 1983 which culminated in the unauthorised bombing of Harrod's in Knightsbridge which killed two policemen and three civilians. The peak of IRA operations came in October 1984 when they blew up the Grand Hotel in Brighton where the Conservative leadership were staying during their party conference.

Thatcher had featured in 'Wanted for Murder' posters in 1981. However Sinn Féin's Danny Morrison[8] says the attack was intended not just to kill her in revenge for her role in the death of the hunger strikers, but also to wipe out a generation of Tory leadership and force a political crisis in Britain. Thatcher narrowly escaped but five Conservatives were killed in the blast. The closest parallel for a fully successful detonation was the destruction of the King David Hotel in Jerusalem by Irgun which started the process leading to the end of the British occupation of Palestine. As it was, the bomb pushed Ireland up the British political agenda and made Thatcher more willing to pay the price of the Anglo-Irish Agreement for Irish government and SDLP support in stabilising the province and isolating the IRA.

Initially the urban northerners had feared that the hunger strike would interrupt their plans to bring Sinn Féin into mainstream politics and that McAliskey or the smaller groups might rob Sinn Féin of any political benefits that flowed from it. As the protest continued it became clear that their hand was instead being strengthened, particularly in the area of electoral involvement which they saw as crucial to their ability to reap the rewards of the movement's other activities. Here Joe Austin found that the strike had unexpectedly moved the planned intervention in elections ahead by perhaps three years: 'the timing was exactly right, which doesn't very often happen in politics, both the conditions and the timing were exactly right to contest elections.'

During the strike normal Sinn Féin organisation had been largely suspended in the rush of H-Block activity and the urban northerners dominated the POW department, which was the key unit of organisation. After some early setbacks this nexus also dominated the deliberations of the broader H-Block movement, keeping a politically clear head when others could not. As Bernadette McAliskey recalled:

> Adams would sit puffing his pipe, surveying the scene, weighing up the arguments and never speaking. When the rest of us had exhausted ourselves arguing across the table it would be left to Gerry Adams to weigh up the balances and to draw up a resolution, a proposition, an idea, that all of us, whatever our differences, would say, 'Well, OK, we'll go along with that.' At the very height of some of the most terrible meetings when the hunger strike was coming to an end and there was a certain, I needn't say a certain, a great deal of bitterness between clergymen and ourselves . . . I have no memory of Gerry Adams ever raising his voice, ever losing his temper, personally insulting anybody. The whole campaign, the H-Block campaign, had been about winning a very limited position on human

> decency for prisoners. We had paid for it with lives and we hadn't got it. To me there was one simple word for that, it was defeat. What separated me from him and all the rest of them was that there was no visible emotion, that total control of whatever emotion they felt was subordinate to the politics, the struggle they were involved in. They could do a balance sheet at that point in time, they could say 'Well, we lost ten volunteers. We did not get the demands but we have immeasurably strengthened the resolve of people and built the anti-imperialist organisation nationally.' There was something in the pit of my stomach at that time that said 'that doesn't balance'.[9]

During the protest the Sinn Féin analysis had been that the H-Block movement had failed to push the mobilisation or the crisis much beyond what flowed from a hunger strike in any case. This strengthened the view that the vehicle for cracking open mainstream nationalism would be a fully politicised Sinn Féin and not a front of what they saw as 'hare brained activists'.

Within Sinn Féin the realisation gradually dawned on the old guard that the POW department, already seen as 'a kind of holy of holies that no ordinary mortal would be allowed into though edicts would come out of it' now functioned as a power base for the urban northern caucus around Adams. The first effects of this were seen in the Ulster executive, a body once dominated by the mainly rural old guard and chaired by the jovial Billy Donnelly from Twinbrook. Stories are told of debates in which one delegate jokingly dismissed socialism with the words 'no bastard is going to get my pigs' and Joe O'Neill of Bundoran was ribbed about the fate of his pub if the ideas gained ground. The executive was a constant thorn in the sides of the urban northerners who lacked the strength to get rid of it. However they were able to place their people on it. Richard McAuley shadowed the traditionalist Tipperary born Pauline McAteer as joint PRO and also functioned as delegate to the POW department and the RACs. Francie Molloy took charge of youth and Mickey Hasson of education.

The Sinn Féin ard fheis itself saw decisive moves against O'Bradaigh and O'Conaill, once the political savants of the movement but now cast as died-in-the-wool traditionalists.

O'Bradaigh later admitted that, although he continued as president, it was at this point that his position became untenable due to the dropping of the federal element from the party's programme, though by an insufficient majority to remove it from the constitution. The other important change was a decision to allow the ard comhairle to decide on involvement in Leinster House, Stormont and Westminster elections to be contested on an abstentionist basis. Carrying the day, Danny Morrison spelt out the new flexible, urban northern gospel: 'Who here really believes that we can win the war through the ballot box? But will anyone here object if, with a ballot paper in this hand and an Armalite in this hand, we take power in Ireland?' It was, as events showed, no rhetorical question.

With that year's ard comhairle, the urban northerners would have been hard put to have carried a vote on a divisive issue and had to consolidate their position through a cumbersome apparatus of specialist sub-committees at national level. However they made some gains. Jim Gibney had moved from his H-Block role to the key position of national organiser, a post which conferred unrivalled contact with opinion throughout the country, making him a vital ear to the ground for his allies in the north. In another key post, that of PRO, Morrison came in to replace O'Bradaigh's brother Sean. POWs itself was headed by Marie Moore, a Belfast woman who had run the H-Block information centre and was to act as Adams' secretary. New faces included the O'Conaillite Kathleen Knowles who joined Joe Cahill as joint general secretary, Phil Flynn and the long-winded Paddy Bolger in education. Previous members to disappear included the ultra-traditionalist Joe Stagg and Sean MacStiofain. A number of the remaining older members were amenable to the urban northern viewpoint, including Belfast-man Joe Cahill and John Joe McGirl from Leitrim whilst the position of some powerful internal movers, including veteran republican Richard Behal, remained floating.

Although the urban northerners had won the decisive policy shifts which were to pave the way for their future success and the 1986 split in the movement, their position was not yet secure. It improved at the 1982 ard fheis when careful preparation on the ground enabled them to carry motions enabling the ard comhairle to abolish and replace bodies like the Ulster executive which was now in the last year of its life and the Belfast comhairle ceanntar, the last redoubt of the city's traditionalists who had tried unsuccessfully to have Rita O'Hare's new women's affairs department abolished. Yet further space for manoeuvre was created by the sanctioning of specialist departments, along the lines of POWs, which would have members who need not join, or be known to, local cumainn. However, given their advantage at army council level and their superiority in urban northern IRA areas the new leaders now had the chance to stand or fall by their new ideas and older members talked amongst themselves of 'giving Adams enough rope to hang himself'. In hindsight this was little more than a policy of letting the grass grow under their feet.

Over the next two years the urban northerners showed consummate ability to turn both adversity and success to their advantage. The pressure from the security forces continued with a new 'supergrass' tactic which could have proved devastating on the political and military levels. Supergrasses, or 'converted terrorists' as police prefer, are paramilitary members or supporters who turn queen's evidence, revealing alleged details of terrorist operations and naming names in court. Except in the case of Kevin McGrady, a member of a CIA linked religious cult, the motives were generally linked to promises of immunity for crimes they had committed themselves, cash or early release to a new life abroad. Often they had been informers and they faced the dilemma of co-operating or risking exposure to the organisations they had betrayed. To date supergrass evidence has not stood up at the appeal stage provided the accused did not sign statements implicating themselves but this did not stop them being detained for months or years, disrupting paramilitary organisation and spreading paranoia and distrust.

The system is an RUC response to the perennial problem of turning intelligence into evidence and taking suspects out of circulation. Earlier efforts were internment and the Castlereagh confession machine. With both the UVF and the INLA the system all but wrecked the organisations by removing key members from circulation and releasing them after long periods when some would go on to cause leadership crises and splits as they struggled to regain their former positions. The IRA weathered the storm and even managed to wring some advantages from it.

The majority of IRA supergrasses came from Belfast and most of the remainder from Derry City, a circumstance which looked bad for the urban northerners with their claim to have improved security. In particular Robert 'Beato' Lean, a reneged Belfast supergrass and former friend of Adams, was portrayed by police as a top-ranking IRA man but was known in republican circles to have got most of his alleged information in pub talk from the Belfast operations officer, not Adams, who was demoted as a result. The scorn of some from country areas was such that one senior IRA man insisted on keeping his back to Belfast members or pulling a snorkel anorak hood over his face so that, whatever they suspected, they would be in no position to identify him.

However, the cell structure did stop supergrass accusations from reaching beyond the local level and ultimately the fear of informers allowed the urban northerners to tighten their grip on the IRA. The fact that most supergrasses were recruited in police custody and some were ex-prisoners meant that after arrest potential dissidents could be frozen out of IRA activity and influence in the interests of security. This ostensibly pragmatic approach prevailed over wild accusations of top-level touting from IRA dissidents and in the end the one real internal security inquiry of these years centered around a supporter of the old guard and not an urban northerner at all.

The person in question was Christine ní Elias, an American of east European extraction living in Rathfarnham. She is an extremely capable woman who wrote extensively on policy in *Republican News* and fulfilled a key role in internal education as well as acting as PRO of the Dublin Comhairle Ceanntar, provincial chair of Leinster and Leinster delegate to the ard comhairle. However her unorthodox background and independent income had laid her open to suspicion and rumour had it that her family had a background in US Intelligence. She was a familiar figure at GHQ and was much favoured by the O'Conaill/O'Bradaigh axis. She had, perhaps on this account, clashed with the younger urban northerners on the way up. Some years previously, at a Saturday education lecture in

Belfast, the most prickly of them, Tom Hartley, shouted her down over an article advocating federalism. Things came to a head in 1983 when they learnt of a number of meetings which she had with a member of the Garda Special Branch and which she had made no particular effort to keep secret. Although it could not be proved that anything had transpired to the movement's disadvantage and it was argued in the subsequent enquiry that the meetings might have been helpful she was dismissed and the case became one of the levers by which the urban northerners, still beset by supergrasses themselves, made their decisive gains at the 1983 ard fheis.

An even more important factor was the party's steady progress in northern elections. After getting rid of the hunger strike, Prior set out to fulfil his pledge of returning political life to the province by attempting to build a power-sharing devolved administration. Since the Unionists would not agree he initiated an ingenious scheme for 'rolling devolution' based largely on the ideas of an Ulster born Tory MP, Dr Brian Mawhinney. Under it a Stormont Assembly had a scrutiny role but might get real devolved powers in specific areas if it could secure 'substantial cross-community support'. This meant the support of the SDLP or other nationalists. The SDLP was still reeling from the hunger strike and scared of being outflanked by Sinn Féin if it was seen to collaborate in Prior's plans. Hume's sights had now been fixed on the other component of the Sunningdale settlement, an Irish dimension, and he was concentrating efforts on an international effort to win support for this. As a result the SDLP followed Sinn Féin's lead in pledging not to take their seats and Haughey, who was again Taoiseach of a minority administration from March to December 1982, poured scorn on the whole idea.

Prior says he was criticised for 'allowing the support for Sinn Féin to become public knowledge' by calling the elections for 20 October. When the votes were in the Provos were 2.5 per cent up on the pro-H-Block vote in the 1981 council elections, notching up 64,191 first preferences. Standing in seven of the twelve constituencies they succeeded in getting Adams (who topped the poll with 8,740 votes in West Belfast, pulling the SDLP's Joe Hendron in on his second-preference votes), Jim McAlister in Armagh, Martin McGuinness in Derry, Danny Morrison in the unaccustomed surroundings of rural Mid-Ulster and Owen Carron (another poll topper) in Fermanagh-South Tyrone elected.

Amidst predictions that Sinn Féin had peaked electorally they upped their vote to 13.4 per cent (35 per cent of the nationalist total) in the June 1983 Westminster elections which returned Thatcher for another term. Most significantly Adams took West Belfast against a divided mainstream nationalist opposition of the former SDLP leader and sitting MP Gerry Fitt and the new SDLP runner Joe Hendron. This signal victory fulfilled the hunger strike pledge to unseat Fitt, and, together with Danny Morrison's narrow 78 vote defeat in Mid-Ulster at the hands of the DUP's Rev. William McCrea, covered Carron's loss of Fermanagh-South Tyrone to Unionist Ken Maginnis.

The Sinn Féin poll had been maximised by three main tactics. Firstly dozens of new advice centres had been opened. Soon after he was elected Adams estimated that he had 38 advice workers in West Belfast alone,[10] to deal with housing and other problems. Secondly there had been a highly professional registration drive aimed at reversing the years of Sinn Féin advice to supporters to disregard elections as well as at young voters and people who had moved in the ongoing housing redevelopment. Thirdly there had been a strong personation campaign, often based on the returns of the registration drive which turned up derelict streets still registered to vote, dead people still registered and voters who would miss the poll. Contributing to this there were instances of double registration of voters and Sinn Féin caravans outside the main polling booths to keep a tally. None of these tactics were new to Northern Ireland politics but all were pursued by Sinn Féin with more vigour and imagination than the other parties.

The election drive was a heavy drain on manpower and financial resources, especially at a time when the successful FBI penetration of American arms networks was forcing the IRA to pay a premium for what equipment it could get and money was lost on a number of continental arms deals. Smuggling continued as an ever more lucrative racket in the south and west of the province but other established means of fund raising were on the decline. Simple extortion in republican areas was out for a party seeking political respectability. Slot machines, which could be illegally but painlessly placed in retail outlets, were being tackled by the RUC's C19 corruption wing, the so-called 'Capone Squad'. The state was also forcing drinking clubs to assume a legal existence and, combined with a general fall in drink sales, this made them less lucrative.

As a result financial structures were tightened in Belfast and some of the less political stalwarts of the movement were moved into areas of business sympathetic to republicanism which were centralised in the Conway Street Mill. This complex is a hive of community and business activities for the Falls area, most of them fully legitimate. It served as the headquarters for the Falls Taxi Association each of whose drivers handed in at least £10 a week at the mill and an Association of Clubs which combined a variety of social clubs whose committee members were often sympathetic. Before the setting up of the Association a typical weekly donation from some clubs would be £200 but a preferred option for the Provos was to have part of the turnover sold outside the books and some club premises used as collateral to raise loans for the development of others.

More direct means of fund raising were armed robbery, largely in the Republic as some financial institutions in the North were persuaded to give loans on favourable terms or even donations, kidnapping and currency forgery. Major IRA counterfeiting of banknotes became apparent from April 1983, shortly before the Westminster election when raids in Shannon uncovered £IR24,000 in bogus £10 notes. Raids in Ballymun on the north side of Dublin in the same year uncovered a further £10,000 and early the next month undiscovered notes, perhaps amounting to £1 million, went into circulation. From 1982 the IRA had been buying forged British £20 from criminal sources in Britain at a discount and, in one form or another the racket has continued as a source of finance of unquantifiable value ever since.

Several early kidnap attempts had already received wide publicity. In 1974 Lord and Lady Donoughmore were unsuccessfully held against the release of the Price sisters. In 1975 maverick republican Eddie Gallagher and Derry girl Marion Coyle abducted Tiede Herrema, the Dutch head of Ferenkas's Limerick plant, surrendering after an eight-day siege. In 1979 the families of several bank managers were successfully held for ransom and another successful heist took place in 1981 when Ben Dunne, heir to a major retail chain, was kidnapped and released in return for a ransom in the region of £750,000.

In 1983 a new chain of kidnaps was started by a recently released prisoner as a freelance bid, in which he had the tacit support of a GHQ officer and the active involvement of a South Armagh family with experience of ransoming smugglers, to solve the movement's cash problems. The first 'victim' was a horse, the Derby winner Shergar, but no ransom was paid, partly because of the large number of people who had a share in the stallion. The animal was killed. This was followed by the August 1983 kidnap attempt on Galen Weston, a Canadian supermarket king with holdings in Ireland and Britain which included Fine Fare, Quinnsworth, Fortnum and Mason, Sunblest, Brown Thomas, Penneys, Crazy Prices and Stewarts. Gardai were alerted to the attempt and four boiler-suited IRA men were captured in a shoot-out and given sentences ranging from ten to fourteen years at a trial which was attended by Adams and Joe Cahill.

In November a Weston executive, Don Tidey, the British-born head of Quinnsworth, was abducted at a bogus Garda checkpoint manned by former Irish army soldier Michael Burke as he drove his thirteen-year-old daughter Susan from their Rathfarnham home to school. After a nationwide manhunt Tidey's abductors, whom Gardai believe included Maze escapees Brendan McFarlane, Kevin Barry and Gerry Kelly, were cornered near Ballinamore, Co. Leitrim where they escaped after shooting Garda Gary Sheehan and Private Patrick Kelly dead. Tidey was recovered but the kidnappers escaped. Earlier the IRA had demanded a £5 million from the Westons and Gardai had intercepted Quinnsworth security chief Des McSherry boarding an Avair chartered flight at Dublin Airport, headed for an unknown destination. After the incident the IRA made further threats to Weston and £2 million was paid into a numbered account in the Swiss Bank Corporation in Zurich. At the time of writing the British government is involved in a Swiss court case designed to force the banking system there to disclose details of IRA cash routes and the Irish government is being challenged in the High Court over its seizure in 1985 of £1.75 million, alleged by the state to be IRA funds, from an account in the Bank of Ireland, Navan, Co. Meath. In the interim the IRA are thought to have been involved in a number of successful attempts to extort money from companies with an interest in Ireland on the strength of the previous kidnappings.

Adams attracted some criticism in republican circles for his stance during the Tidey affair when he had commented, 'I would not condone the kidnapping though I would also refuse to condemn it', a variation on his normal line on embarrasing IRA actions that whereas he would not be prepared to condemn them publicly he would be making his comments privately.

When the 1983 ard fheis opened on 11 November, Tidey was still unaware of what lay in store for him and Adams was riding high on the northern election victories. The conference put dents in the policy of abstentionism with a decision that Sinn Féin should contest the forthcoming EEC election on the basis of taking their seats if elected. The ard fheis also voted by a two-thirds majority that 'no aspect of the constitution and rules be closed to discussion', a change aimed at the prohibition on discussion of abstentionism, and to replace the constitutional commitment to 'Christian principles' with 'Irish republican socialist principles in accordance with the Easter Proclamation of 1916 and the democratic programme of the First Dail'.

The old guard had left it too late to put up an effective fight, though desultory efforts were made to re-introduce federalism and reaffirm the ban on abstentionism. Outflanked, O'Bradaigh, O'Conaill and Behal declined to stand for their posts of President, Deputy President and Director of Foreign Affairs respectively. In a bitter resignation speech O'Bradaigh revealed that he had been defeated in ard comhairle sub-committees and on the ard comhairle itself on a number of policy issues including the decision to stand in the EEC elections and a commitment in principle to contest all future Dail elections. He said a paper he had written on abstentionism was rejected and that with policies he had championed for ten years in tatters the credibility of the office of president was being called into question. 'During my fourteen years as head of Sinn Féin' he said 'there have been no splits or splinters. Long may it continue so — as it will provided we stick to basic principles.' If anything O'Conaill was more scathing, saying that in dropping federalism Sinn Féin 'threw away an original, positive and progressive element of policy' and that it now had a leadership that was 'not representative of the organisation as a whole.'

Adams was elected as president, protesting his reluctance to let his name go forward because he believed that the emphasis from now should be on the south. His speech was a model of temperance and conciliation. He denied that his election represented a northern takeover or a move towards Leinster House saying, 'we are an abstentionist party; it is not my intention to advocate change in this situation'. However he did raise Sinn Féin's 'almost total concentration on the constitutional question', trying to reclaim the 'social and economic spectrum' of issues which characterised the 1960s republican movement, advocating mundane political work on the ground and an eventual planned economy, all issues which fed speculation amongst diehards that Adams had set foot on the 'sticky slope' which they had split the movement to avoid in 1969. However in phrases more redolent of de Valera's stricture that 'labour must wait' than the Workers' Party he stressed that the 'securing of Irish independence is a prerequisite for the advance to a socialist republican society'.

After the ard fheis he countered suggestions that the course he had now embarked on had always split the movement in the past with the words:

> One of the major elements is that the struggle has continued without really stopping. The whole struggle has been going on for about thirteen years without really stopping . . . and that has meant, in effect, that people are always re-examining in a real context. If you are having talking shops or having debates, having discussions in a vacuum then that has a tendency to lead to splits. People have arguments and dialectical discussions where at the moment what we are trying to do is to shape the Republican philosophy to meet the needs of the struggle and to broaden the struggle to meet the needs of the people and you can do that concretely because the struggle is still going on and you can evidence the fact that you need to do this, that or the other because that's dealing with the reality of the ongoing struggle.

Military expediency was the justification and cover for political development and IRA activity the means of holding the movement together through any stress that this imposed on it. In this agile mind the apparent contradictions of acting both within and outside the democratic process were reconciled to produce further opportunity for change.

Increasingly old timers in the north had found new faces in their local cumainn, often released blanketmen who, they joked, must have 'been fed little white mice' in prison, coming up with fresh ideas and gradually supplanting those they considered to be dead wood. In Lurgan Brendan Curran had emerged from jail to oust Liam Haddock and Peter Corey in the local Sinn Féin office. In Andersonstown it was Paddy Wilson and in Belaghey Ben McIlwee was seen in the same way. A disgruntled old timer quipped 'are these the people we tramped the streets for when they were in jail?'

After the ard fheis this process continued in a far reaching reorganisation in which the real strength of these youngsters combined with the almost unassailable national superiority of the urban northerners. In Belfast, for instance, the old comhairle ceanntar was decentralised until there were three and one in nearby Lagan Valley where Richard McAuley was the main figure. These smaller and more easily controlled units were united under a new Belfast comhairle limistear. The crucial West Belfast comhairle ceanntar meeting in the Felons' club in Andersonstown had, as part of its platform party, a group known as the 'RPG 7 Gang' after the rocket launcher. One observer commented:

> There had been so much anticipation of opposition from Andersonstown in particular that the meeting had to be well stacked with army people who had probably never been to a Sinn Féin meeting in their lives before. C******* even got a position as organiser though it never appeared in *AP/RN*. They expected a backlash from people like Drumm, McAirt, Seamus McCotter from Lenadoon, all old '50s men with some local standing who didn't approve of the changes, who didn't approve of people like Ruadhri and Dave who they'd idolised all their lives being thrust aside and who were a bit peeved at Johnny-come-latelies

like Alex Maskey and C******** taking up the key positions. These people had a view of republicans as fine upstanding citizens and Maskey, Adams, Morrison and Paddy Wilson didn't fit that. They were brash, they were bullying and they were prioritising the political side of things. Any money available during '80-'83 was going into the H-Block campaign and subsequently the elections. The number of operations had fallen; apart from the RPG 7 there hadn't been any serious military activity in Belfast for a long time. They saw this as a major departure and they resented it.

At that meeting you had people like Alec Maskey as the up and coming mouthpiece of Adams. Very abrasive, very rough, just the man to implement a policy that needs to be done. Barbara Brown, or Bairbre de Brun, who came in through H-Block, Padraig Wilson, the released blanket-man as well. The blanketmen were highly politicised. A lot of them got absorbed into the structures, Fra Browne for instance. Kieran Nugent, the first blanketman, was absorbed into the civil administration at the time of the onslaught on hoods and was known as the 'Chief Constable'.

This sort of process was mirrored unevenly around the country and, after the next ard fheis, the entire Sinn Féin organisation in Britain was disbanded, in favour of creating closer links with the Labour left and working through the emerging Irish organisations in that country.

Now the hold of the urban northerners was so strong that despite the falloff in IRA operations, particularly marked in the areas they controlled, their position seemed invincible. Yet hair-line cracks were beginning to show in the jewel of their crown, the seemingly unending succession of electoral victories.

At the end of 1984 they stood in the EEC poll, with the Northern candidate Danny Morrison predicting victory over John Hume and Behal surprising everybody by contesting one of the southern seats, but succeeded only in reducing their vote to a still substantial 13.3 per cent in the North and around 2 per cent in the south. In the northern local government elections of 1985, elation at the total number of seats won, fifty-nine, concealed a fall in their share of the vote to 11.8 per cent, though this was admittedly on the basis of contesting only selected seats.

The approach of the Sinn Féin councillors was by and large to try and work the system. In Fermanagh, where there was a clear nationalist majority, for instance, they declined to second an IIP motion banning the flying of the Union Jack on council property and in Omagh, where a mix-up in Unionist voting gave Sinn Féin's Seamus Kerr the chair, they went out of their way to avoid confrontation. In Derry, where one Sinn Féin councillor Gerry Doherty, had last entered the Guildhall with a bomb in 1972, a motion calling for the selling off of council-owned Orange memorabilia for charity was tactfully withdrawn once the point was made. Such pragmatic efforts to make local government work for their constituents would, in the normal course of events, have brought Sinn Féin up against the fundamental ballot and armalite contradiction of on the one hand taking part in the electoral process and accepting any gains which it brought and on the other resorting to force to undermine it. However this contradiction had little opportunity to surface thanks to the immediate and violent reaction of the unionists who first tried various legal ploys to drive Sinn Féin out and ended by closing many councils rather than sit in the same chamber as Provos.

The NIO ministers, now headed by Douglas Hurd, also played their part by refusing to meet Sinn Féin elected representatives. The potentially troublesome question of Provo participation in institutions of the state which they sought to destroy was transferred from the narrow ground of explaining the deaths of council officials at the IRA's hands and reaching voting agreements with people they regarded as legitimate targets to the broader and more favourable terrain of whether Sinn Féin, and the people whom they represented had a right to be heard. With under 12 per cent of the popular vote they were immediately placed at the centre of political debate. It was a situation of confrontation in which they could only thrive, and all created in the name of 'Smashing Sinn Féin'.

The real forces which could smash, or at least damage Sinn Féin, were massing elsewhere, both in their own ranks and in the range of interests which were coming together to give birth to the Anglo-Irish agreement.

NOTES

1. Interview in *Andersonstown News,* 22 November 1986.

2. William McQuistan in an interview with the author. I am also indebted to Sam Walker of Loyalist Prisoners' Aid for copies of a large number of communications and reports from UDA prisoners.

3. The Hennessy report of 26 January 1984.

4. During the hunger strike itself 64 people died violently: 12 RUC men, 3 RUC reservists, 8 members of the British army, 7 UDR men and 34 civilians. The total of deaths was the lowest for any previous year except 1976 and 1980 but higher than any subsequent year. An opposite trend is visible in relation to the amount stolen in the province. The total in 1981, £894,929, was higher than any previous year but lower than any subsequent year. By comparison 221 died in road accidents in Northern Ireland in the same year.

5. *The Politics of Irish Freedom,* p. 64.

6. Saturday 5 September 1981.

7. *Magill,* November 1981.

8. In an interview with TV South.

9. In Granada TV's World in Action production, 'The Honourable Member for West Belfast'. McAliskey later apologised to the republican movement and, indeed, the people of Ireland for her comments in this programme.

10. Interview with the author.

11

Riding Two Horses

When a government has come to power with popular participation, whether fraudulently or not, and preserves at least the appearances of constitutional legality, then the seeds of guerilla warfare can never germinate.

Che Guevara.[1]

Even if it costs me friends and maybe votes, I will not be a hypocrite and condemn the IRA.

SF Councillor Brendan Lewis, Newry and Mourne.[2]

During and after the hunger strike the Provisionals did their best to whip up a narrow war psychology in order to maximise support amongst nationalists. There were constant predictions of an imminent loyalist holocaust and, in the final weeks, these were supplemented by visits to interface businesses advising them to employ security staff. The backlash did not come until the assassination of Bradford, when two Catholics were murdered, and was not long lived.

A major escalation of sectarian tension and state repression would allow the IRA to present themselves as, and perhaps to actually become, the defenders of the Roman Catholic community. In such a crunch situation there would be a much higher ceiling on the Sinn Féin vote and support than the 11 per cent to 14 per cent in the north and 1 per cent to 3 per cent in the south they now enjoyed. These circumstances would also ease the ballot and armalite contradiction, allowing them to be more widely accepted as complementary aspects of a fight for communal survival.

The lesser degree of tension, hatred and repression which existed meant that IRA operations could be counter-productive to the drive to reach beyond the hard core of their support into a less committed nationalist constituency. Yet a visible lessening of IRA activity, especially if it was combined with a slowing down of the electoral bandwagon, would create internal problems and undermine the very basis of the organisation. The dilemma was underlined at an IRA meeting in Andersonstown in Spring 1983 during which members of Active Service Units were addressed by a leading urban northern strategist and agreed to give the new approach a two year trial.

Another factor affecting Sinn Féin's success was the competition which constitutional nationalism was able to mount. For some years after the hunger strike the SDLP were seen to offer little alternative to the IRA campaign. Since both parties were boycotting the Prior Assembly, the only political show on the road, many nationalists concluded that the smart money should be with the player who had the military ace up his sleeve.

Hume's answer was to lift his sights beyond the Northern Ireland sphere to all Ireland, Europe and the US. In March 1983 the New Ireland Forum was announced as an Irish government sponsored effort by the constitutional nationalist parties in the island to hammer out a common approach. Over the next eighteen months it heard evidence, commissioned reports and presented an appearance of movement which did much to discourage mainstream northern Catholics from seeing the IRA as a way forward. Despite considerable internal difficulties in balancing the views of Fianna Fail, Fine Gael and at least two discernible wings of the SDLP it did succeed in producing a final document with three options, a unitary Irish state, joint sovereignty and a confederal solution. If nothing else, the document represented one victory for the IRA analysis: it posited the terms of political debate firmly in the constitutional and religious sphere, bringing in economic and social considerations only as backup and rejecting the gloomy findings of the economic studies which it commissioned on the three constitutional models.

In November Margaret Thatcher ruled the three models 'out' and before he heard this Garret FitzGerald shot himself in the foot by saying the report had been well received. Despite the unpromising tone of Thatcher's initial response the hunger strike and the Sinn Féin advances had focused British minds on the need to offer some legal way forward for nationalists. This need was underlined by the increasingly favourable international response to the Forum, the inability of the unionists to offer, or the SDLP to accept, any movement towards an internal devolved government solution and the Brighton bombing in which the problems and grievances of Pat Magee's New Lodge Road reached into the heart of the Tory cabinet, threatening to wipe it out.

The option of simply continuing the Assembly in Stormont in the hope of something turning up was removed first by nationalist refusal to take seats and then by the recurring threats of the OUP to pull out of it. The only parties working it were the middle of the road Alliance, with a smaller vote than Sinn Féin, and Paisley's DUP who saw the possibility of forming a cabinet and feared something worse if it failed. Thatcher had never given it wholehearted support because of her rivalry with Prior. Her lukewarm approach allowed the maverick right-wing MP for South Down, Enoch Powell, and his cabinet contact Ian Gow to hope, and to convince Jim Molyneaux, that if the Assembly failed then complete integration with the UK would be forthcoming and the threat of a united Ireland would be gone forever.

Molyneaux was mistaken and Hume and Paisley were correct. The failure of the Assembly meant the end of attempts at an internal political solution for the foreseeable future and a possible weakening of the union. Prior found Thatcher the 'strongest unionist I have ever met'[3] and although she maintained the policy of keeping Northern Ireland as far from mainstream British politics as possible she would do nothing to imply a surrender of territory. After a period of lowering nationalist aspirations to take account of this fact, keeping the Assembly on a drip feed and trying unsuccessfully to smash the IRA by security means, she did business with Dublin, though not on the basis of the Forum options.

The talks between the two governments were shrouded in secrecy as far as the public and the unionists were concerned but were disclosed to the SDLP. In November 1985, just a year after Thatcher's 'out, out, out' speech, they culminated in the Anglo-Irish agreement, a document flexible enough to allow the possibility of change in more than one direction. Its essential provisions were a guarantee of the status of Northern Ireland as long as the majority wanted to remain in the UK; a rejection of violence for political ends; the establishment of a conference of ministers from both states with a brief to consider security and legal matters; the establishment of a permanent secretariat of eighteen civil servants from the two jurisdictions; a commitment to a power-sharing devolved administration in the north; a commitment to recognising the rights of both nationalists and unionists and to the prevention of discrimination; a commitment to the harmonising of some undefined areas of law in the two jurisdictions; security force co-operation against terrorism; the establishment of an inter-parliamentary tier including members of the two sovereign parliaments and the Assembly; and a review of the legislation in three years time.

The document had two clear intentions; to isolate Sinn Féin politically as a prelude to the military isolation of the IRA and to split the unionists until a section could be found who would accommodate the SDLP. Shortly before the report some of its provisions were floated to unionists by NIO officials, amidst claims by Molyneaux that they were out to topple him as party leader. At the time a senior DUP source told me that Paisley had been asked his feelings on an inter-parliamentary tier which would be open to Assembly, Dail and Westminster members but which would have no executive or legislative clout. The suggestion was that the lure of seats on this body would get the SDLP into a rejigged Assembly after the next election. The DUP reaction was that though they would object and wouldn't take part 'we wouldn't go on the Carson trail about it'. It was, in short, a price worth paying for SDLP participation in some form of devolved administration.

Bearing such soundings in mind, the NIO were surprised at the breadth of unionist opposition. When, in the immediate aftermath of the agreement, Thatcher met Paisley and Molyneaux they expressed less than total opposition both to her and, a little later, to the press. However the unionist leaders changed their tune back in Belfast and were left in the difficult position of trying to lead an opposition which they did not initiate. If their gradual withdrawal from public bodies has made it impossible to get the necessary local participation for an inter-parliamentary tier the mass across the board endorsement of the agreement at Westminster meant that they have had no effective means of pressure on Thatcher. This left them uncomfortable in the knowledge that it might take the UDI option favoured by some sections of their parties to shift the agreement but that their grass roots are not desperate enough to contemplate such a step. In this position of weakness a remaining hope was that an outside force, in the shape of a new southern government, would wreck the agreement and rescue them from their dilemma. A series of initiatives ranging from a midnight invasion of Clontibret, Co. Monaghan by Peter Robinson and other DUP supporters to actual firebombings of towns in the Republic by the paramilitaries were designed to make the agreement less popular in the south and maximise opposition to it by raising the threat of an overspill of northern violence.

The Provisionals, who had done so much to initiate all this change, were, as ever, unable to reap the rewards. In their unremitting efforts to force a crisis in nationalism they had instead forced the mainstream to get its act together. The agreement was the fruit of pressure on Britain in which they had played a part but instead of dividing their enemies they had succeeded, for the time being at least, in uniting them. Seeking to force the SDLP into a corner they had instead pushed it through the door onto open ground where it had more room for manoeuvre than ever.

Their own battlefield, broadened at such dreadful cost to themselves and others, was again showing signs of narrowing, even though they had temporarily tapped a vein of support that had not been visible for generations.

After the 1983 ard fheis they increasingly compared themselves to the African National Congress on the grounds that, like it, they were using force to achieve their conception of freedom. The difference was that for the ANC the use of force was a last resort after generations of constitutional agitation in which not even a limited or gerrymandered franchise could be achieved. Force came in when all else had failed, and was accepted by most South Africans to have failed, to shift a government based on a minority of the population. For the Provos, force was the first resort and electoral politics only arose when force was seen to flounder. For this reason it could command the support of only a small and fluctuating minority, yet because it was the uniting factor in the movement it could not be rationally debated, much less abandoned, without crippling repercussions.

The south became crucial as the northern vote passed its peak, yet here too support slumped. In the 1982 Dail elections their vote in the crucial constituencies of Louth and Cavan-Monaghan was less than half of the H-Block total; and in the local government poll of 1985 it barely passed 3 per cent. Urban northerners who canvassed for Sinn Féin in the Republic found themselves being told that it was no use voting for them because they would not go to the Dail. It was also apparent that their policies did not address themselves to southern needs and, as one Sinn Féin member put it, 'we were not going to get votes in Ballymun because the Brits were battering down doors in Ballymurphy.'

Once again they were hitting against one of their movement's basic tenets of faith, the belief that elected or not, accepted by the people or not, the Dail was a treasonable assembly and that those who entered it were themselves guilty of treason against the first and only true Dail. It was an article of faith that was well enough known in the north, but was not strongly felt. There the reasons for joining the Provos lay in internment, house searches and grievance within living memory while policy arose in response to immediate pressure. Southern Provisional founding fathers worked on another time span, putting principles of legitimacy at a higher premium than opportunities for immediate advance. For them breaking the laws of a legislature you voted in was immoral. They reasoned that as this contradiction matured the armed struggle would suffer in the quest for Dail seats. It was a process which had taken place in Fine Gael, Fianna Fail, Aontacht Eireann and the Officials and they believed they saw it starting again now.

Other potential trouble spots existed in country areas of the north, areas where, in the words attributed to Dominic McGlinchey, "they don't know anything about Mandela but they see the Brits in their fields and they don't like it.' Even in the urban northern ghettos years of being told that politicians were collaborators were not sloughed off like an old skin. Besides, Adams' generation of leadership no longer represented youth. Young recruits were coming forward, eager for action, only to be directed into the 'mundane political work' which Adams constantly recommended or, if they were allowed to join the IRA at all, often being given weapons classes on video and little opportunity to operate. Some joined the INLA as a result and a haemorrhage of trained men was only prevented when, in 1983, a former Belfast operations officer was kneecapped for defecting.

The declining size and activity of the IRA, particularly in urban northern areas, and the clear moves of the leadership towards electoral participation was bringing all these strands together. Their cohesion was sapped by favourable election results, by dramatic IRA operations like the Brighton bombing or the halting of work on police stations in the 1985 'year of the mortar', as well as by the organisational measures taken to isolate them in the new structures, and security force tactics like the alleged shoot-to-kill policy. However they could not be forever submerged.

The 1983 warning that the new methods could have two years was a disturbing sign of trouble amongst the Belfast Active Service Units, the core of urban northern support and hand picked to be ultra loyal to the new leaders. The night before the 1983 general election they bombed Andersonstown RUC station in the very heart of Adams' constituency to make the point that the momentum of their campaign would not be interrupted or its character fine tuned for political considerations. It was a massive blast in an area surrounded by houses. Fortunately there were no civilian casualities but the next day Sinn Féin activists cut a strange figure advising the owners of damaged homes of their rights to compensation from the Northern Ireland Office. It was said that Adams, seeing the unit returning from the bombing as he walked along canvassing, shook his fist at their car.

Difficulties were compounded, in 1984, by a string of instances in which IRA weapons seem to have been tampered with. One of the RPG7 rocket launchers had to be abandoned after it misfired three times, on one occasion missing a Saracen and sending a rocket into a classroom where it smashed the blackboard, on another wrecking a greengrocer's shop and on a third taking the wheel off a coal lorry. A consignment of sub-machine guns were also found to be faulty. A clue to what may have happened was provided when an informer, James Young from Portaferry, was interrogated by the IRA before being murdered. He told them that police had placed a bug in the stock of an IRA machine gun which he brought them and asked him to return it. The weapon eventually turned up in a dump where two IRA men, Declan Martin and Henry Hogan, were shot dead whilst trying to lift it.

The killing of IRA members and the discovery of IRA dumps in this period was far from rare, giving rise to fears of high level infiltration. It also pointed to a fundamental weakness of the cell system and the new slimmed down IRA: once the state agencies had adapted to the new situation it presented them with a far more limited number of targets for their improved intelligence and surveillance methods than had the more spontaneous all-out campaign of the early seventies. The smaller number of more specialised operators also meant that the IRA was less able to sustain its previous levels of attrition. Between December 1984 and April 1985, for instance, no less than thirteen IRA members were killed in action, nine at SAS stakeouts, two in incidents involving explosives and one, Belfastman Sean McIlvenna — the Director of Operations for the North — was killed in Armagh shortly before Christmas 1984. In the same period Don Tidey was found and a huge shipment of arms were discovered aboard the *Marita Anne* off the Kerry coast. Before that E4A had been able to track members of the British bombing unit through Ireland, England and Scotland and to tip off the Glasgow police who lifted them. New RUC flak jackets were proof against low velocity fire, military vehicles were improved to reduce landmine damage and patrols had started to operate in parallel covered by 'heli-teli' airborne surveillance cameras making ambushes both more difficult and less likely to succeed.

In this difficult situation dissent had plenty of room to grow and there was an organised push to call a new IRA army convention to review strategy. The army convention is a delegate conference of all IRA formations with the powers to elect an army executive. The convention did not normally meet in 'time of war' and the last one had been in 1970. In its absence its powers were vested in the executive who could select the army council and, if necessary, replace it. The AC had charge of the overall running of the campaign, selecting a chief of staff and a

GHQ staff who in turn selected the various directors of operations. This structure meant that a convention need only be called if it was proposed to question the stewardship of the collective leadership or to push for a fundamental change of policy.

Some of the urban northerners became increasingly worried about their own personal security because of the apparent shoot-to-kill units in the security forces, the increasing anger of loyalists and the internal divisions which were opening up. Adams regularly travelled with two bodyguards and in March 1984 it was shown that his fears, at least in respect of the loyalists, were not groundless. After a court appearance on a charge of obstruction on 14 March Adams' car was riddled with twenty bullets by the UFF (UDA) as it drove through the rush hour traffic towards West Belfast. Three other republicans (Sean Keenan, Joe Keenan and Kevin Rooney) were also injured and a fifth man, Bob Murray, escaped unhurt, earning himself the nickname 'hit the deck' after his reaction as the bullets started flying. His presence of mind continued at the nearby Royal Victoria hospital where he alerted staff and ensured that the four injured men were promptly treated.

Those calling for a convention included several figures in the southern old guard but also a number of key northerners. In March 1985 four of them were expelled from the IRA for what was described as 'factional activity' and told that they would be 'executed' if they attempted to form a new organisation or join an existing one. Three of the four had been strong Adams supporters at an earlier stage. The first was a former member of the army council who had taken part in peace negotiations with the British; he was one of the best-known IRA men in the country and had broadcast the fact that he had no confidence in the leadership. The second had recently been the adjutant of the Belfast Brigade and had become embittered when his OC, another dissident, was arrested and apparently wrongly convicted in connection with the murder of a woman in South Belfast. The OC was promptly replaced by a man in whom the deputy had no confidence and whom he believed to owe his position to nepotism. The third, from the Lagan Valley area, was also a senior operator. The fourth, a woman, was the common law wife of the former army council member and a strong supporter of Sean McIlvenna. The last two unsuccessfully appealed the decision and the first had his case taken up by one of the best-known members of the old guard who also supported the recall convention proposal.

Amongst their main criticisms had been the low level of IRA activity in Belfast, the exclusion of tried members like themselves from the inner circle and the diversion of funds into political work. Partly thanks to their pressure the IRA had refused to grant Sinn Féin £250,000 towards its council election expenses, one of the reasons why the number of candidates had had to be scaled down.

The criticisms continued after the expulsions and were joined by a former trusted Adams aide, Bob Murray, Sinn Féin's Belfast head of finance and the man who had been with Adams when he was shot. Although the expulsions did not halt the criticisms they did give the leadership time to conciliate a key member of GHQ staff and a number of other individuals throughout the country. The level of IRA operations also rose dramatically after May when a 1,000 lb trailer bomb at Killeen near Newry killed four police officers who were guarding a cross-border cash consignment. By December the IRA were able to boast that they had used the largest amount of explosives of any year of the campaign.

In this period of consolidation and reassurance Adams did not publicly back a motion at the 1985 ard fheis advocating dropping the principle of abstentionism. Given his speech at the 1983 ard fheis he could hardly do otherwise and in any case the debate was useful as a toe in the water which allowed the issue to be aired and the various degrees of opposition to be assessed. A number of other prominent urban northerners including Danny Morrison, Tom Hartley and Richard McAuley did enter the debate portraying abstentionism as a matter of tactics rather than one of principle. Hartley, now a joint general secretary, summed up the pragmatic and flexible urban northern approach in the words 'there is a principle riding above all principles and that is the principle of success.' The motion was defeated by a margin of twenty votes.

Another motion was passed at the ard fheis affirming 'a woman's right to choose' on the matter of abortion but this time the urban northern ard comhairle advised voting against it, characteristically on grounds of expediency rather than principle.

After the dry run 1985 debate the urban northerners had a fairly accurate map of the opposition and in the coming year they put as many as nine organisers on the road to convince the doubtful and seek accommodation where practicable.

By the summer of 1986 it was clear that the price would involve the dropping of abortion, a recall army convention, the dismissal of claims that they intended going in over the heads of local activists to contest Dail seats themselves and a number of changes in the IRA command in Belfast. The OC of the Belfast Brigade was dismissed as were two successive adjutants and there was apparent a softening on the emphasis on socialism in favour of the traditional physical force roots of the movement.

The main Sinn Féin publication of the period was a pamphlet by Danny Morrison entitled *The Good Old IRA* which consisted of a catalogue of the goriest operations of the Tan War period, stressing a continuity between the IRA of those years and the present day Provisionals. This built on the appearance on the 1985 ard fheis platform of war of independence veteran Dan Gleeson with Gerry Adams and the appearance of Adams himself at a number of old IRA gatherings.

Strenuous efforts were made to expand the level of IRA activity and to allow hard-line elements a freer hand in the name of local autonomy. Between May 1985 and the end of July the IRA claimed to have used 6,000 lbs of explosives in a concentrated blitz in the border strongholds where the campaign now largely took place. At the end of July mortaring techniques were improved. Previous mortar attacks on the province's 151 operational police stations which were undergoing a £150 million rebuilding programme had resulted in a large number of near misses. The tubes had been sometimes mounted on vehicles whose suspension recoiled when they were fired but now a stabilising steel sub-frame overcame this difficulty, though the weapons remained hazardous to civilians. A seaside bombing campaign had also been planned for Britain but this fell through when the majority of the personnel involved were captured.

On 16 December the unionists resigned their Westminster seats in protest against the Anglo-Irish agreement and by-elections were called for 23 January. The Sinn Féin results were down by 18,231 votes in the four constituencies they contested whilst the SDLP total in the same constituencies was up by

11,371. SDLP deputy leader Seamus Mallon took the Newry and Armagh seat from a sitting Unionist, reflecting the ability of the Anglo-Irish agreement to pluck back marginal nationalist votes for Hume's party and undermining Sinn Féin's pre-election claims that nationalist seats would be lost if the SDLP did not form a pact with them. The four constituencies (Newry and Armagh, Fermanagh-South Tyrone, Mid Ulster and South Down) which Sinn Féin fought bore the brunt of the IRA mortar campaign against police stations both before and after the election, emphasising that IRA actions were now neither tied to electoral considerations nor popular with the electorate.

Throughout this period of heightened activity the IRA was careful to claim that none of their operations were aimed against the Anglo-Irish agreement, preferring to rely on the unionists to bring it down. Their line was that far from being an impediment to peace IRA activity was actually forcing the British to make concessions to the SDLP but that all attempts at reform would perish of their own accord on the rock of unionist intransigence. There was even a noticeable lowering of the tempo of operations in the run up to a one-day loyalist work stoppage in May.

A string of sectarian murders of Catholics in North Belfast[4] allowed the IRA to intervene by first encouraging street committees and the stockpiling of supplies and then by assassinating the UVF man they thought to be responsible for the killings, John Bingham, on 14 September. After the killing two more Catholics (Raymond Mooney and Joseph Webb) were murdered by the UVF.

The apparent decline in organised loyalist opposition by August and the large amount of rebuilding work which was necessitated by the mortar attacks on police stations led the IRA to broaden their target list to include civilian suppliers of police installations. The tactic was not new. In August 1985 Seamus McAvoy was killed, ostensibly because his building firm worked on police contracts. But the murder was thought to be linked to an extortion attempt against a pub he owned in the republic. In the same month an entirely innocent man, David Mallon, was shot dead in a Strabane pub in mistake for another contractor. In November 1985 a Derry businessman, Kurt Konig, was killed on the grounds that he had been providing catering services to the local police station but here again the motivation was obscured by claims of extortion.

The new list of targets included milkmen and shopkeepers as well as contractors and seemed designed to give the IRA scope to operate more widely than ever before. The Irish Congress of Trades Unions estimated that 40,000 people were potential targets on the basis of the IRA list. The first two victims were builders, Terence McKeever who was working on Cloughmills RUC station and John Kyle from Greencastle. However the attacks came to an end when the UFF (UDA) issued a parallel threat against people who were 'supporting the republican war machine' in any way, down to using black taxis or buying *Republican News*.

The threats were seen to be provoking the loyalists into a new tit-for-tat campaign as well as undermining one of the few buoyant areas of the declining building industry. However they had their effect and several contractors withdrew, binmen in some areas refused to collect security force refuse and the IRA was seen to be affecting a vital and hitherto untouched area of life.

All this made up the background for the local IRA conventions which were meeting throughout the country to elect representatives to the army convention and hammer out their attitude to the leadership. The convention eventually took place on 20 September, just six days after Bingham's murder.

The gathering comprised upwards of sixty IRA activists who pledged in advance to abide by the collective decision and not to split. Kerry was opposed to the change as was Tyrone and the vital areas of South Armagh and Dundalk were divided down the middle. However a final statement was hammered out and issued on 14 October:

> Recently, and after much careful planning, IRA delegates from all over Ireland secretly met in a General Army Convention for the first time in sixteen years. At this meeting were members of the outgoing Army Council and representatives of the Army Executive, GHQ Staff and Departments Northern and Southern Command Staffs, Brigades and Battalions and Units, all of whom were elected by their own conventions to attend.

The Convention opened with a unanimous pledge of rededication to the armed struggle and confidence in the armed struggle as being the means to breaking the British connection and bringing about Irish independence.

Several sections of the Constitution of *Oglaigh na hÉireann* were amended and, by more than the required two-thirds majority, the delegates passed two particular resolutions. The first removed the ban on Volunteers discussing or advocating the taking of seats. The second removed the ban on supporting successful republican candidates who take their seats in Leinster House.

Also reaffirmed was General Army Order No. 8 which prohibits offensive action against the administration in the twenty-six counties or its forces.

The Constitution was modernised so that it reads in non-sexist language.

The objective of restoring the Irish language as the everyday language of the Irish people was reaffirmed.

The present strategy of the Irish Republican Army was discussed and endorsed, although the volume of resolutions made it impossible to deal with every issue.

By secret ballot, the delegates then elected a twelve person Army Executive, which in turn elected a new Army Council. The Army Council, the Chief of Staff it has appointed, and the Army Executive will study the outstanding resolutions which relate to how best to prosecute the struggle for freedom.

On the face of it the leadership had the mandate they wanted and even those who held IRA office were now free to advocate entry to the Dail, or for that matter Stormont and Westminster.

The price of adopting a policy which urban northerners believed would bring them into line with what voters wanted had been to conciliate a body of opinion, the hardline elements in the IRA, who were not representative of voters' feelings. The reaffirmation of the armed struggle, and the unannounced commitment to escalating it, seen at the time of writing in a return to car bombing, was something which was not going to win votes in anything but a near civil war situation and which seemed bound to come into conflict with their hoped for positions as TDs. As

Ruadhri O'Bradaigh was to put it[5] the northern leadership had committed itself to a policy of riding two horses.

There was immediate evidence that at least one of the steeds would prove unruly, for old-line republicans could, and had in the past, look to a more mystical authority than the decisions of the sixty or so men and women who made up an army convention. In 1969 the IRA had also backed the dropping of abstentionism and had continued its campaign for some time, but still the movement had split. What is more, one of the strongest advocates of change, Seamus Costello, who went on to become the Official IRA director of operations, had split the movement yet again when the leadership attempted, after a decent interval, to wind down the violence. Although the ground had been more thoroughly prepared this time, the threat remained like a sword of Damocles, ready to be dislodged by any movement onto the head of Gerry Adams.

Despite the electorally damaging appeasement of the hardliners dissenting voices appeared in the run up to the Sinn Féin ard fheis on 1 November. O'Bradaigh pledged to fight the change 'tooth and nail'. Cumann mBan (a women's IRA formation) also came out against the motion to remove abstentionism, saying it 'would mean accepting the right of Britain to rule in Ireland.' Key units throughout Ulster were bitterly divided on the proposal. The leadership's concern was to prevent a split in the IRA or the growth of any new nationalist paramilitary force which could threaten their control of the campaign, emerge as an alternative pole of attraction for the disgruntled or even become involved in a feud with them. It was to this end that four people expelled from the IRA had been warned against forming or joining any other terrorist organisation. Martin McGuinness went on to launch a series of public attacks on the rival INLA, already with problems of its own, accusing it of gangsterism and urging the competing group to disband. The calls for a dissolution of the INLA were repeated through private contacts between the two terror groups and were eventually taken up by one of the INLA's dissident factions who, from January 1987, engaged in a war of annihilation against the organisation's GHQ staff and its supporters.

In Louth, the area where local blanketman Paddy Agnew took a seat during the hunger strike and where Sinn Féin seemed best placed to enter the Dail, the likely candidate, Councillor Fra Browne, indicated his support for abstentionism. Agnew, after release from prison, did not immediately rejoin Sinn Féin.

Outside the Provisionals, Jim Sullivan, a former adjutant of the Officials' Belfast Command and later a City Councillor, publicly challenged Gerry Adams to explain why he joined the Provos in the first place, recalling that he had not been amongst those who walked out in the ard fheis when the movement last split.

Two more figures entered the ranks. General Tom Maguire, the last surviving member of the 1920's first Dail who was now in his 90s, had performed a useful function for the early Provisionals by conferring the legitimacy of that Dail on them when they defied the army council in the split. Now he repeated the performance, saying: 'I do not recognise the legitimacy of any army council styling itself the Army Council of the Irish Republican Army which lends support to any person or organisation styling itself as Sinn Féin and prepared to enter the partition parliament of Leinster House.'

Finally Bob Murray rounded on Adams when, in a letter to the Belfast nationalist *Irish News*, he described the current republican leadership as 'discredited' and asked Adams, 'what happened Gerry? Where did it go wrong?'

These and a dozen other straws were in the wind as the ard fheis opened but it was by now too late seriously to consider turning back. In the Republic, the Fine Gael-Labour coalition was on its last legs and an early election was expected. Internal estimates of Sinn Féin's chances aimed at five seats, a target set publicly by Martin McGuinness, and Provo hopes of holding the balance of power in a hung Dail were highlighted by the media. Such an influential position would cut the ground from under the begrudgers once the hurdle of the ard fheis was passed. Right up to the last week Adams was predicting that there would be no split and attempting to play a temporising role, meeting O'Bradaigh and the other dissidents, but with little success.

As the conference unfolded it became evident that things would not go smoothly. Sinn Féin general national organiser Pat Doherty, uniquely placed to gauge the mood of the country, set the tone of the debate by describing the leadership as the 'people who, along with others, were doing all the things that were required to be done on the ground at local level during the years 1969 to 1975', adding that 'there are no long rifles or armchair generals amongst them'. More pointedly he reminded delegates that 'they were the people who after the disastrous 1975 truce moved into the middle leadership and the national leadership and started to push the movement forward once again.' Martin McGuinness and Alex Maskey were more pointed still. Maskey made what was judged to be a personal attack on O'Bradaigh and was booed as a result. After hearing a string of speakers slamming the proposed change as a sellout of republican principles McGuinness concentrated his fire on the very integrity of the old leadership whom he described as 'elitist'.

> The reality is that the former leadership of this movement has never come to terms with this leadership's criticisms of the disgraceful attitude adopted by them during the disastrous eighteen month ceasefire in the mid 1970s. Instead of accepting the validity of our case, as others who have remained have done, they chose to withhold their wholehearted support from the leadership which replaced them. Some of the former Leadership have already gone. They were not squeezed out, they left us. Some stayed and will stay after this debate. If those who remain leave this movement it will not just be because of abstentionism.

In a final contemptuous thrust he told the dissidents: 'If you allow yourself to be led out of this hall today the only place you are going is home. You will be walking away from the struggle.'

Hearing this O'Conaill was livid, recalling that McGuinness himself had been part of the 1972 delegation to negotiate with the British and had been a senior republican implicated in the conduct of both truces. However he was unable to speak as he had already resigned from Sinn Féin and was reduced to arguing the point with his old adversary Seamus Twomey, as ever a firm supporter of the younger talent he had nurtured.

Other old timers spoke in favour of the change. Joe Cahill admitted he had been wrong to leave the movement in 1965 and mistaken in his opposition to entering Leinster House. John Joe McGirl said he too had changed his mind about abstentionism since 1969, saying that if it was not dropped 'we will be passing on the fight to our children and the children of a future generation'.

O'Bradaigh was neither so constrained as O'Conaill nor so penitent as Cahill and McGirl, but fluffed whatever chance he had in the set piece debate by confusing mixing procedural points with an unsupported affirmation of principle.

Adams, who had stretched out his hand to O'Bradaigh as he rose to speak (O'Bradaigh said, 'I'll shake hands with anyone' as he clasped it) closed the debate with a last minute call for unity. Nobody should walk out but if they did they should think about it and return to the movement later. Defending his own record as a conciliator and shifting the blame to the other side he said: 'If I bend backwards any further I'll go up my own arse.' Appealing to traditional loyalty he recommended the example of Dan Gleeson. Gleeson had upset plans by declining to put in a repeat appearance on the platform this year. Adams said that Gleeson had told him: 'I'm voting against the ard comhairle but I'm not walking out.' A personally religious man, Adams had already spoken against abortion and succeeded in having the 'right to choose' removed from party policy.

The abstentionism motion got its two-thirds majority but despite Adams' best efforts to bring unity the walkout took place and a new organisation, Republican Sinn Féin, was formed.

At the time of writing it claims 85 cumainn and appears to be building a network of the pure and faithful, ready for their chance in the event of disaffection within the IRA. RSF also aims to stand abstentionist candidates in future elections and although its prospects of emerging as a significant political force in its own right remain remote its areas of strength do not bode well for Sinn Féin. They include Mid Ulster (where Morrison narrowly missed an Assembly seat but has been replaced as the candidate), Louth, Donegal, John Joe McGirl's Leitrim, and South Armagh where former Sinn Féin councillor Eamon Larkin now chairs RSF and a decline in the standard of mortaring suggests further defections. In the north Bob Murray is the organiser and in West Belfast any defections at all must threaten Adams' hold on the seat now that Fitt is gone and the mainstream nationalist vote is again concentrated in SDLP hands.

After the ard fheis there was an immediate scaling down of Sinn Féin's electoral predictions and its left-wing rhetoric. The keynote in both was provided by Adams who asserted that although it was the duty of the left to support Sinn Féin, Sinn Féin was not itself a socialist organisation.[6] Electorally he said that he wouldn't be disappointed if the party took no seats, though hopes remained of victory in Cavan, Louth and Dublin Central.

Adams' caution was justified by the results. After fielding 29 candidates, two in some areas, Sinn Féin lost 24 deposits and were nowhere in serious contention for a seat. Their share of the vote was under 2 per cent, not only down on the H-Block total but also lower than the 1983 EEC elections and the 1985 local government poll. Charles Haughey's Fianna Fail was indeed short of an overall majority but those in a position to give it to him were the Workers Party (4 seats), the Democratic Socialist Party (1 seat) and three independents.[7]

Republican News's immediate reaction was that Sinn Féin is not yet relevant to the electorate in the Republic and is seen as a 'Brits Out' party, attuned to the north at a time when southern voters are concerned with their own economic future. The task ahead, in this analysis, is to build the party, using the canvass returns as a guideline and tailoring policies to make them more relevant to popular needs.[8] However true this may be, such realism sits uneasily with the movement's claims to historic legitimacy, calling into question the assumed right to wage war on behalf of the nation and the centrality of the 'national question'.

In full flight from such contradictions, later analysis lapsed into wishful thinking, fixing the main blame on handicaps outside the movement's control. Section 31 of the Broadcasting Act, which bans Sinn Féin from appearing on Radio Telefis Eireann, and lack of media interest became the scapegoats for the poor showing, this despite the fact that until opinion polls gave the game away in the immediate run-up to the election Sinn Féin was taken very seriously indeed by the print media. Even after that they featured prominently in BBC and ITV broadcasts which were received in the main target constituencies.[9] In what is a counsel of despair for a party seeking fundamental political change the political system was also blamed for Sinn Féin's failure to make an impact.

If Sinn Féin can adjust to its position as a fringe party with an electoral floor of 2 per cent rather than maintaining the grand illusion that it represents the Irish nation it may be able to become a significant force by dint of judicious change over a period of years and plenty of the mundane and tedious work which Adams recommends. However all attempts to do so tend to undermine the legitimacy of its use of violence, allowing RSF or some new grouping to bid for the mantle of the legitimate inheritor of the physical force tradition and undermine the movement's ability to fund itself both by domestic rackets and foreign donation.[10] To make matters worse, further electoral erosion is likely in the north. Yet the conciliation of internal dissent by upping the terror campaign will not only come up against the increasing efficiency of the security forces north and south but will, more importantly, appal the broader constituency whose support is necessary for political advance. In such a situation Sinn Féin could again find that other parties with cleaner hands will reap any rewards arising from the IRA campaign.

The signs are that the ballot and armalite strategy, after a dramatic five year run on the backwash of the hunger strike may, like abstentionism, have outlived its usefulness. The battlefield which was broadened by Sands and his colleagues inside and outside the jail has again contracted, leaving the Provos with the task of finally choosing between the options which it opened up for them. If the choice is not managed rationally O'Conaill may be correct in predicting a crunch over money as the IRA competes with Sinn Féin for available resources.

NOTES

1. Quoted in Regis Debray, *A Critique of Arms* (Peregrine 1977).

2. *Irish News,* 2 December 1986. The statement was made at the council meeting following an IRA mortar attack aimed at Newry RUC station which overshot, injuring thirty-seven civilians, including four-year-old Aveen Lynch.

3. Interview with the author.

4. The victims were Leo Scullion (14 January), Martin Quinn (31 January), John O'Neill (14 March), Margaret Caulfield (the only Protestant victim who was killed on 7 May, apparently because she was married to a Catholic), Brian Leonard (12 July), Colm McCallan (16 July), Martin Duffy (19 July) and Paddy McAlister (20 August).

5. *Sunday Tribune,* November 1986.

6. See *The Politics of Irish Freedom,* p. 132 where Adams asserts that 'those on the left in Ireland who regard themselves as socialists and as representing the working class should be the most uncompromising republicans' but that 'the republican struggle should not at this stage of its development style itself "republican socialist". This would imply that there is no place for non-socialists.'

7. Tony Gregory (a community candidate in Dublin Central), Neil Blaney and Sean Treacy.

8. See *An Phoblacht/Republican News,* 19 February 1987, p. 1, 'No Short Cuts', in which Sinn Féin's previous position is seen as one of standing on 'the pedestal of patriotic chauvinism'.

9. Sinn Féin had a better publicity tailwind than any of the other parties outside the political mainstream. Several papers ran articles speculating that they would hold the balance of power and both the Taoiseach and the Health Minister, Barry Desmond, warned that this was a danger.

10. At the time of writing there is speculation that financial problems may be solved by Libyan aid. In *The Observer* of 1 March 1987, Qathafi announced that he would be increasing aid to the IRA. There had been similar pledges in 1985 and in October 1986. Qathafi said that Irish young people should 'join the struggle for liberation'. However evidence that Qathafi actually helped the IRA has been harder to find. A cache of weapons worth £1m found in Cavan and marked 'Libyan Armed Forces' were thought by police to have come from France and a small quantity of Czech-made Symtex plastic explosive found at a dump in Cheshire is more likely to have come from the Lebanon where it is used by Iranian backed suicide bombers. Sinn Féin maintains contact with Iran, two of whose diplomats, Hojatoleslam Hadi Ghafaril and Sabah Zamgemah, have visited Ireland to meet them. Further allegations of Libyan aid were produced by the *Sunday Times*'s Chris Ryder. In 1986 it was alleged that William 'Blue' Kelly was being sought by the police as a linkman to Libya. However Kelly was living in Belfast at an address known to the RUC. In 1987 Ryder claimed a joint Libyan-IRA plot to spring several prisoners, including Dickey Glenholmes who turned out to have been released from jail in August 1986.

Appendices

APPENDIX 1

(Smuggled prison communication from Bobby Sands, August 1970. The pseudonym 'Marcella' was used in all Sands' prison writings.)

Saturday 4th August H-6 Comrade. There'll be another communication along with this one, so you can read that also to give you a better indication of what I am saying here.

This will be pretty long, so get comfortable cara. Well, first of all I'll try to outline this thought here with regard to what way we view things and what way we should go about doing what we haven't done. Also I'll include some of the ideas that have come up so far to give you an indication of what we are at and what can be done. As you know, we have failed to reach a broader base of support, therefore we have failed to engage any active support outside of our immediate hardcore, friends, relatives, etc. The reason why we haven't done this doesn't matter anymore, so we are now going full steam ahead to rectify this. So I'll just get on with the new thought. There are two major things we have got to do. One, we must make more people aware and engage their help. Two, to get to these other people, we must organise our own people effectively and massively on the ground. Just not the RAC but the movement when we have organised our own people then we move into second gear. As you will see from the other communication, we in here have set about to organise and urge our own people, friends and relatives, to become involved more actively in the RAC or Sinn or whatever. The logic being, if they won't do it, then we can't expect anyone else to do it. For this, the experienced must lead the timid — we from in here, be in conjunction with you organising them, supplying them with ideas etc. We are preparing an army of propagandists on the ground. It will depend on you and your team comrade to ensure their co-operation at a later date, whether through the central body of the RAC, or whoever. For when they are ready to move we must move in a massive co-ordinated attack. Show you what I mean in a minute, you'll see why when I reach the ideas, you'll have to direct and monitor the whole operation.

You can box off a meeting with all the RAC and Sinn Féin or whoever can give them a rundown on the crack, some of them should already know as things are beginning to roll. The idea to reach people is to pass a simple message to them. Our simple message to everyone will be 'smash H-Block' that is what we shall build around. If it is a poster also contain short run down of the blocks, and call for action. When we go to the people we shall go through our own people, our 'workers on the ground'. They shall make it very hard for anyone to refuse to help (come back to this later) this wee message then 'Smash H-Block' will be what we will build around. We want to get this message to everyone, we want to make it impossible for people to forget it, no matter who they are or where they are, they shall see it, hear it, backing this will be material on H-Block to stir people's emotions and to arouse them and activate them. Now to tackle this broad spectrum of people in which we'll be plunging we must create our own mass media. The Brit mass media being unreliable but we can use it wherever possible and through time they'll be forced to cover us, through what we are going to stir up, now as you'll see in other communication passing the message can mean or be through painting a smash H-Block on a road or wall or sticking a poster on the side of a bus or lorry that is stopped at traffic lights or whatever, now I'll be giving you ideas on this later, but consider those two wee things I mentioned — A Paint and Poster Campaign. A massive effort on a national basis, through organised workers on the ground (this also brings in the co-ordination aspect). In one weekend we move and distribute one million posters both North and South — a million is not aiming too high, we stick them everywhere on roads, bridges, walls, trees, windows, we want one in every window in a nationalist area, we must work on people to get them to put them up, we must put them on everything that moves to carry them for us, at traffic lights we stick them on vehicles, they'll be carried into towns, loyalist and upper-class areas. There are any amount of ways and ideas to spread them.

Shortly afterwards we back this up with another massive co-ordinated painting spree (Smash H-Block) cover the countryside with it — there are many ideas on this also, we can cover everywhere with it. We can keep repeating this every three or four weeks. By doing this we create our own mass media, we can advertise forth from us 'Big Parades' in this manner, we must work hard and make it big, we want people to see H-Block everywhere. We'll do a door to door canvassing in every area, our people being armed with facts and details of H-Block. They give our material and put our case, emotionally breaking people down into giving a commitment, put them on the spot there and then, offer them ways in which they can help, come to a march, put a poster in their window, buy a paper, do the whole lot, join the RAC etc. We want parades the like of which have never been seen before. By continuing pushing 'Smash H-Block' we believe we are pushing a small message and making people aware through their wee jobs and those who they reach will learn something if it's only that H-

Block exists. They will help and support. We'll pick up as we progress!! We must also emphasise political status as a political prisoner's right so we must broaden into avenues we have not been before, to simplify it, everyone has a target, we must get to everyone in order to jerk the consciousness of the people — it sort of boils down to this Cara:

1. Organise the people that we have already got.
2. Attack through mass media propaganda, through an army of propagandists, you out there and we in here, cages etc.
3. Make our message simple — Smash H-Block, some details, a call for action and plenty of emotion.
4. Broaden our battlefield, locally — nationally and internationally, the field is limitless, everyone is a target whether approachable or not. As I said if we do this and approach a massive amount of people, it helps us pass the message, pick up support, as I said it also helps the progress of politicising in a simple fashion. It opens up avenues of contact between us and everyone who is anyone and at the same time it's politicisation on both sides.

Those doing the work by the nature of it, by answering questions or whatever of those who are directing them will become aware at the same time, they are putting the message across to the target. We believe that that is making people aware. You outside can take this further, you know what can and cannot be done. It is possible we may need some things to spur us back into people's minds, but if we do our work right we'll be doing just that comrade. The best example of what I'm trying to get across may be seen from some of the ideas, nothing is impossible for us and nothing too big for us to attempt or do. We must think positively, work hard and constant . . . here's the ideas of several men in one wing following an hour's discussion, what the thought and action of the whole movement could do is unimaginable. We need a list of names, a who's who, what's what in Ireland, all those who have influence, here's a few to start with, trade unions, we want the people in the North & South of the most influential in them — e.g. secretary, chairperson, social conscious groups, left wing groups, churchmen Catholic and Prod, with influence, newspaper and tv and media list of people who write or produce political or social programmes and articles, etc. Anybody who's anybody — also a list of people who have already made some form of statement on the H-Block favourable to us ranging from organisations leaders to important individuals those doctors made statements last year, etc!! The idea is this, one of us in here can write to one of those above or whoever, in a very emotional and distressing letter (in the case of an organisation our workers outside can back it up with a publicity brief, where possible give us as much background so that we can make the letters individual. The RAC where possible will deliver these humble letters and also where possible wait for a reply. Also to answer any questions that may arise, in other words, put their foot in the door and make a commitment to hold, there are many ways that they can help, like direct a statement or action at the 14th September. Also, comrade, we would like you to start choosing people in the RACs with leadership quality or in the movement. In fact do it through new comrades. Even the neighbours of prisoners, etc. who are local. Don't approach them let us know what sort of area they cover, we're thinking of people we can rely on for the best work and for the future ideas. What we want is to take those with interest and supply them with an idea that will suit them and therefore getting the best out of them, we'll approach them, need all this data before we start making major moves, when we do move we can move in all directions at the one time, personally I envisage creating an atmosphere of mass emotion trying to use it as best we can and as soon as we can. To assert pressure from all angles on the Brits, all this data can you keep it small and on thin paper, preferably send it through the cages to us, we'll box them off...

The door to door canvassing as I said must be done we'll herd our people into the RACs & Sinn Féin and they can do it, the massive poster & paint campaign is another good idea. The posters must be eye catching, thick black type with 'Smash H-Block' small run down on blocks and the call for action (you'll probably need about 10 million for what we've planned). Deadly serious comrade, sort of brings me to expenses, hopefully the Appeal Fund will rise with the reaction and progress!! Poster with a child on it, emotional The Year of the Child 'Don't let my Daddy Die in H-Block'. Get them up everywhere (I'm wrecked). Get those Smash H-Block posters up everywhere for Pope coming on the vehicles we can do it on the continent and USA. Also England. Paint Smash H-Block all over the major motorways in Britain — God knows how many will see it before it's obliterated. We want H-Block more common than Shamrock and we can do it (read on Cara). Black hacks — we want posters stuck on every door so as we have Smash H-Block sailing in and out of every District every minute of every day up and down the Falls so that thousands see them and every time someone gets in or out of a hack they see it. Also leaflets in the taxis for passengers to read, if Brits interfere we can exploit that too. Posters can be put on moving trains, half a dozen on the outside of a train coming into a crowded station carries a message on bridge on motorways. There's thousands of ways, 75,000 people in A/Town. We want most of them on our side and at parades, we want them all, how about a thousand letters of H-Block in as many languages and countries as possible like a chain effort. Post the thousand to people and ask them to copy and pass on as many copies as they like to their friends or what about a small transmitter radio station in Dublin and Belfast and Derry or more if we can do it if we make it our business — school kids refusing to attend school 'cause of H-Block, like during internment — small token industrial strikes build them up to bigger things. A double page poster in *An Phoblacht/RN* for people to put in their house and shop windows. Attack every crowd that can be found with leaflets and H-Block propaganda, get at GAA and immediately try for a major H-Block publicity coup at the All-Ireland, like a woman wearing a blanket throwing the ball in, Smash H-Block poster on her back or half a dozen women walking around the park also consider getting at the players, Kerry men if they are in final. We hear that the Pope is saying mass for the youth of Ireland in Phoenix Park — send all our kids in blankets — small insertions in the *R/N* and *Irish News*, eg Marcella POW H-Block 'Don't let my daddy die', Liza aged 4 or 'My big brother' or whatever gets to the peoples' emotions and arouses them. All local papers and community ones etc. will be flooded with H-Block material from here and cages, Portlaoise Armagh and Crum. What about an H-Block flag — get them flying everywhere (booby trap a few in Crossmaglen) form an International Committee for the push H-abroad form it from those relatives who have been abroad and who have experience and contacts — link them with people like Faul and Murray and others and we have a good team, to stir it up abroad. Get them to encourage Yankee action, also Yankee personalities and film stars and singers or whoever to come over and speak on Smash H-Block platform. We'll be attacking unions to a state of taking action — students, doctors the head, as I said to the lads, anyone from a schoolchild to a President is a target. There are hundreds of small ideas that we will pass to the RACs or whoever? All that I have written here came out of an hour's discussion from one wing. By next week we'll have more when we discuss it deeper. I have one more idea to add to all this — I'll give it to you in the minute (we're still thinking on it.) But to achieve all that you'll need a lot of help, there's no good in your doing half of this we need to do it big. Anyway, I hope that you got it all that I was trying to say, there's so much that I must put down as it came out of my head. We are very enthusiastic and we intend to waken everyone else up, about time someone lent a hand to you and your team. I'm sure you've a million ideas of your own and when the rest of the blocks and cages get going, the place will be alive with them. You can box off everyone involved outside on our thought, because this is all it is unless its done. Let us know what you's think also you should give consideration to approaching relatives of loyalist Blanket men — prompt them into action. Well here's the last idea for the time being — going on the supposition that our massive push sparks off a large emotional reaction. We gauge the three best areas, say for the sake of talk, Crossmaglen, Bogside and Short Strand, we call on people to show their opposition to H-Block end Brits representation in Ireland which means Brit repression. By coming out and voting for a Blanketman as being the representative of the people, just a wee local election with no opponents we need to do it right. We must have it I/O'd right before hand. We want at least 70 per cent or 80 per cent of each area turning out (the Blanketman must be a sensible effort. Fairly well known in their area) the idea will be that he is and those voting, the oppressed, make him not a figure head but the representative of the people in that area. This is a launching pad to community councils. The Blanketman cannont administer the local affairs of the area where he is and while he is in H-Block, the people have decided to run their own affairs and undermine the oppressor — the best a substitute can stand in for him while he remains in H-Block, preferably an RAC person or tenant association chairman, who must be red minded or at least nationalistic. Their main task will be to bring down H-3 Block to get their representative status, then freedom. When the time is ripe, we build & move to other areas doing the same thing.

We bring all these standing together and form a provisional type government, we move south to places like Leitrim & Kerry and Wexford and do likewise, we seek international recognition similar to what Arafat done, we get Basques, Bretons and every other person and group to back and recognise these Blanketmen as the true representative of the nationalist oppressed people. We undermine the Brits, Fitt, Loyalists etc. We get our substitute representatives to disrupt the House of Commons, things like that for publicity, well just another idea, we're still formulating and refining it, but it is quite feasible and very suitable, take everything that I've said and tie it in with the IRA and the War effort and we are on the right track comrade. That's about it on that for now!!

Cara, can you take a copy of the other communication for H3, H4 and H5. Also for Crum, cages, Portlaoise and Armagh and get it to them. This week, what we want is them to do the same. I have six articles ready for you you'll have them on Tuesday or Wednesday. They're very simple and a complete change of style — can you read them? — give them to the paper reports and ask for a pace for them — one a week — if you think they're sound. I'll do some more to back them up if they're alright.

I've a man doing a diary for one week. We'll see how it turns out, think it will be sound. Can you urge priests to bring lots of pens into us, also cages — to send as many as possible. Well, that's about it, the screws are throwing buckets of disinfectant under the doors at the minute so I'll see ya!! Regards to all — Marcella

'Smash H-Block' YAHOO!!

Cara, there's also going to be 3 communications in this for Block O/C to T. McG — will you put them to them with the other copy for the PROs.

Can you get word to Tom to ensure he knows that the other Report is Red okay?

APPENDIX 2

(Copy of IRA standing orders for special category women prisoners in Armagh, 29 December 1976. At the time there were only four non conforming prisoners in Armagh.)

1. Any volunteer found guilty of undermining the Staff will be dealt with severely.
2. Anyone found guilty of loose talk will be dealt with severely.
3. Smuggling of letters (in or out) of court will not be tolerated unless permission is granted before hand by the staff.
4. Any volunteer applying for Compassionate Parole must get permission from 'A' Coy Staff. If permission is granted and she wishes an extension she must work through Sinn Féin outside.
5. All statements going to the papers must go through the Bat PRO via A Coy PRO (J McElhinney).
6. On the day of a funeral of a volunteer, all radio, TV, record players and recreation will be suspended for the day (except for the News). Until after the funeral (there will be a Commemoration Parade on the first Sunday after the burial of a volunteer) full dress will be worn (BLACK).
7. News, Irish political and National Music programmes will have first preference on radio and TV.
8. Aggro with screws or Loyalists will not be tolerated (if a volunteer has any complaints against any of these two parties she must report to her Coy Staff immediately).
9. All volunteers must have cells cleaned out by 10.00 am.
10. All volunteers reporting sick must remain in bed until the following morning (unless called for a visit).
11. There is to be no noise after twelve midnight.
12. Anyone wishing to see the Welfare must have prior permission from Coy OC. Any welfare matter the OC deals with will be kept in strict confidence.
13. All volunteers must be ready on the day of their visit, this is to ensure that visitors are not kept waiting.
14. No property within the Coy is to be destroyed or damaged and all Coy notices are to be obeyed.

15. All volunteers are to be locked in their cells 10 mins after the meals are brought into the wing to enable the check to be made. All volunteers are to be locked at the time decided by the OC and Staff of the Prison.
16. All volunteers must make the best of possible use of Education Facilities in the gaol. This is to ensure the volunteers do not waste their time.
17. All volunteers must duly elect their OC twice a year in the months of January and July. Coy Staff (Adj FO, TO, IO, PRO)[1] must also be elected.
18. It must be stressed that PIF work is an important point of the Republican Movement. By helping the Green Cross Volunteers will be helping families of prisoners who might otherwise be in need.
19. Drill is an important part of discipline in the gaol, but the time and regularity of the drill will be left to the discretion of the TO and Staff of the gaol, anyone with a genuine complaint or reason why they cannot partake in drill can obtain permission to absent themselves from the OC.
20. Staff meetings will be held once a month unless it is an emergency.

Note

1. Adjutant, Finance Officer, Training Officer, Intelligence Officer and PRO.

APPENDIX 3

('Yellow Card' instructions on the use of firearms issued to all British soldiers serving in Northern Ireland since 1971).

INSTRUCTIONS BY THE DIRECTOR OF OPERATIONS FOR OPENING FIRE IN NORTHERN IRELAND.

1. These instructions are for the guidance of commanders and troops operating collectively or individually. When troops are operating collectively troops will only open fire when ordered to do so by the commander on the spot.

General Rules

2. Never use more force than the minimum necessary to enable you to carry out your duties.
3. Always first try to handle the situation by other means than opening fire. If you have to fire:
   a. Fire only aimed shots.

b. Do not fire more rounds than are absolutely necessary to achieve your aim.

4. Your magazine/belt must always be loaded with live ammunition and be fitted to the weapon. Unless you are about to open fire no live round is to be carried in the breech and the working parts must be forward. Company Commanders and above may, when circumstances in their opinion warrant such action, order weapons to be cocked with a round in the breech where appropriate and the safety catch at safe.
5. Automatic fire may be used against identified targets in the same circumstances as single shots if, in the opinion of the Commander on the spot, it is the minimum force required and no other weapon can be employed as effectively. Because automatic fire scatters it is not to be used where other persons not using firearms are in or may be close to, the line of fire.

WARNING BEFORE FIRING

6. A warning should be given before you open fire. The only circumstances in which you may open fire without giving warning are described in paras 13 and 14 below.
7. A warning should be as loud as possible, preferably by loud hailer. It must:
   a. Give clear orders to stop attacking or to halt, as appropriate.
   b. State that fire will be opened if the orders are not obeyed.

YOU MAY FIRE AFTER DUE WARNING

8. Against a person carrying what you can positively identify as a firearm but only if you have reason to think that he is about to use it for offensive purposes and he refuses to halt when called upon to do so, and there is no other way of stopping him.
9. Against a person throwing a petrol bomb if petrol bomb attacks continue in your area troops and civilians or against property, if this action is likely to endanger life.
10. Against a person attacking or destroying property or stealing firearms or explosives if his action is likely to endanger life.
11. Against a person who, though he is not at present attacking has:
    a. in your sight killed or seriously injured a member of the security forces or a person whom it is your duty to protect; and
    b. not halted when called upon to do so and cannot be arrested by any other means.
12. If there is no other means to protect yourself or those whom it is

your duty to protect from the danger of being killed or seriously injured.

YOU MAY FIRE WITHOUT WARNING

13. Either when hostile firing is taking place in your area, and a warning is impracticable, or when any delay would lead to death or serious injury to people whom it is your duty to protect or to yourself; and then only:
    a. Against a person using a firearm against members of the security forces or people whom it is your duty to protect or
    b. against a person using a firearm if you have reason to think he is about to use it for offensive purposes.
14. At a vehicle if the occupants open fire or throw a bomb at you or others whom it is your duty to protect, or are clearly about to do so.

APPENDIX 4

(Provisional reorganisation document found by the Gardai in a search on a flat occupied by IRA Chief of Staff Seamus Twomey in December 1977. It is generally believed to have been produced by a commission headed by Gerry Adams as a report to General Headquarters Staff).

STAFF REPORT

The three-day and seven-day detention orders are breaking volunteers, and it is the Irish Republican Army's fault for not indoctrinating volunteers with the psychological strength to resist interrogation.

Coupled with this factor, which is contributing to our defeat, we are burdened with an inefficient infrastructure of commands, brigades, battalions and companies. The old system with which Brits and Branch are familiar has to be changed. We recommend reorganisation and remotivation, the building of a new Irish Republican Army.

We emphasise a return to secrecy and strict discipline. Army men must be in total control of all sections of the movement.

1. A new rank of Education Officer must be created. GHQ must have a department of Education Officers available for Lectures and Discussions at Weapons Training Camps. Anti-interrogation Lectures must be given in conjunction with indoctrination lectures. The ideal outcome is that no Volunteer should be charged unless caught red handed.

It should be pointed out to new recruits the failures of our past structures — the number of men who have been arrested and signed their freedom away. The common sense methods of personal security should be thrashed out. Any new recruit mixing with known volunteers should be suspended pending discipline.

We must gear ourselves towards long term armed struggle based on putting unknown men and new recruits into a new structure. The new structure shall be a cell system.

2. Ideally a cell should consist of four people. Rural areas, we decided, should be treated as separate cases to that of a city and town Brigade/Command.

For this reason our proposals will affect mainly city and town areas where the majority of our operations are carried out and where the biggest proportion of our support lies anyway.

As we have already said, all new recruits are to be passed into a cell structure.

Existing Battalion and Company Staffs must be dissolved over a period of months with present Brigades then deciding who passes into the reorganised cell structure and who goes into the Brigade controlled and compartmentalised Civil Administration (explained later).

The cells of four volunteers will be controlled militarily by the Brigade's/Command's Intelligence Officer.

Cells will be financed through their cell leader who will be funded through the OC co-ordinator. That is, for wages, for running costs, financing of operations. (Expenses etc will be dealt with through the OC.)

Cells must be specialised into IC cells, sniping cells, execution, bombing, robberies etc.

The cell will have no control of weapons or explosives, but should be capable of dumping weapons overnight (in the case of a postponed operation).

The weapons and explosives should be under the complete control of the Brigade's/Command's QM and EO respectively.

Cells should operate as often as possible outside of their own areas: both to confuse Brit intelligence (which would thus increase our security) and to expand our operational areas.

Brigades should be made use of in all operations.

The breaking up of present structure into administration sections and operational cells will make for maximum military effectiveness, greater security, a more efficent back up structure to increase support and cater for our people's problems.

Thus our operations officer can go straight into an area and deal exclusively with Military Operations and problems.

All present volunteers under old structure must be reeducated and given up-dated lectures in combating new interrogation techniques.

Sinn Féin should come under Army organisers at all levels. Sinn Féin should employ full time organisers in big republican areas. Sinn Féin should be radicalised (under Army direction) and should agitate about social and economic issues which attack the welfare of the people. SF should be directed to infiltrate other organisations to win support for, and sympathy to, the movement, SF should be re-educated and have a big role to play in publicity and propaganda depts, complaints and problems (making no room for RUC opportunism). It gains the respect of the people which in turn leads to increased support for the cell.

APPENDIX 5

Rules of the Belfast Central Relatives Action Committee for the retention of political status for Republican and Republican Socialist prisoners of war in the six occupied counties of Ireland.

1. The Relatives Action Committee was set up on Easter Monday 1976. The committee was established to defend the political status for Republican and Socialist P.O.W.s. Our immediate demand is that political status should be retained and extended to all prisoners who are in jail because of their opposition to British interference in Irish affairs. We further demand that there should be a total amnesty for all Irish political prisoners. We finally demand the withdrawal of all British troops from Ireland and the re-establishment of a 32 county Republic as proclaimed in Easter 1916. In making these demands we are asking that Irish and World opinion recognise that a war of national liberation is being waged in Ireland. The demands for British withdrawal and amnesty are therefore an inseparable part of a campaign to secure Irish freedom.
2. The R.A.C. should concern itself with all matters concerning the arrest, interrogation, trial and sentencing of prisoners and their rights and conditions pending a general amnesty. Recognising that all these matters relate to the British policy of 'CRIMINALISATION'.
3. The R.A.C. seeks to mobilise National and International opinion behind these objectives.
4. The R.A.C. is organised in local branches which will carry out the agreed tasks of the organisation. Membership is open to people who support the aims and objects of the R.A.C. Branch meetings are held weekly and voting at branches is left to the discretion of local committees. Branches where attendance at meetings falls below 3 over a period of one month should inform the centre and

ask for help to build up local branch. If however strengthening is impossible then the branch should amalgamate with its nearest branch.

5. The Central committee shall consist of not more than two voting delegates from each area branch plus elected officers and shall organise and co-ordinate activity to secure the aims and objectives of the R.A.C. The officer board shall consist of Chairperson, Secretary, Treasurer and P.R.O. who will carry out the usual duties of such officers. The officers will be elected for a period of six months. They will be elected by the central committee. Only branch delegates and elected officers shall be entitled to vote at central meetings.
6. The central committee may appoint sub-committees, as may be deemed necessary, to carry out particular tasks. Each sub-committee shall report on their activities to each centre meeting.
7. Political parties who support the objectives of the R.A.C. are permitted to send an observer as liason officer without voting rights.
8. The officer board are responsible for maintaining effective contact with other R.A.C. groups and any other groups and parties who support the struggle for political status.
9. Responsibility for carrying out the decisions of the Central Committee rests with the chairperson and officer board.

Central Relatives Action Committee

APPENDIX 6

PRISONERS' STATEMENT OF 4 JULY 1981

We, the protesting republican prisoners in Long Kesh, having replied in short to H. Atkins' statement of June 30th, wish to expand our view on this statement.

Responsibility

1. The British government are responsible for the hunger strike in Long Kesh. The ending of special category status was a political tactic used by the British government in its attempt to criminalise the republican attack on British imperialism in Ireland

   The existence of special legislation, special courts and criminal interrogation, plus the British administration's refusal to acknowledge a special category of prisoners, all contribute to the placing of the responsibility for this issue on the administration's shoulders.

   Furthermore, the British government have had ample opportunities during the course of this issue to avoid the occurrence and reoccurrence of hunger-strikes. The Cardinal O'Fiach/NIO talks, and the refusal to honour the December 18th agreement, are prime examples of this.

Legal Credibility

2. Lord Gardiner, like so many other Brit appointed examiners, was sent to Ireland to do a specific job: to recommend the ending of special category status so that legal credibility could be attached to the criminalisation policy.

Five Demands for All

3. It is wrong for the British government to say that we are looking for differential treatment from other prisoners. We would warmly welcome the introduction of the five demands for all prisoners. Therefore, on this major point of British policy there is no sacrifice of principle involved.

Dignity Restored

4. We believe that the granting of the five demands to all prisoners would not in any way mean the administration would be forfeited control of the prison, nor would their say on prison activities be greatly diminished; but the prisoner could have his dignity restored and cease to occupy the role of establishment zombie.

Flexibility

5. The European Commission on Human Rights criticised the British government for being inflexible and for allowing an impasse to develop. Flexibility is in not perpetuating the protest but, rather, trying to remove or resolve the cause of dissent which foments such protest.

Work

6. Mr Atkins outlines the present routine under the title 'prison activity'. It is a crude system which Mr Atkins disguises with flowery jargon. Yet, it should not be a major point of contention between the administration and outselves. What the British government recognises as 'prison work' we do not. Therefore, with goodwill 'work' and the achieving of a compatible arrangement should be available without loss of principle. Besides self-education, which would be the main prop in any agreement, we are prepared to maintain our cells, wings and blocks, and participate in any activity which we define as self management.

Free Association

7. Mr Atkins is either misinformed or exaggerating the free association demand.

Free association means that there would be freedom of movement within the wings. Supervision need not be restricted. That is a matter for the regime's discretion. There would be no interference with prison officers who would maintain their supervisory role. It must be remembered that H Blocks are control units, and each wing is built to accommodate 25 prisoners. So it is rather a red herring to speak of the regime losing control of the prison if the prisoners had freedom of the wing.

Equally, it is misleading to quote of one hundred prisoners presumably associating together. We believe there should be wing visits but we do not envisage ourselves (although Mr Atkins does) running around the blocks as we please in large numbers.

It is unrealistic to expect loyalists and republicans to integrate satisfactorily together. Forced integration, or the deliberate creation of confrontation between those who bear arms in respect of their highly conflicting political ideologies is wrong and can only lead to trouble. Even Mr Paisley recognised this several weeks back.

If studied carefully it will be seen that our definition of free association is far removed from what seems to be Mr Atkins'.

Clothing

8. Prison clothes are prison clothes. It is illusory to minimize the wearing of prison clothes to half the week. Prisoners, like everyone else, sleep, and for most of the other half are forced to wear prison clothes. The women of Armagh wear their own clothes, and there is no objective reason why all prisoners should not be allowed to wear their own clothes.

Parcels

9. If we accept that toiletries, and to a lesser extent reading material are essential, then the weekly parcel amounts to 4 lbs of fruit. That speaks for itself.

Remission

10. Lost remission is a result of the protest and is not connected with the cause of it. As the British government says, the machinery exists to reclaim it — yet, for some reason the British government is being ambiguous on this matter. What constitutes a 'subsequent period of good behaviour'? What does one fifth return of remission mean?

This should not be an area of disagreement, for it does not

directly affect the running of the system. But it is of mutual benefit to all whom it affects that full remisssion is given back to the prisoners.

Conclusion

In giving our views on what Mr Atkins said, we have outlined what should be the basis of a solution, without loss of principle to either side of this conflict.

It could well be that Mr Atkins has been misinformed about our demands. It certainly appears that from his June 30th statement that this is so. We ask all parties involved to study this statement closely. We particularly ask the British to study it. It should not be taken lightly.

By asking the British administration to come to discuss a resolution we ask nothing unreasonable. It is common for officials from that administration to visit this prison and converse with prisoners. It has been done before.

Comrades of ours have died and eight of our other comrades presently face death on hunger-strike. Our people on the outside have died and more may die. That is why we seek immediate talks with the British administration to seek a solution to the H Block protests. It is a reasonable request.

Select Bibliography

Books

Ackroyd, Carol; Margolis, Karen; Rosenhead Jonathan and Shallice, Tim; *The technology of Political Control* (Pelican 1977)

Adams, Gerry; *The politics of Irish Freedom* (Brandon 1986); *Falls Memories* (Brandon 1982)

Adams, James; *The Financing of Terror* (New English Library 1986)

Arnold, Bruce; *What Kind of Country — Modern Irish Politics 1968-1983* (Jonathan Cape, 1984)

Asmal, Kadar; *Shoot to Kill — Report of International Lawyers Enquiry into the Lethal use of Firearms by the Security Forces in Northern Ireland* (Mercier 1985)

Barzilay, David: *The British Army in Ulster* (Century Books, 4 Vols, 1973-1981)

Bell, J. Bowyer; *The Secret Army — The IRA 1916-74* (The MIT Press 1974)

Bew, Paul; Gibbon, Peter and Patterson, Henry: *The State in Northern Ireland* (Manchester University Press 1979)

Bloch, Jonathan and Fitzgerald, Patrick; *British Intelligence and Covert Action* (Brandon 1983)

Boulton, David; *The UVF: 1966-1973* (Torc 1973)

Boyle, Kevin; Hadden, Tom and Hillyard Paddy; *Ten Years On: The Legal Control of Political Violence* (Cobden Trust 1980)

Bradford, Norah; *A Sword Bathed in Fire* (Pickering and Inglis 1984)

Buckland, Patrick; *A History of Northern Ireland* (Gill and Macmillan 1981)

Cathcart, Rex; *The Most Contrary Region — The BBC in Northern Ireland 1924-1984* (Blackstaff 1984)

Clarke, A. F. N.; *Contact — the brutal chronicle of a Para's war on the Battlefield of Ulster* (Pan 1984)

Collins, Tom; *The Irish Hunger Strike* (White Island Books 1986)

Coogan, Tim Pat; *On the Blanket — The H-Block Story* (Ward River Press 1980), *The IRA* (Fontana 1980)

Cronin, Sean; *Irish Nationalism — A History of its roots and Ideology* (Academy Press 1980)

— and Richard Roche (ed); *Freedom the Wolfe Tone Way* (Anvil 1973)

Curtis, Liz; *Ireland and the Propaganda War* (Pluto 1984)

Dibray, Regis; *Critique of Arms* (Peregrine)

Devlin, Bernadette; *The Price of my Soul* (Andre Deutsch, 1969)
Devlin, Bobby; *An Interlude with Seagulls* (Information on Ireland 1986)
Dillon, Martin and Lehane, Denis; *Political Murder in Northern Ireland* (Penguin 1973)
Darby, John; *Dressed to Kill — Cartoonists and the Northern Ireland Conflict* (Appletree Press 1983); (ed) *Northern Ireland — The Background to the Conflict* (Appletree Press 1982)
de Paor, Liam; *Divided Ulster* (Penguin 1979)
Downey, James; *Them and Us — Britain and the Northern Question 1969-1982* (Ward River Press 1983)
Eveleigh, Robin; *Peace-keeping in a Democratic Society — the lessons of Northern Ireland* (Hurst 1978)
Fairweather, Eileen; McDonough, Roisin and McFadyean, Melanie; *Only the Rivers Run Free — Northern Ireland — The Women's War* (Pluto 1985)
Faligot, Roger; *Britain's Military Strategy in Ireland — The Kitson Experiment* (Zed 1980)
Faul, Fr Denis and Murray, Fr Raymond; *The Hooded Men — British Torture in Ireland, October 1971, The Flames of Long Kesh, Corruption of Law, The Shame of Merlyn Rees — 4th Year of Internment in Long Kesh 1974-1975, The RUC — The Black and Blue book, Violations of Human Rights in Northern Ireland 1968-1978. The Sleeping Giant — Irish Americans and Human Rights in N. Ireland, The Castlereagh File - Allegations of RUC Brutality 1976-77, The British Dimension — Brutality, Murder and Legal Duplicity in N. Ireland, The H Blocks, Danny Barrett — A British Army Murder* (Published by the authors)
Feehan, John M.; *Bobby Sands and the Tragedy of Northern Ireland* (Mercier 1983)
Flackes, W.D.; *Northern Ireland — a Political Directory* (Ariel 1983)
Geraghty, Tony; *Who Dares Wins — The Story of the SAS 1950-1980* (Fontana 1981)
Goldring, Maurice; *Faith of Our Fathers — The formation of Irish nationalist ideology 1890-1920* (Repsol 1982)
Hamill, Desmond; *Pig in the Middle — The Army in Northern Ireland 1969-1985* (Methuen 1986)
Irish Freedom Movement; *The Irish War* (Junius 1985)
Jardine, Rev David; *Belfast's Bleak House — Faith Behind Bars in the Crumlin Road Jaol* (Marshall's Paperbacks 1985)
Joyce, Joe and Murtagh, Peter; *The Boss — Charles J. Haughey in Government* (Poolbeg Press 1983)
Kelley, Kevin; *The Longest War; Northern Ireland and the IRA* (Brandon 1982)
Kelly, Henry; *How Stormont Fell* (Gill and Macmillan 1972)

Kitson, General Frank; *Low Intensity Operations* (Faber and Faber 1971); *Bunch of Five* (Faber and Faber 1975)
Lyons, F.S.L.; *Ireland Since the Famine* (Fontana 1979)
McCann, Eamon; *War in an Irish Town* (Penguin 1984)
McClean, Dr Raymond; *The Road to Bloody Sunday* (Ward River Press 1983)
McGuffin, John; *The Guinea Pigs* (Penguin 1974); *Internment* (Anvil 1973)
McKeown, Ciaran; *The Passion for Peace* (Blackstaff 1984, withdrawn from circulation)
Mac Stiofain, Sean; *Memoirs of a Revolutionary* (Gordon Cremonesi 1975)
Maloney, Ed and Pollak, Andy; *Paisley* (Poolbeg 1986)
Mitchell, Tom; *Jail Journal* (Dublin University Press 1984)
Morgan, Austin, and Purdie, Bob (eds); *Ireland: Divided Nation, Divided Class* (Ink Links 1980)
Mullin, Chris; *Error of Judgement — The Birmingham Bombings* (Chatto and Windus 1986)
National Council of Civil Liberties; *The Prevention of Terrorism Acts of 1974 and 1976* (Cath Scorer); *The Special Powers Act of Northern Ireland; Strip Searching*
National Graves Association; *Belfast Graves* (National Graves Association 1985)
Nelson, Sarah; *Ulster's Uncertain Defenders — Loyalists and the Northern* Ireland Conflict (Appletree 1984)
O'Dowd, L., Rolston W. and Tomlinson, M.; *Northern Ireland: Between Civil Rights and Civil War* (CSE Books 1980)
Patrick, Derrick; *Fetch Felix* (Hamish Hamilton 1981)
Pearse, Peter Gerard and Matesn, Nigel; *Ken Livingstone — or 'The End of Civilisation as we know it'* (Proteus 1982)
Prior, James; *A Balance of Power* (Hamish Hamilton 1986)
Republican Publications; *The Politics of Revolution — The main speeches from the 1986 Sinn Féin ard fheis including the presidential address of Gerry Adams* (Republican Publications 1986)
Sands, Bobby; *One Day in My Life* (Mercier 1982); *Prison Poems* (Sinn Féin 1981); *The Writings of Bobby Sands* (Sinn Féin 1981); *The Diary of Bobby Sands* (supplement to *Republican News)*
Segaller, Stephen; *Invisible Armies — Terrorism into the 1990s* (Michael Joseph 1986)
Smith, Raymond; *Garret: The Enigma* (Aherlow 1985)
Taylor, Peter; *Beating the Terrorists — Interrogation in Omagh, Gough and Castlereagh* (Penguin 1980)
Uris, Leon; *Trinity* (Corgi 1977)
White, Barry; *John Hume — Statesman of the Troubles* (Blackstaff 1984)

Periodicals and Pamphlets

Republican News and the occasional *Iris* are both Sinn Féin publications. *Belfast Bulletin* once produced by the Workers Research Unit, carried a number of well researched articles on prisons, civil liberties, the economy and other aspects of northern life from a left republican viewpoint. *Lobster* (Hull) is a useful occasional digest of information on the British Intelligence services with frequent articles on their activities in Ireland. Republican Sinn Féin publishes *Republican Notes*. People's Democracy published *Unfree Citizen* and the IRSP *Saoirse*.

Mainstream publications which have been particularly useful have included *Irish Times, Irish News, News Letter, Belfast Telegraph* (all daily) *Magill, New Hibernia* (monthly) and *Hibernia* (defunct, weekly).

Two NIO publications, *H-Blocks — The Reality* and *Day to Day Life in Northern Ireland Prisons* are also worth seeing as are the series of briefings on IRA and related subjects prepared by the NIO for foreign journalists.

A wealth of other H-Block and republican pamphlets and propaganda material from a variety of groups has been collated in the Belfast Linenhall Library's invaluable political ephemera collection.

Index